W9-BEO-012

An inlet in
Bohuslän,
on the west
coast

Insight on ...

Information panels

Travel Tips

Places

THE SPIRIT OF SWEDEN

No longer an inward-looking nation, Sweden is making

its mark on the international stage

A subtle change in Swedish attitudes has been emerging in recent years. Not so long ago the country was an introverted Fortress Sweden perched uneasily on the edge of Western Europe. Indeed, many Swedes still talk about travelling "to Europe" as if it was on a different continent. If they are travelling further afield they sometimes say rather quaintly they are going "out into the world".

The country's admission to the European Union in 1995 was hardly given an overwhelming welcome by the Swedes, but they are beginning to realise that they have to be good Europeans, too, and are now presenting a much more positive international image. Perhaps the ultimate symbol of this "internationalisation" is the opening in 2000 of the Öresund bridge and tunnel across the straits separating Sweden from Denmark, emphasising the fact that Sweden really is part of Europe now.

As such, Sweden is attracting many more visitors, not just to the bustling big cities and cultural centres of Stockholm, Göteborg (Gothenburg) and Malmö, but also to the rural regions and the vast wilderness areas of Lapland and the Far North. Where else can you stay in an hotel made entirely from ice, play golf under the midnight sun or dance with abandon around a maypole at Midsummer? It is an ideal country for those who like the great outdoors and activities such as angling, golf, riding, fell-walking, sailing or canoeing.

Sweden is also becoming a popular year-round destination. The winter climate is usually much less harsh than many people imagine and the period around Christmas, with its traditional markets, brightly decorated streets and St Lucia processions, is a magical time of year. Sweden is also achieving international recognition as a winter-sports destination, with skiing centres to rival the best Alpine resorts.

Culturally, you can take your pick from well-preserved sites like the island remains of the Viking capital of Birka, state-of-the-art museums, and the homes of artists such as Carl Larsson who inspired the clean lines of contemporary Swedish design. On the musical front, Göteborg's Symphony Orchestra is in the top rank of world orchestras, and Sweden has even become a centre of gastronomic excellence, with many restaurants now earning Michelin stars.

For such a large country with a comparatively small population, Sweden offers the visitors immense variety. ❑

PRECEDING PAGES: Royal Marines Music Corps at Nynäshamn Annual Tattoo; pedal power; telephone time at Smögen, Bohuslän; Swedes learn to swim early.
LEFT: Sami dressed appropriately for the rigours of the Lapland climate.

Decisive Dates

THE FIRST SWEDES

From 10,000 BC Hunters and food gatherers follow the melting ice northwards, establishing settlements and farming communities.

1500 BC Trade routes are forged through the rivers of Eastern Europe to the Danube.

400 BC–AD 400 Trade extends south to the Roman Empire. In the 1st century AD the Roman historian Tacitus describes the Sveas (Swedes) who inhabit what is now central Sweden.

AD 500 the Sveas conquer the Goths living in what is

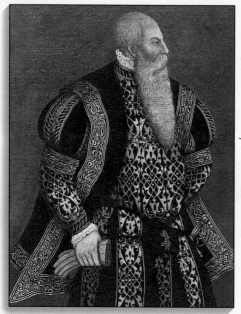

now southern Sweden. Lake Mälaren becomes their power base.

THE VIKING ERA

AD 800–1060 Scandinavian Vikings earn a reputation as sea warriors. In 862, at the invitation of the Slavs, Prince Rurik leads the Swedish Vikings (Varangians) east to bring order to the principality of Novgorod. They soon extend their rule south to Smolensk and Kiev, controlling trade routes along the River Dnieper to the Black Sea and Byzantium.

THE ARRIVAL OF CHRISTIANITY

AD 830 A Benedictine monk, Ansgar (801–865), lands on Björkö in Lake Mälaren, and founds a church.

12th century Christianity finally replaces paganism with the conversion of King Erik Jedvarsson (St Erik, patron saint of Sweden). Sweden colonises Finland.

13th century Trading ports such as Visby become centres for the powerful Hanseatic League of German merchants. In 1252 the regent, Birger Jarl, builds Stockholm's city walls.

1397 Sweden, Norway and Denmark are united under Queen Margareta of Denmark's Kalmar Union.

1434 Swedes rise up against Margareta's successor, Eric of Pomerania, and nationalism spreads.

1477 University of Uppsala founded.

1520 Kristian II of Denmark invades Sweden and massacres the nobility in the "Stockholm Bloodbath". Gustav Vasa drives Kristian out of the country. The Kalmar Union is disbanded.

VASA DYNASTY 1523–1720

1523 Gustav Vasa (1523–60) becomes king of an independent Sweden and declares Stockholm his capital. Vasa strengthens central authority, banishes the Hanseatic League, and adopts Lutheranism as the state religion (1544). He curbs the power of the nobles and makes the monarchy hereditary.

1560–1611 Vasa is succeeded by his eldest son, Eric XIV, who is imprisoned by his brothers, Johan and Karl, and succeeded by Johan III (1569–92). Johan marries the daughter of the King of Poland. When he dies, his son Sigismund III of Poland, becomes king of Sweden and tries to impose Roman Catholicism. In 1599 he is deposed by Vasa's youngest son, who becomes King Karl IX (1607–11).

1611–32 Karl's son, Gustav II Adolf, turns Sweden into a great European power, aided by his chancellor, Axel Oxenstierna. He gains control of the Gulf of Finland from Russia and Livonia from Poland. In the Thirty Years' War (1618–48) he presses south into Poland. He dies on the battlefield at Lützen, Germany.

1632–54 Six-year-old Queen Kristina succeeds her father with Oxenstierna as regent. She grows up to preside over a glittering baroque court and earns a reputation as patron of the arts. In secret, Kristina turns to Catholicism and in 1654 abdicates and leaves for Rome. The Peace of Westphalia, 1648, ends the Thirty Years' War and makes the Swedish monarchs princes of the Holy Roman Empire.

1654–97 Karl X recovers southern Sweden from Denmark. Karl XI (1660–97) sets about reducing the power of the nobles.

1697–1718 The reign of Karl XII, the "warrior king", his defeat by the Russians in 1709 and his death in the Great Northern War (1700–21), marks the decline in Sweden's power.

THE AGE OF FREEDOM

1718–71 The Riksdag (parliament) becomes more powerful and two factions, the Hats (nobles) and Caps (urban traders) dominate politics. Mining and manufacturing develop. In 1739 the Swedish Academy of Science is opened.

1771–92 Gustav III restores absolutism. Fine arts flourish and Swedish drama, in particular. He is assassinated at a masked ball.

1792–1809 Gustav IV Adolf loses Finland to Russia in 1808 and is deposed by his uncle, Karl XIII.

IN THE FOOTSTEPS OF BERNADOTTE

1810–44 Jean Baptiste Bernadotte, French marshal

THE TWENTIETH CENTURY

1932 The Social Democratic Party is elected to government and establishes a welfare state. Under the Saltsjöbaden Agreement (1938) trade unions and employers agree to co-operate on labour relations.

1914–49 Sweden remains neutral in World War I and II. It does not join NATO in 1949.

1950 Gustav V (reigns 1907–50) is succeeded by Gustav VI (1950–73).

1951–76 Social Democrats hold office. In 1969 Olof Palme becomes prime minister. He reduces the Riksdag from two chambers to one (1971) and removes the monarch's constitutional powers. Economic growth slows, unemployment rises.

of Napoleon, is elected crown prince and succeeds to the throne as Karl XIV Johan in 1818. Sweden is united with Norway (1815–1905).

1844–1907 The reigns of Karl XIV's heirs, Oskar I (1844–59), Karl XV (1859–72), Oskar II (1872–1907), witness liberal reforms, industrial development and the building of the railways. In 1866 the Riksdag is reformed and the monarch's role is reduced. Compulsory education is introduced, trade unionism takes hold, and the foundations are laid for the Social Democratic Party, which dominates 20th-century politics.

PRECEDING PAGES: Viking raiding party, 9th century.
LEFT: King Gustav Vasa, reigned 1523–60.
ABOVE: King Carl XVI Gustaf and Queen Silvia.

1973 Carl XVI Gustaf ascends to the throne.

1976–82 Palme is defeated on the issue of taxation in the 1976 election and power moves to the Centre Party under Thorbjörn Fälldin.

1982 Social Democrats regain power, but in 1986 their leader, Olof Palme, is assassinated.

1991 Social Democrats are defeated. Carl Bildt heads a centre-right coalition, which introduces austerity measures to combat the recession of 1992.

1994 Ingvar Carlsson leads the Social Democrats to power. Fifty percent of the ministers are women.

1995 Sweden joins the EU. Welfare benefits are cut to curb spending. Göran Persson succeeds Carlsson.

1998 An election sees the Social Democrats returned with a reduced majority. ❑

GLACIERS, GRAVES AND VIKINGS

Ten thousand years ago, as the glaciers began to retreat, Sweden's first inhabitants arrived to occupy the newly revealed land

Sweden's history is a patchwork, with periods of economic and political greatness contrasting with longer periods of decline in international importance. One factor has remained constant: the significance of the sea and of the country's inland waterways.

From prehistoric times, the distant ancestors of today's Scandinavians were seafarers who used the sea, lakes and rivers as a means of transport through their densely forested lands. Later, as Vikings, their voyages ranged over every part of the then known world.

Not for Sweden the glories of the early Christian church, when earnest monks chronicled the doings of kings and prelates. Sweden did not become Christian until the 11th and 12th centuries, so the country's written history began late. If there were triumphs, they were remembered only in legend and saga.

The Vikings were Sweden's first conquerors and traders, followed by the monarchs of the Vasa dynasty, who extended this small country's boundaries far into Europe. At that time its leaders looked over their shoulders to Russia in the east, the traditional source of threat. Not until the 19th century did Swedish preoccupations shift towards the west. Abruptly, the government renounced all pretensions to conquest and has since lived within its own boundaries. In the 20th century, its hardest fought campaigns have been for peace among nations.

But long years of war had left a legacy of poverty and hardship, and Sweden entered the 20th century as a poor, backward nation. In less than 100 years, however, the country has transformed itself into a model of peace, prosperity, neutrality and good living.

In the beginning

Sweden's known history began 10,000 years ago. As the melting ice crept north, a peninsula of land grew on the northern edge of the Euro-

pean Continent. This was land in the raw, a turmoil of melting glaciers and seas. A thousand years later, a single great cataclysm severed what became Sweden from the land that is now Denmark.

As life became possible, Stone Age hunters followed the melting glaciers north. Modern

archaeological finds of implements and camp sites witnessed the slow establishment of settlements and agriculture, as these primitive people began the long evolution from hunters and gatherers to farmers.

Already, these unknown people had established a rapport with the sea and, by 1500 BC, their trade routes extended to the Danube. Bronze began to appear in Scandinavia, thanks to these early traders who almost certainly brought back the raw materials as well as the knowledge. Sweden's own rich deposits of copper and tin were not discovered for many centuries, and it was some 500 years later that the Swedes began to make iron for themselves.

LEFT: examining rock carvings at Tanum, Bohuslän.
RIGHT: Viking runestone at Täby, near Stockholm, bearing the Christian hallmark, c.11th century.

One of the earliest chroniclers to mention these northern tribes was the Roman historian Tacitus, who visited northern Europe during the 1st century AD. He wrote briefly of a people who appear to be from Scandinavia called *fenni*, but his successor Procopius gave the more evocative description of the people of Thule (Scandinavia) as skiing hunters.

Tales and tombs

The pace of history began to pick up about AD 500, when the fertile valley surrounding Lake Mälaren grew into a centre of power. This was the start of unending minor wars and feuds,

the site of Sweden's last heathen temple. The *Ynglingatal*, a 10th-century Norse poem about 6th-century Uppsala, claimed that these grave mounds belonged to three members of the ruling family, Aun, Egils and Adils. Another member of the same ruling family, Ottar, was killed at Vendel, north of Uppsala, which has a mound known as Ottar's Mound.

More came to light about the society of these times when excavation of the mounds began in the 19th century. Archaeologists unearthed not only the burned remains of humans and animals but also precious objects and utensils, which indicate an ordered way of life in

a tradition inherited by the later Swedish nobility, as the Svea tribe began the struggle to supremacy over its neighbours. The Svea tribe gave its name to Sweden or *Sverige* (the Realm of the Sveas) and its base was Uppland (then called *Svitiod*), centred on Old Uppsala.

The contemporary Anglo-Saxon *Beowulf* saga, more historical fiction than history, describes with awe the exploits of several Swedish "kings", or tribal chieftains. According to *Beowulf*, they fought in great horned or winged helmets, slashing at one another with jewelled longswords and spears. The impressive burial mounds of three of these kings are now major tourist attractions at Old Uppsala, near

Uppsala in the 6th century. What is certain is that, by the beginning of the early Viking era, the militant Sveas had expanded into territory to the west and south, covered by the present-day provinces of Västmanland and Södermanland. They were the power in the land.

The marauders

During the next 500 or 600 years, the Scandinavians entered the European theatre in the role of marauders. Their first recorded appearance was in the late-8th century at the rich abbey of Lindisfarne on the northeast coast of England. It was attacked, plundered and burned by "vicious barbarians from Outer Tule. So primitive they are, they spared not the library from the torch nor the timid monks from the sword." By the year 1000 the Norsemen had learned the value of books in barter and destroyed no more libraries.

Such lamenting reports of the destruction of one of European civilisation's major centres of book illumination and learning were not taken seriously by the court of Charlemagne. The idea of unexpected, pillaging savages was preposterous – at first. They soon learned their error for, within a few years, Charlemagne was defending the long coastline of civilisation against the repeated incursions of the Norse.

Overpopulation at home seems to have been the primary reason for the sudden appearance of the Vikings, a name derived from the Nordic word for bay or shallow inlet. At first they were simply summer raiders but, as this became more organised and part of the way of life, superior ship-building technology, superb seamanship, and a lack of respect for the European Continent's established moral code were the reasons for their success in ravaging Europe.

Their methods of construction allowed their longships to withstand heavy seas by twisting through surging waves, and the ship's shallow draught made it possible to beach the craft in extremely shallow waters for surprise attacks on unsuspecting settlements. The Viking strategy depended heavily on hit-and-run tactics, but later many Vikings came to trade and settle in the lands they had terrorised.

Sailing east

Swedish Vikings directed their longboats eastwards across the Baltic, first to the Baltic coasts, then deep into present day Russia along the rivers Volga and Dnieper. The rivers, and short portages across flat lands, in slow stages at last brought the Swedes to Constantinople, or as they called it, Miklagård – the big city. The attraction of the east was tremendous.

The Swedes developed trade with the Byzantine empire and the Arab domains, and set up short-lived principalities in Russia such as Rurik at Novgorod. Many Norsemen remained

LEFT: ruined fort on the island of Björkö, near Stockholm, the site of Sweden's first "city", Birka.
RIGHT: an 11th-century bronze fertility god.

> **INVASION THREAT**
>
> In the 9th century the standard prayer of the English included the plea, "Protect us, Oh Lord, from the wrath of the Norsemen."

in Byzantium as an elite imperial guard, described by an Arab chronicler as "huge mustachioed angels, of evil disposition and smell."

Throughout Sweden, but especially in Skåne, Gotland, Öland and Uppland, these proud travellers raised large flat stones inscribed with serpents, legends and inscriptions which give insights into Viking society. "Commemorating Wulf and Alderik who died fighting out east in the big City. This stone was raised by their mother, Bodil."

The profitable trade in furs, honey and amber

in the east led to the founding of Kiev by Swedes around AD 900. The Swedes brought back from the Black Sea and Constantinople gold, silver, luxury cloths, and trinkets such as the small gilt bronze Buddha found at the excavations of the early town of Birka, on Björkö.

This island on Lake Mälaren (the lake where Stockholm now lies) was the site of Sweden's first "city" – a crowded, dirty but rich trading centre, with an interest in luxury items and precious metals. At Birka coins from countries as far away as Arabia and Ireland have been found, a tribute to the skilled seamanship, ruthlessness and endurance of these Norse trading-warriors (*see pages 24–5*). ❑

SWEDEN'S MARAUDING MERCHANTS

The legacy of the Vikings isn't all murder and mayhem. Excavations on the island of Björkö have revealed evidence of a rich trading culture

In June 793, the peaceful prosperity of 8th-century Europe was shattered by the arrival of a new menace from the sea. The image of the bloodthirsty Viking plundering all in his path is one that was to haunt medieval Europe for the next 300 years. But archaeological finds have forced us to re-evaluate the image of the rampaging Viking: none more so than the discoveries at Birka – Sweden's first Viking town, on the island of Björkö west of Stockholm.

The finds at Birka illuminate the elaborate trading networks of the Viking Age, pointing to a society of traders, merchants and skilled craftsmen. The coins, silks, beads, pottery, glass and jewellery found in the graves that surrounded the town reveal connections with countries as far afield as the Byzantine Empire and China.

For nearly 200 years Birka flourished as the northernmost mercantile centre in Europe. More than 700 people are thought to have lived in the town, which was a major marketplace for the people around Lake Mälaren. No one knows why Birka was abandoned. The emergence of trading towns such as Sigtuna is thought to be behind its demise. A thousand years on Birka has risen again, this time as part of Sweden's cultural landscape, with its own museum and a place on UNESCO's list of World Heritage sites.

▷ WARRIOR TRADERS
The Vikings opened up new lands for settlement and established trade routes that were to shape history.

▷ BURIED TREASURE
Vikings were buried with their possessions, the quantity and quality of which, such as this pendant, were a reflection of their status in life.

△ VIKING JEWELS
This brooch of gilt bronze was found in the grave of a wealthy woman. Chains of beads were often hung between the brooches.

△ GRAVE OBJECTS
Tools were among the items unearthed by archaeologist Björn Ambrosiani between 1990 and 1995.

▽ HAIR STYLING
Antlers of elk and deer provided Birka's comb-makers with raw material. Most of the excavated graves contained combs.

THE APOSTLE OF THE NORTH

Sweden was, by the 9th century, one of the last outposts of paganism in Europe. Missionaries feared the Vikings, while in Birka the people attributed their own success to their pagan gods, and so they saw no reason at all to renounce them.

The arrival from Germany of the Benedictine monk, Ansgar, in AD 830 transformed Birka into a spiritual battleground, as paganism and Christianity vied for souls. Ansgar was a man of burning faith whose tireless work to bring Christianity to Scandinavia eventually earned him a sainthood.

He was welcomed in Birka, probably because the people believed it would help to promote trade with the Christian continent. However, Birka was never evangelised. Christianity would not defeat the pagan gods for another 250 years. Its advent brought the Viking Age to an end, for the new Christian god refused to tolerate rival divinities.

▽ **FAR-FLUNG FINDS**
A bishop's crosier from Ireland is proof of Birka's long-distance trade with south and west Europe.

△ **MODEL TOWNSHIP**
A large model town can be seen at the Museum of National Antiquities (*see page 182*), along with many of the finds from the excavated graves.

▷ **FOREIGN CURRENCY**
Danish, Frankish and Arabic coins have been found on site, but no coins were ever minted by the Birka kings, despite their prosperity.

CHRISTIANITY AND THE MIDDLE AGES

By the 14th century Sweden had emerged from the Dark Ages and formed a turbulent alliance with its neighbours

Once the Vikings had drawn Europe's attention to Scandinavia, the continent could not leave its northern neighbour alone. The first purpose was to spread the Gospel, in the pious hope that Christianity might change the Viking temperament.

In the 9th century, the first notable Christian missionary arrived. He was Ansgar, who landed on Björkö in Mälaren. Here he founded a church and converted some islanders before returning to Germany as Bishop of Hamburg. Sweden's conversion was only skin-deep and in AD 936 another missionary, Bishop Unni of Hamburg, was murdered in Birka. Sweden had to wait until the second half of the 11th century for true conversion.

Pagan rituals

The clerical scholar Adam of Bremen left a picture of Norse paganism when he included Scandinavia in his history of his own bishopric. The temple at Uppsala, Adam wrote, was the very heart of paganism. Here was a structure covered in scales and wreathed with serpents and dragon heads. A heavy golden chain girt the heathen temple to contain the evil of the idols Thor, Odin and Frej. Even more fearsome was the sacred grove alongside the temple, its branches hung with the sacrificial remains, "seven males of every species from man to the lowly cat."

By the middle of the 12th century, paganism was officially out of fashion. King Erik Jedvarsson, later Saint Erik, the patron saint of Sweden, had been converted and with "sword and word" saw to it that his subjects bowed to the word of the Lord.

While the Christian church struggled for souls, the kingly families of Erik and Sverker struggled for temporal power. From this time, Sweden began to emerge gradually as a coun-

try separate from Norway and Denmark and to turn its attention to the idea of conquest. Swedes living along the Baltic had long had trading and raiding links with the east Baltic coasts, but now they began a serious colonisa-

tion of Finland. This led to the eventual absorption of that country almost as part of Sweden itself, a state that lasted for some 800 years.

The German centuries

German traders had become a familiar part of life on the small island that became Stockholm at the mouth of Lake Mälaren. But the 13th century brought the turn of the German Hanseatic trading cities, grouped under Lübeck, eager to get a foot into the Swedish door.

The German merchants conquered through commerce and eventually gained almost total control of Swedish foreign trade and its domestic economy and politics. Many new towns

---

LEFT: the god, Thor, as seen by early Scandinavians.
RIGHT: Christian artefact, 10th-century silver crucifix.

grew up to accommodate the lively commercial activity instigated by the Hansa and the German traders lived alongside their Swedish neighbours. They were particularly strong on the Swedish island of Gotland where they left medieval walls and part of their trading city.

During the next few centuries Germany dominated the Swedish world. German manners were *comme il faut*, German architecture was fashionable. Even the Swedish language assimilated many of its pre-

CIVIL RIGHTS

Sweden's system of rights for the ordinary person was brought to England by the Vikings. It was later adopted in the United States in the form of "bylaws", from the Norse for "village ordinances".

ers", and were descendants of the early chiefs. Now, true nobles began to make their appearance. Many of these families still exist, such as the once royal Bondes (meaning Farmer), Svinhuvuds (Pigheads), Natt och Dag (Night and Day), and Bjelke (Beam). Feuds were endemic and ballads and chronicles record the bravery and the treachery of these struggling families.

By the 14th century, the shadows of the Dark Ages had lifted. Monasteries and convents flourished in Sweden and

sent linguistic forms from the Platdeutsch of the Hanseatic traders.

The concentration of interests on Stockholm, the country's political centre, led to the advent of a noble class in Sweden. As early as 1280, King Magnus Ladulås had introduced a form of European feudalism. To some extent, this countered the old Viking democracy, where the chief was but first among equals, but the ordinary farmers held tightly to their ancient rights and privileges. These verbal rights were written down during this period to form Europe's oldest body of written law.

Up to this point, the important families of the country were known familiarly as "big farm-

brought medical knowledge where had previously been only home remedies. Saint Birgitta founded her order of Catholic nuns and the convent of Vadstena. Her mystical *Revelations*, often on political and religious themes, were Sweden's first major contribution to European thought. Guided by one revelation, she eventually went to Rome, where she worked to establish her order. She was canonised in 1391.

A new union

By this time, Sweden and the rest of Scandinavia had acquired enough sophistication to object to the heavy political and economic control of the Hansa and, in 1397, the three countries formed the Union of Kalmar. It involved an undertaking that all Scandinavia should have one and the same monarch, Queen Margareta of Denmark.

Margareta's new, loose-knit domain was enormous and not easily ruled. But she maintained the union, especially at times when external threats were serious. Her greatest success was in using the danger of such incursions to strip the Hansa of some of its power.

The Miners' revolt

As the most advanced of the three Scandinavian states, Denmark dominated the Kalmar alliance, but the union was marked by conflict between the monarch on the one hand and the high nobility and intermittently rebellious burghers and peasants on the other.

In 1434, intolerable Danish tax demands coupled with general social anxieties led to a revolt against Margareta's successor, Erik of Pomerania, by Sweden's first great national hero, Engelbrekt Engelbrektsson. A minor noble, he raised the peasants and miners from his native Dalarna, and stormed towards Stockholm. There, it is said, Engelbrekt forced the council to support him by taking one member, a bishop, by his collar and threatening to throw him out of the castle window.

Despite his successes, Engelbrekt was murdered by Magnus Bengtsson Natt och Dag, the son of one of his enemies, but his legend lived on. The political might of ordinary people had become evident.

King Erik was deposed but nationalism spread. The struggle continued between powerful families who were for or against the union. The Hanseatic League conspired, more often than not now with the complicity of the Swedes, and the Danes threatened.

Victory over the Danes

Against this background, another national hero emerged. Sten Sture changed Sweden's history, and yet he was not of royal birth. Through his leadership in 1471 at the Battle of Brunkeburg just outside Stockholm, Sture gained a decisive victory over the Danes. Although the Kalmar Union still had nearly 50 years to run, this fierce victory – and later Sten

Sture's actions as statesman rather than soldier – saved Sweden from being reabsorbed completely into the northern union.

First parliament

By this time Sweden had a national assembly (the Riksdag) of four estates – nobles, clergy, burghers and peasants – the first step towards parliamentary government. Swedish nationalism and a renewed alliance with the Hansa, as well as a struggle emerging between church and state power, led to more Danish attacks.

In the early 16th century, the Riksdag voted to burn the fortress of the Archibishop of

Sweden, a pro-Dane, Gustav Trolle. In the event, Trolle was merely imprisoned.

In 1520 the Papal Court excommunicated Sten Sture the Younger for this act and Kristian II had his justification for invading again. In the hope of saving their city, the burghers of Stockholm opened the gates, and Kristian retaliated with a feast in the palace where he gathered together Sweden's leading nobles.

On the pretext that the Papal excommunication released him from any promises of safe conduct, Kristian chopped off the heads of 82 of Sweden's finest and of many innocent bystanders, too. This "Stockholm Bloodbath" was the catalyst that raised the nation. ❑

LEFT: an early Swedish wall hanging.
RIGHT: 12th-century bronze warrior's head, Sigtuna.

FOUNDER OF A DYNASTY

Gustav Vasa, the first of the Vasa monarchs, ousted the Danes, introduced the Lutheran Reformation and gave Sweden its national identity

Young Gustav Eriksson Vasa (1496–1560) was fortunate to escape the Stockholm Bloodbath in which his father, two uncles and a brother-in-law were killed. He was in Denmark at the time, held hostage by King Kristian, who had been trying to force talks between Sweden and Denmark. By the time

administration and the army. Nothing escaped his attention. He ran Sweden as though it were his family estates and set the country on the road from the Middle Ages to a national state. Today, Gustav Vasa could have been an innovative manager or enlightened landowner.

Gustav Vasa's reign merely coincided with

Kristian was killing his kin, however, this resourceful young man had already escaped from Denmark, slipped into Sweden to rouse the countryside, spurred on by news of what had happened in Stockholm.

After hard fighting, Gustav Vasa subdued Kristian and the Danes, who retreated south, killing and burning as they went. In 1523, a grateful nation invited Gustav to take the Swedish throne.

Though Gustav still had many further struggles against dissident factions in his own country, centred on the Sture family, he set about enhancing the power of the king and reorganising the government, the monetary system, the

the Swedish Reformation, and did not bring it about, but he was quick to make use of it. His struggle against the Danes was also a struggle against the Roman Catholic Archbishop Gustav Trolle, whose accusations of heresy had led to the Bloodbath.

Trolle had fled into exile at Gustav Vasa's victory and the Pope refused to consecrate a successor, but the bishops were still unruly and it suited Gustav to support the Reformation. Though he was not particularly religious, like Henry VIII of England, Gustav needed money and less interference from Rome.

His success against the Danes cost money, however, as did his internal struggle against rival factions, which continued throughout his reign, and later foreign campaigns. He was also in debt to the Lübeckers, who had continued to involve themselves in Swedish affairs by providing funds to fight Kristian.

In his great need, the wily young king was not slow to see the rich pickings in the churches and monasteries. He confiscated Roman Catholic property and prepared the ground for a state Lutheran religion.

An enlightened ruler

Gustav's achievements were remarkable and long-reaching. He not only succeeded in bring-

great orator, he had charm, he was not uncultured, and he both loved and played music. He was also a successful trader, who became the country's richest man, with treasure hoards in Gripsholm and Stockholm castles. But his greatest strengths were his skills as organiser and manager, his ability to give Sweden a sense of nationhood.

When he died in 1560, Gustav Vasa had welded his country together, made it strong and had not neglected his duty to the dynasty. In three marriages he produced 11 children, and thus secured the Vasa rule for more than a century ahead. ❑

ing about the supremacy of state over church in order to curb the power of the nobles, he also strengthened the monarchy by making it hereditary. When he recalled the Riksdag in 1544, it was to reform it, and to plan what became a form of national military service, to make Sweden the first European country to have a standing peacetime army.

Though he curbed some traditional Swedish liberties and ruled firmly, Gustav Vasa was more than a straightforward autocrat. He was a

FAR LEFT: an early portrait of Gustav Vasa.
LEFT: Gustav Vasa's statue at Mora, Dalarna.
ABOVE: Vadstena Castle, one of many built by Vasa.

OLAUS PETRI

Olaus Petri was one of Gustav Vasa's closest advisors. A man of humble birth, he was known as the Father of the Reformation in Sweden, and the country's first "modern" writer. He translated the New Testament into Swedish and was a fearless preacher of Lutheran doctrines, He was chancellor to Gustav for two years. Inevitably, the two strong characters quarrelled, and in 1540 Petri was sentenced to death for alleged complicity in a plot against his master. In fact, his only crime was in refusing to divulge a secret of the confessional. Gustav reprieved his old counsellor, who then produced his most famous work, *A Swedish Chronicle*, a history of Sweden up to 1520.

A GREAT EUROPEAN POWER

The 16th and 17th centuries were dominated by two military geniuses, Gustav II Adolf and Karl XII, whose conquests shaped the nation

After the death of Gustav Vasa, his eldest son Erik (XIV) succeeded him according to the decision by the Riksdag in 1544. Erik's brothers, Johan and Karl, supported him in the beginning. But, after he had married a simple guard's daughter and even murdered two noblemen in a burst of insanity, they turned against him and a civil war broke out. Erik was imprisoned and Johan III succeeded him.

Under the Vasa prosperity, Sweden grew in ways other than conquest. The University of Uppsala, which had been founded in 1477, flourished. The Vasas encouraged immigration by Belgian Walloons, Scots and Germans, who were knowledgeable in the working of iron into swords and cannons. Sweden, fortunately, was abundantly endowed with deposits of pure iron and copper.

With weapons and a standing army, Sweden had become a military power. The Vasa sons now looked for expansion in trade and territory in what became the Seven Years War of the North, after which Denmark accepted the *status quo* and renounced claims to the independent state of Sweden.

Family infighting

Johan had married the daughter of King Sigismund I of Poland and, on Stefan Bathory's death in 1586, Johan's son, Sigismund, was elected King of Poland. When Johan died in 1592, Sigismund tried to turn Sweden into a Roman Catholic country. His uncle, Karl, Gustav Vasa's youngest son, opposed this strongly and, at a meeting in Uppsala in 1593, it was decided that only if Sigismund accepted the Lutheran state religion would he remain as King of Sweden.

But Karl's ambitions aimed higher than being a duke and a subject of his nephew Sigismund. Once again, Sweden was involved in a bitter civil war. Sigismund left for Poland, but he never renounced his claims to the Swedish throne – an attitude which was to affect Sweden's relations with Poland and be the cause of a war that would last long into the 1600s. The tests of strength continued, but Karl asserted his authority with cruel force and curbed the nobles' power by executions and banishments.

Military leader

With the accession to the throne in 1611 of Karl's son, Gustav II Adolf, Sweden acquired a military genius. Gustav Adolf was intelligent, his education was thorough and, having a German mother, he spoke both German and Swedish. He had all the strength, determination and enthusiasm of his celebrated grandfather, Gustav Vasa. One difference was Gustav Adolf's belief in the Lutheran faith. His piety induced him to hold regular prayers for his army in the field.

Gustav Adolf was backed by an equally robust chancellor, Axel Oxenstierna. The two believed that Sweden was circled by enemies

LEFT: Swedish monarchs of the 16th–19th centuries, from Gustav Vasa to Oskar II.
RIGHT: Gustav II Adolf's statue in central Göteborg.

who thought themselves stronger and that its friends didn't understand Sweden's problems.

In the War of Kalmar, which Gustav Adolf fought at the beginning of his reign, the Danes captured the only port to the west, Älvsborg. To regain this vital port, Sweden had to pay the enormous ransom of 1 million Riksdaler. Even the king himself contributed by melting down some of his plate.

Gustav Adolf was luckier, however, in the war against Russia, and in the Peace of

SPOILS OF WAR

Gustav II Adolf, the "Lion of the North", sent back treasures from Europe that are now to be found generously spread throughout Sweden's palaces.

Stolbova, reached in 1617, Sweden was left in sole control of the Gulf of Finland.

Wider conflict

The start of the Thirty Years' War in 1618 involved Sweden in the wider conflict. Over the next years, Gustav Adolf's army drove far into Europe and south to the rich trading area of the Vistula. After the defeat of Sigismund at Mewe, it marched into Poland, where Gustav Adolf defeated the Polish cavalry at Dirschau, to give Sweden a strong presence in Europe.

After these successes, Gustav Adolf spent several less satisfying years of intense diplomacy with Denmark. He also tried to bring together the Scandinavian countries and the participants in the Thirty Years' War.

In 1630, the king sailed again to Pomerania on what was to be his last campaign. Gustav Adolf had the satisfaction of knowing that he had brought low the power and prestige of his Danish rival, Christian IV, and had the support of his Riksdag and people.

Yet the sense of foreboding was strong in his last speech to the Riksdag, almost as though he knew his fate.

The Swedes marched firmly across Europe and crossed the Elbe. The decisive battle of this year was Breitenfeld which lasted five hours, with the Imperial cavalry charging and charging again. By sunset, it was a clear victory for Gustav Adolf and his veterans, thanks to the new military tactics he had perfected with his well-trained army.

Gustav Adolf's aim was to unite all the Protestant countries and his diplomacy-on-the-march continued until just before the final battle, at Lützen, near Leipzig. The November day was misty as Gustav Adolf's Swedish and Finnish troops fought the Catholic Imperialist army. Few saw Gustav Adolf's death because the mist had again swirled low. He was shot three times and died immediately. As rumours of his death whispered along the lines, the Småland companies almost wavered until Gustav Adolf's chaplain, Fabricus, began to sing the hymn "Sustain Us By Thy Mighty Word". Inspired to vengeance, the Swedes won a battle so fierce that one-third of the army fell alongside its king.

Gustav II Adolf was Sweden's most successful military leader. He made Sweden a great power, captured huge territories in the Baltic, the east, and south as far as Poland. He also made his country for the first time more powerful than Denmark. His military innovations, advanced techniques and trained army won battle after battle but they did not stop the fatal bullet at Lützen in 1632.

Infant heiress

When Gustav Adolf fell, his daughter Kristina, whose name figures in many Swedish towns and institutions, was only six years old. But she had the advantage of her father's chancellor, Axel Oxenstierna, who became Regent during her minority. Oxenstierna continued the king's policies at home and overseas. The formidable army in Europe subdued more German and Slavic domains and, by 1645, Denmark had ceded to Sweden some of the provinces in south Sweden which had traditionally been part of Denmark.

Oxenstierna and the foremost nobility soared high in the see-saw of power between throne and council by introducing a new constitution which placed effective power in the hands of the nobles.

When she came of age, Queen Kristina presided over a shining baroque court filled

in Rome she announced her conversion. And so the daughter of one the great champions of the Protestant faith renounced it. As a final irony, with her to Rome she took many of the same treasures her father had plundered from the Catholic rulers of Europe.

Continued greatness

Although Kristina had gone, Sweden's power continued to grow. In 1658, Sweden astounded Denmark by a surprise attack, partly due to Karl X Gustav's luck. The winter of 1657–58 was one of the coldest in a century and froze the sea between Sweden and Denmark, and

with massive silver furnishings and dark intrigues. She had been well educated and gathered around her the brilliant young minds of the age. But, by now, the relationship between Kristina and her elderly chancellor was not sympathetic and the country stagnated.

In one of history's unexplained decisions, she decided to abdicate, probably because she was drawn to the Roman Catholic faith. After she stepped down in 1654, she travelled through Europe and shocked her former subjects when

LEFT: the battle of Lützen (1632), at which the great military leader Gustav II Adolf was fatally wounded.
ABOVE: Skansen Kronan, Gustav II's fort at Göteborg.

between Denmark's first and second main islands. Though two squadrons of horses and riders fell through the ice, an army of 1,500 cavalry and 3,500 foot soldiers came safely across and overran the island of Fyn almost before the Danes knew what was happening. The Treaty of Roskilde gave Sweden all the provinces in the south Swedish mainland which Denmark had traditionally ruled.

The last decades of the 17th century saw the tentative start of an Age of Enlightenment. This came to maturity in the 18th century, as it did in many parts of Europe, as a time of scientific discovery, a flowering of artistic talent, and of freedom of thought and expression. One of its first exponents was Olof Rudbeck. From Uppsala, he became Sweden's first internationally recognised genius, contributing significantly to medical and scientific advancement, with discoveries such as the human lymphatic system.

But, as the 17th century ended, with the country still at the height of its political rather than intellectual powers, Sweden produced its greatest romantic warrior king, Karl XII. Every European country has its royal figure of romance and how much Karl's reputation derived from

WHO KILLED KARL?

Swedes still argue about whether it was a Norwegian bullet or one from the gun of a disaffected Swedish soldier which killed the romantic warrior king, Karl XII, in 1718.

the fact that, of his 21 years as monarch, he spent 18 away at the wars is not clear. To many, he is Sweden's greatest king – certainly to those of a romantic and nationalist temperament.

The warrior king

All Karl XII's successes and failures were inextricably mixed with European issues, the struggle between Protestant and Catholic, and the race for trade and sea routes. His strong personality brooked little opposition and, three years after he came to the throne as a minor, he first showed his military skills by landing on the nearest main Danish island of Sjaelland. This led to an early peace treaty and left Karl

free to turn to the east. Meanwhile, Tsar Peter of Russia had declared war on Sweden and Karl hurried through Estonia to relieve Narva. Soon Poland was involved in the war, and Karl's victorious army swept through Poland, taking Warsaw and Krakow, as well as Danzig. By 1705 Poland had signed an alliance with Sweden against the Russians.

In his mission to save Europe from the Russian bear, over the next few years Karl rampaged over Germany and Russia. However, in 1709, at one of the most important battles of the 18th century, the Swedes met their match. Everything conspired against the Swedish army. Karl had already been wounded in the foot and had to command from a litter. At the end of a day of victory and defeat, the Swedes retreated to Perevolotjna, where the king was at last persuaded to cross into Turkey.

From his distant "court" in Turkey, the frustrated Karl attempted to guide his realm and, at times, almost persuaded the Turks to go to war against Russia. By 1714, Karl realised that he must return to Sweden, and he made a journey of more than 1,300 miles by horseback across Europe to Stralsund in Germany. That he did the journey in 15 days with just two companions says much for the king's determination and endurance.

Only Stralsund and Wismar remained of the vast Swedish European Empire. At Stralsund, Karl was still not safe from the alliance which had formed against him, and eventually he fled secretly to Sweden. Fifteen years after his first triumphs, Karl devised plan after plan to defeat his traditional enemies, the Danes. In 1718, he invaded southern Norway to besiege the border fortress of Fredriksten. On 30 November, he went out to inspect his troops, when a bullet struck his skull and he died instantly.

Next to Gustav II Adolf, Karl was undoubtedly Sweden's greatest military genius. But while the former left Sweden powerful, Karl left the country divested of all its conquests except Finland. From the moment the fatal bullet found its target, Sweden ceased to be a great fighting power. ❏

LEFT: Queen Kristina (by David Beck, 1650) presided over a glittering court before abdicating.
RIGHT: Karl XII, Sweden's most romantic warrior king.

THE AGE OF FREEDOM

Great advancements in science and the fine arts, under the patronage of enlightened monarchs, characterised life in the 18th century

The death of Karl XII in 1718 and the end of long exhausting wars left Sweden shrunk in size, weak, and forced to negotiate from an inferior position. The council and Riksdag were tired of absolute monarchs and warfare. The lack of an obvious heir provided their opportunity. In 1719 the Riksdag introduced a constitution which again curbed the royal prerogative and stated that the monarch was obliged to endorse all laws passed by the Riksdag. So began the "Age of Freedom".

At first the crown went to Ulrika Eleonora, the dead king's sister, whose husband, Fredrik of Hesse, was close enough to the army to make a successful bid for the throne on behalf of his wife. Under the new constitution her powers were curbed and the Riksdag refused to recognise her husband as king. Her short reign was marked by a parliament determined to assert itself and, after a tense year, she stepped aside in 1720, enabling her husband to take over as Fredrik I.

He, too, was threatened by rival claimants to the throne and, over the years, Sweden's cautious path was plotted by the Finnish politician Arvid Horn, who trod a delicate diplomatic road to compensate for Sweden's weakness. When Fredrik died in 1751, the Swedes had the satisfaction of knowing that the successful claimant, Adolf Fredrik, had at least a few drops of Vasa blood.

As democracy began to gain a foothold, the estates of the Riksdag took on the job of nominating the members of the council and, though its own proceedings were still a well-guarded secret, the Riksdag passed a Freedom of the Press Act in 1766, the world's first attempt at press freedom which is still in force today.

In political terms, this era was dominated by two factions, the Hats (mercantile nobles or Whigs) and the Caps (liberal commoners and urban traders similar to Tories). In diplomatic

terms, Sweden was lucky in having a leader whose cautious temperament suited the age. During the 1720s and 1730s, Arvid Horn continued to steer Sweden through dangerous foreign shoals. Despite minor alarms and Russian inroads and the swings in the allegiances of the Caps and Hats to foreign powers, he con-

trived to keep an insecure peace with the old enemy, Denmark, as well as Russia and Prussia.

Trading opportunities

In 1718 the wars of Karl XII had killed not only the king but also many of the strongest young men in Sweden and Finland. Bad harvests added to the economic problems. Although Sweden remained primarily an agricultural country until late in the 19th century, the Age of Freedom saw the start of a transformation into a trading nation.

The government encouraged mining of iron in the many small works, and copper from the great mine of Falun. Hand manufacturing of

LEFT: the botanist, Carl von Linné (Linnaeus), in Sami dress after his expedition to Lapland in 1732.
RIGHT: King Gustav III, patron of drama and fine arts.

many kinds also began. Swedish ships carried Swedish goods all over Europe and further, through companies such as the new Swedish East India Company, which lasted into the next century. The ships carried iron and returned with luxury items such as silk and provided young Swedes with an adventurous challenge.

Scientific pioneers

Away from these affairs of politics, diplomacy and trade, the Age of Freedom was also an Age of Science which produced a royal flush of

> **FEELING THE HEAT**
>
> In 1742 Anders Celsius invented the Celsius scale of temperature and the 100-degree thermometer. He set up Sweden's astronomical observatory at Uppsala.

analysis, Wallerius and Cronstedt and, most famous of all, C.W. Scheele, the first man to analyse air as oxygen and nitrogen.

This outpouring of science and scientists, many of whom worked closely together, led to formal co-operation in 1739 when the Swedish Academy of Science was opened in Stockholm, with Linnaeus as one of its founders. Sweden began to gain prestige abroad, and many botanical pilgrims came to Linnaeus's garden in Uppsala.

At home, scientists used their talents to

original thinkers. High among them was Emanuel Swedenborg, a scientist who edited the first Swedish scientific journal but is also known for his studies on the human brain and his religious writing. Nils Rosén was one of the earliest to study and practise paediatrics. He was also an anatomist and a pioneer of inoculation against diseases.

Carl von Linné (Linnaeus), a student of the first great scientist, Olof Rudbeck, developed his theories that plants, like animals, reproduced sexually. It became the basis for his great work *Species Plantarium*, which classified 8,000 plants. Sweden also produced good chemists: Bergman, the founder of chemical

advise the new industrialists and the farmers – practical scientific work that laid a foundation for prosperity and future study. Although it continued into the reign of Gustav III, it was inevitable that such a flood could not continue at the same volume indefinitely. In any case, Gustav III did not encourage freedom but another form of enlightenment. His sphere of interest was the arts and the encouragement of a national Swedish culture.

Autocracy returns

During Gustav III's reign, the Age of Freedom gradually faded, though study of science and economics continued. He was influenced by his mother, Louisa Ulrika, sister of Frederick the Great of Prussia, a strong-minded woman who had spent her life in political schemes and in grooming her son for the monarchy. At the age of 25, Gustav III started out as a golden figure. He was proud of being the first Swedish born king since Karl XII, and was well educated for his role. He loved France and the theatre, where he both wrote and acted, and his sense of drama loomed large throughout his 21-year reign.

In the Riksdag, the Caps were supreme, moved by common cause against the Hats, who represented the nobility. Gustav III was beset by threats from Russia and Prussia; in the countryside, two bad harvests had raised political discontent. In 1772, the king organised a bloodless *coup d'état* that condemned the aristocracy and demanded a return to the ancient constitution, but, essentially, gave him absolute power.

War and peace

Like his predecessors, Gustav did not escape conflict with Russia. In 1788, he declared war, partly in the hope that external strife would allay the unrest caused by his growing despotism, partly to make the most of Russia's pre-occupation with a Turkish war. At first, Gustav succeeded in pushing far into Finland but the support of his Finnish officers could not be guaranteed and a group of more than 100, the Anjala Confederation, made contact with the Empress Catherine in an attempt to restore the Finnish boundaries of 1721. When a Danish-Norwegian force invaded near Göteborg, Gustav returned to Sweden and a surprising naval victory at Svensksund, when the Swedish fleet sank 50 Russian ships, which led to peace and, against all the odds, left Sweden with its reduced territory intact.

A king of many talents

This unlikely victory did not make Gustav III a notable warrior, and his fame lies not in his political or military skill. He is remembered for the upsurge he encouraged in all the fine arts. Though the king loved France, he was a patriot who founded Swedish drama when he built Stockholm's Dramatic Theatre, replaced the French actors in his mother's theatre at Drott-

ningholm, and hired Swedish actors and writers to develop a native theatre.

The most important of the arts in the Golden Age was opera and, in 1782, Gustav opened the magnificent Royal Opera House alongside Strömmen, where Lake Mälaren pours into the beginnings of the sea. Gustav commissioned the first opera in Swedish at the Dramatic Theatre, followed three years later by *Thetis and Peleus*, which he planned, and staged six major tragedies and other plays, in four of which the king himself took part.

Gustav's old tutor Olof Dalin was one of the earliest of this age of writers with his popular

LEFT: Gustav III's court at Drottningholm Palace.
RIGHT: a performance at Drottningholm Court Theatre, founded in 1766 and still in use today.

critical essays in *Then Swänska Argus* (The Swedish Argus). Most unusual of the early writers was Carl Bellman, a troubadour who wrote poetry about the ordinary people of Stockholm's taverns and markets. Another in the same mould was Jakob Wallenberg, whose robust words were Bellman's prose equivalent, Carl Cristoffer Gjörwell described nature, and another distinguished poet, Johan Kellgren, helped Gustav to translate his plays into Swedish – the king

replaced them with more pliable commoners and the newly-great *parvenues*.

So much of Gustav's energies had been centred on his artistic protégés that he may have been lulled into a false sense of political security. As with so many Swedish monarchs, he had become more autocratic, and this was the era of the French Revolution.

The curtain on Gustav's drama came thundering down at an opera masquerade in 1792. A group of conspirators formed the plot and a disgruntled minor nobleman, Jakob Anckarström, shot Gustav III. The king died from an infection two weeks later. The Golden Age was at an end.

Afterthoughts

The Gustavian era trailed on for another 17 years under the young king, Gustav IV Adolf. His one real achievement was land reform which resulted in larger farming units. Earlier, the land had been split up in smaller units after every division of inheritance, thus leaving farmers with small and widely dispersed fields.

There was also one last gasp of territorialism. The Swedes had already fought an unsuccessful war over Pomerania, but this was the time of the Reign of Terror in France. Gustav Adolf embarked on a campaign against France which eventually found him in opposition to Russia. Russia immediately abrogated the Treaty of Armed Neutrality between the two which had left Finland as part of Sweden. In 1808, Tsar Alexander invaded Finland. For the Swedes, the campaign was disastrous. The Finns were disillusioned, and the Swedes forced to retreat to the Gulf of Bothnia.

Under the Treaty of Fredrikshamn, 1809, Sweden lost Finland for the last time. Gustav IV Adolf had already abdicated in April and, by 1810, Sweden had made peace with all its enemies. Old Duke Karl (who had once been regent to his nephew Gustav IV Adolf) resumed the role under a new constitution as Karl XIII. This allowed power to move gradually from king to Riksdag, the end of autocracy and the start of Sweden's democratic monarchy. ❏

knew French so well that he always wrote that language better than Swedish.

Many more poets and prose writers clustered round Gustav when he founded the Swedish Academy of Literature in 1786. Gustav also founded the Musical Academy in 1771, the Literary, Historical and Antiquities Academy, and the Academy of Art.

Gustavian life was rich in culture and the court went to the theatre and opera in silks and brocades. The middle classes also prospered in the atmosphere of expanding commercial contacts abroad. Only the old noble families felt neglected. Gustav III had manoeuvred them out of their traditional roles and political power and

LEFT: troubadour Carl Bellman by Tobias Sergel.
RIGHT: the Royal Dramatic Theatre, Stockholm.

A CENTURY OF CHANGE

Agricultural and political reform, and growing industrialisation, were not enough to deter 19th-century Swedes from emigrating in large numbers

Once the last faint link to the great Vasa dynasty was gone, Sweden elected the French Marshal Jean Baptiste Bernadotte as Crown Prince. By 1810, the new prince had converted to Lutheranism on his way north to Sweden, taking the name Karl Johan.

The election of a Frenchman as heir to the throne and the loss of Finland to Russia the year before turned Swedish eyes away from the east. As Sweden's interests and identity became more and more involved in Western Europe, foreign policy lost much of its preoccupation with its great eastern neighbour, though that did not preclude treaties with Russia.

At the time, many believed that a French marshal was bound to be no more than an emissary of Napoleon, but Karl Johan soon proved them wrong. A few weeks after his arrival, he took over state affairs when the elderly Karl XIII had a stroke, and later became the legal regent. The Swedish aristocracy remained hostile, but Karl Johan steered a quiet course through the tangle of European diplomacy. By 1812, Sweden had broken its long-held treaty of alliance with France and in 1813, after campaigning in Europe, Karl Johan allied Sweden with Russia and Prussia against his former leader, Napoleon. In return, Karl Johan was allowed to prise Norway from Denmark and unite it with Sweden.

An uneasy union

Athough Denmark agreed in the Peace of Kiel (1814) to the transfer of Norway, and received in exchange Swedish Pomerania (which was later "sold" to Prussia), the Norwegians were less than delighted at being handed over like a parcel and wrung many concessions from the Swedes before agreeing to a loose-knit union under the Swedish king. The new union struggled on for almost a century but had the effect of arousing Norwegian nationalism still further

---

LEFT: King Gustav IV Adolf, the agricultural reformer.
RIGHT: the former French Marshal Jean Baptiste Bernadotte became King Karl XIV Johan in 1818.

until, in 1905, Norway's separation into a sovereign state became inevitable.

Curbing the monarchy

In 1818, the former French marshal became King Karl XIV Johan under the 1809 constitution drawn up during the *coup d'état*, which

separated and rebalanced the powers of government and monarch. Though Karl XIV Johan was himself a conservative, a liberal opposition began to form during this period and expanded during the reigns of his son, Oskar I, and his grandson, Karl XV.

By 1862, Sweden had local self-government and four years later the reform of Parliament abolished the four estates which had formed the Riksdag for over 400 years and reduced it to two chambers.

From this time until 1974, the monarch's power was only marginally greater than it is today and history has become a chronicle of Riksdag and people. In 1971, the Riksdag

Exodus to America

At the end of the 19th century and the start of the 20th, more than 1 million Swedes – that is, one quarter of the population – left the country. So many came from the poor agricultural areas of Småland, Bohuslän and Värmland that some found themselves exchanging a Swedish village at home for a small American community in Minnesota or Wisconsin whose population also spoke only Swedish.

Their story is best summed up in the emigration trilogy of the 20th-century writer Vilhelm Moberg,

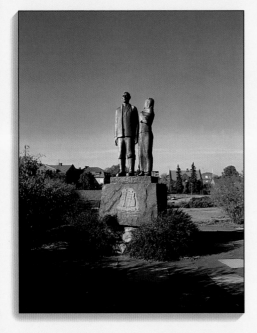

The Emigrants, Unto a New Land and *The Last Letter Home*. Moberg was a Smålander and he wrote about his own people who left the county's stony ground for a better future.

The motives of the Swedish emigrants were not simple. Unlike the Highland Scots, forced out in the Clearances by their own chiefs, who found sheep more profitable than people, the Swedes were not obliged to leave. But changes in agriculture from communal crofting villages to individual farms had split the old communities. Some moved first to the city, and then to America; others went direct to build a new life for themselves, encouraged particularly by the United States Homestead Act of 1862 which gave land almost free to

settlers who dared to travel west. To the United States, the Swedes took their virtues of hard work, thrift and honesty and, given the wide open opportunities of the New World, many made their fortunes. The new settlers sent back glowing accounts of their lives in America, and a great deal of money to support those left behind. These signs of prosperity encouraged others.

The movement became highly business-like. Shipping companies used agents to recruit new settlers and so provide passengers for their ships, and introduced a system of pre-paid tickets for emigrants to send home for a younger sibling. Some agents were rogues who preyed on the would-be settlers and disappeared with their money. But most emigrants prospered and added to the success of their adopted country.

In Sweden, this mass movement of people coincided with the start of the country's Industrial Revolution, just when the new mills were beginning to attract workers to towns and cities. Gradually, the administration realised that Sweden was in danger of losing too many of its youngest and most able citizens. In the early years of the 20th century, the Riksdag began to encourage people both to stay and to return, and compiled a survey of what had brought about the exodus. It revealed a sorry tale of oppression, poverty and discontent with life in Sweden.

Around one-fifth of all those who had emigrated came back to Sweden, many of them bringing their new riches to put money into the poorer areas. Swedes have always had a great love of their country and the opportunity to better themselves was the real lure of America. When they had done that, they could sometimes afford to come home.

In 1968, a group which included Vilhelm Moberg founded the Emigrant Institute – the House of the Emigrants – in Växjö in the centre of Småland. The largest European archive on emigration, it has 2,000 Swedish-American church and club record books and a library of 25,000 volumes.

More than anything, the emigrants helped those who remained behind through the realities revealed in the 1908 survey. These alerted the powerful to the ills and indignities of a system that was still far from egalitarian. Many of the sweeping democratic reforms of the 20th century owed much to the insights provided by those 19th-century Swedes who left for a better life. ❑

LEFT: the Emigrants' Statue at Karlshamn, Blekinge, a memorial to the many Swedes who went overseas.

became a single chamber and a new constitution in 1974 gave the present king, Carl XVI Gustaf, purely ceremonial functions.

Population doubles

The Napoleonic wars and the loss of Finland left Sweden low in morale and poorer than it had been for a century. The earlier growth in agriculture and trade stagnated and meant poverty and even starvation for the large numbers who earned a living from the land.

The greatest potential for disaster was the population explosion, which took numbers in Sweden from less than 2½ million in 1800 to

vented the sub-division of land into ever smaller, uneconomic portions, Maclean had already reformed his own estate into manageable lots and abolished some of the near-feudal duties of his peasants.

At first, this reform met with bitter hostility: if an independent farmer failed, he was usually reduced to the status of landless labourer. Maclean persisted and, when he died in 1816, most of his tenants were able to buy their farms. Maclean's example took a long time to filter through, but the greater productivity it brought did something to put food in the growing number of stomachs.

more than 5 million by 1900, due in part to a much reduced death rate.

Land reform

In the first decade of the new century Gustav IV Adolf had begun agricultural reform, but the real father of the Swedish agricultural revolution was an estate owner in the southern province of Skåne, Rutger Maclean. Some 20 years before Gustav Adolf introduced his land enclosure laws of 1803 and 1807, which pre-

ABOVE: Hagdahl's painting of emigrants leaving Göteborg in southern Sweden, lured by the promise of land and employment in America.

Transport revolution

By the second half of the century, Swedish transport, which had changed little since the days of Gustav Vasa, began to improve. Water had always provided trading and travelling routes and Baltzar von Platen's Göta Kanal, which opened in 1832, made full use of Lakes Vänern and Vättern to link east to west.

In 1853, the engineer Nils Ericsson took charge of railway building and began the construction of a part-state, part-private network. Rail transport encouraged the new forest industries to make use of Sweden's endless wooded acres for sawmilling and later wood-pulping, and, by the last decades of the 19th century, the

first glow of the Swedish inventive genius had begun to show in men like Gustav Pasch, who invented the safety match; Lars Magnus Ericsson, whose invention of the table telephone led to the start of the company which bears his name today; and Alfred Nobel, the inventor of dynamite. The economic stage was set for the country's swift industrial development in the next century.

The Riksdag introduced compulsory education and elementary schools in 1842 and better

FIRST TRADE UNION

The first Swedish union, started in 1874 for tobacco workers in Malmö, was founded by Danes, afraid that the unorganised Swedes might move into Denmark and lead to lower wages there.

medieval guilds of craftsmen in 1846 led to new associations which were the beginning of trade unions. The start of unions led to many inconclusive strikes. The first notable confrontation happened in 1879 in Sundsvall where the sawmill owners proposed a 15 to 20 percent reduction on already minimal wages. Oskar II sent his troops to face several thousand strikers and, though no violence occurred, many were alarmed at the official high-handedness. Workers began to realise that they must organise to win and militant socialist trade unionists were soon taking over these "liberal" unions.

Birth of the Social Democrats

Other popular movements included the formation of free churches and a crusading temperance league. The co-operative movement was very strong in 19th-century Sweden. Most far-reaching of all were the beginnings of what later became the Social Democratic Party. Its progenitor, August Palm, converted to socialism in Denmark; a radical and eccentric trouble-maker, he was expelled from Germany and imprisoned when he returned home. He started a radical newspaper and, from prison, launched the congress that founded the party.

But Palm was a wayward founder and a steadier guiding hand for the new party came from Hjalmar Branting. He had been an early associate of Palm but realised that the latter's disruptive influence would kill the infant party before it could walk.

In 1892, Branting succeeded in having Palm declared unfit to lead the party and took over himself. For a long time, he was the only party-affiliated Social Democrat in the Riksdag, but between 1895 and 1905 party membership multiplied and returned 13 to the Riksdag.

This new Social Democratic Party expressed the hopes and aspirations of an industrial population that exploded in size before and during the Industrial Revolution.

With the workers behind it, the party could scarcely fail and, more than anywhere else in Europe, the 20th century was to belong to the Swedish Social Democrats. ❏

education led to many popular movements. Frederika Bremer was one of the founders of the women's movement, and wrote many books, from her early *Sketches of Everyday Life* to her polemical novel *Hertha*, which put forward the women's cause. Late in the century another writer, Ellen Key, shocked polite society with her support for free love. In the country, where sex was considered natural and marriage after the conception or birth of a child was customary, these ideas were less startling.

Workers' rights

Growing industrialisation created a new social class of workers, and the abolition of the

LEFT: August Palm, founder of the Social Democrats.
RIGHT: King Carl XVI Gustaf and Queen Silvia.

THE INDUSTRIAL MIRACLE

Sweden's transformation from an impoverished rural economy to a leading
industrial nation was its most striking feature in the 20th century

Few nations have experienced such a rapid development as that of Sweden from 1900 onwards. Just a century ago Sweden was one of Europe's poorer countries with an economy entirely based on agriculture. Today it is a highly industrialised nation, which for many years topped the European gross domestic product league.

It was Sweden's natural resources, such as timber and iron ore, that formed the basis of its new-found wealth. Industries including paper and pulp, steel and engineering all relied on these resources and as demand grew for their products following the two world wars so exports increased. Sweden was also able to draw on skilled workers and an entrepreneurial spirit. New companies were born and Sweden's industrial output diversified.

Rapid expansion

At the beginning of the 20th century, Sweden experienced a mass emigration to the United States. There was not enough work to go around and farming could not feed a growing population. Those that remained turned to the cities for work. New companies such as the telecommunications firm LM Ericsson, the bearings company SKF, and the electrical experts ASEA were expanding as export orders grew and provided sought-after employment.

At the outbreak of World War I, Sweden had achieved the same per capita income as Great Britain. Although the country remained neutral during the war, it nevertheless experienced the post-war depression of the late 1920s and early 1930s. Industrial empires – including that of the famous match-king Krueger – crashed and brought unexpected poverty to the new middle-classes. Bankruptcies were followed by political unrest and strikes.

The election of the Social Democratic Party in 1932 eased the unrest and marked the begin-

ning of an electoral love-affair that would not end until 1976.

After World War II – during which Sweden again remained neutral – there was a change in emphasis. Employment in traditional industries such as mining and manufacturing peaked around 1960 and Sweden, like many other

Western countries, veered towards a service-based economy. The public sector expanded rapidly on the back of the welfare society. Between 1960 and 1995 the numbers employed in the public sector rose by 800,000, while the increase in the private sector was only 250,000.

Telecommunications boom

The 1990s saw a shift in Sweden from manufacturing based on domestic raw materials to a wider variety of goods. Engineering had expanded rapidly and accounted for almost half of manufacturing output. The strongest growth was in the field of telecommunications, where Ericsson is now one of the world's major play-

---

LEFT: wood pulp mill – timber products are important in a country half covered by forests.
RIGHT: fish are a valuable food resource in Sweden.

ers. The pharmaceutical sector is another field in which a high level of investment in research and development has paid off. Sweden is among the world's top countries in terms of industrial research and development, the bulk of which has been undertaken by the 10 major industrial groups – with Ericsson, the engineering group ABB and motor manufacturers Volvo ranking the highest.

Partnership for industry

Swedish Social Democracy has many similarities to British New Labour of the 1990s. The welfare state has been built with the aid of industry, and industry has been allowed to prosper with the blessing of all the post-war governments. The door of each post-war prime minister has always been open to the representatives of the leading industrial families.

Göran Persson, prime minister in the late 1990s, nurtured an open relationship with Sweden's industrial barons, and some Social Democrats of the old order accused him of being too cosy with the establishment. His predecessor, Ingvar Carlsson, was more detached in his dealings with industry, as was Olof Palme in the 1970s and '80s. During the two post-war periods when the opposition was in power there

SWEDEN'S NUCLEAR DILEMMA

Sweden is considered to have the safest nuclear reactors in the world. In 1997, the nation's 12 reactors had a capacity of 10,439 megawatts, 45 per cent of its electricity production. Yet by 2010 Swedes will scrap all their reactors; and this is their dilemma. They need cheap energy, but for many nuclear energy is not an acceptable solution.

Nuclear energy became a political hot potato in the 1970s, and the issue helped to topple the Social Democrats in 1976. The nuclear programme was put on hold and in a referendum in 1980 the majority voted for an expansion of nuclear reactors, but with the proviso that all would be decommissioned by 2010. The debate has recently focused on two reactors at Barsebäck near Malmö. In 1998, the government decided that one reactor should close down that year and the other by 2001. Sydkraft, the electricity distributor, opposed the decision and the fight moved to the law courts. Sydkraft won a reprieve for the second reactor.

The debate has now moved on: nuclear reactors are not now seen as an environmental risk, though nuclear waste still is. Expansion of hydro-electric power is not a viable alternative according to environmentalists. The decision to abandon nuclear power stands until there is a shift in public opinion. So far a majority of 56 percent still want all nuclear reactors to be decommissioned.

was very little difference in the constructive co-operation between the state and industry.

Swedish democracy is based on equality. It has been so ever since the two chambers of Parliament were introduced in 1866 to replace the four estates (assemblies) to which the aristocracy and clergy were automatically invited. Women were given the vote in 1921, but although today almost half the members of parliament are women, not one has yet made it to prime minister.

The openness between state and industry has

TOP OF THE EXPORTS

Engineering products, including aircraft, motor vehicles, electrical and electronic equipment, and specialised machinery, make up 80 percent of Swedish exports.

Federation was the common way to solve disputes until the early 1980s.

One reason for relative peace in the labour market was low unemployment. This changed in the late 1980s. Swedish manufacturing exports lost more than 25 percent of their global market share between 1970 and 1992, and the Government was forced to depreciate the currency several times to increase Swedish competitiveness. The official unemployment rate hovers around 8 per cent but the true figure, when training and

also coloured the relationship between employers and employees, allowing Sweden to experience generally peaceful labour relations during the post-war era.

Pay bargaining

The Swedish labour market is characterised by a very high degree of unionisation; some 80 per cent of employees belong to a trade union. Centralised bargaining between the Swedish Trades Union Council and the Employers

LEFT: Forsmark Nuclear Power Station, Uppland.
ABOVE: farm workers are given a lift – about 3 per cent of the labour force is employed in agriculture.

public schemes are taken into account, is much nearer to 12 per cent.

Depreciating the currency is a cure no longer viable to Sweden since it became a member of the European Union in 1995. Instead, the comparative weakness of the krona against other EU currencies has helped to increase exports. In addition, productivity has been on the increase since the recession in the early 1990s when Swedish management was forced to slim down any corporate over-weight.

Industrial profitability is high, but that does not mean that Sweden is out of the proverbial woods. Increased global competition and rampant merger-mania has led to some startling changes. National icons such as Volvo and Saab are now in foreign hands. Unlike Great Britain and other European countries, which take these sales to foreigners with equanimity, the Swedes find it difficult, and each loss has been followed by furious hand-wringing. Equally disturbing is the flight of companies moving abroad. Ericsson, the telecom giant, moved its headquarters from Stockholm to London in 1999. Others are expected to follow.

During 1998, mergers worth more than £30 million swept through Swedish industrial corridors, a sum greater than that of Germany where the economy is 10 times larger. Much of

Swedish Industries. The same picture emerges in the financial sector.

The government is proud of its low corporate tax rate – only 28 per cent – but it is unable to lower personal taxes and still provide a cradle-to-grave security. The Social Democrat government of the late 1990s earned respect for tackling a burgeoning public debt, yet the core of its philosophy was still *trygghet*, the Swedish word for comfort and security.

As more Swedish companies end up in foreign hands there is a growing concern that jobs will be lost. This has not happened yet: new companies in technology and services have

the merger rush was due to restructuring within the Wallenberg empire, Sweden's leading industrial family. Many analysts see this shake-up as just an appetiser. More is to come.

If the industrial exodus continues it will put pressure on Sweden's government. With tax rates touching the ceiling, entrepreneurs including the founders of the successful IKEA home-furnishing empire and the equally prosperous fashion chain, Hennes, have moved abroad.

Today's generation of well-trained young people are attracted by higher salaries and lower taxes elsewhere. In 1997, 800 engineers, roughly a quarter of the year's graduates, left the country, according to the Federation of

entered the marketplace, and the Internet explosion has delivered hundreds of fast-growing enterprises. Which of these will be tomorrow's Ericsson is too early to forecast.

Inventors mean business

One Swede who is famous worldwide and whose memory is celebrated each year on 10 December is Alfred Nobel (*see pages 62–3*). He invented smokeless gunpowder and dynamite and made his fortune. Most of today's

ABOVE: vehicle test track near Arjeplog, Lapland.
RIGHT: making Scania trucks at Södertälje.
FAR RIGHT: Olof Palme, Social Democratic leader.

industrial conglomerates have their roots in a simple invention.

In 1876 – the same year that Alexander Graham Bell invented the telephone – Lars Magnus Ericsson set up a workshop for repairing telegraph equipment. A few years later he started the production of an improved telephone and in 1882 he introduced the world's first table-top model. Ericsson was quick to see the importance of exports and he set up a UK subsidiary 1898.

AGA was built on the invention by Gustaf Dalén of the sun valve, which switches lighthouse beacons on and off. Today, the company

mostly produces industrial gases. Its world-famous AGA cookers were sold to a British firm many years ago.

SKF was for many years the world leader in industrial ball-bearings, another Swedish invention, and Electrolux refined the vacuum cleaner and is now the world-leader in white goods.

TetraPak is the world's largest liquids packaging company. It was based on tetrahedron-shaped paper packaging, an invention by Ruben Rausing, and is still in the ownership of the Rausing family.

Alfa-Laval is built on the invention of the separator, in which cream can be quickly

WHO'S WHO IN PARTY POLITICS

Anyone can establish a political party in Sweden. Political donations are illegal and the state and the parliament contribute £20 million a year to support the political parties. The country has a system of proportional representation, which with seven main parties vying for power has led to a succession of coalition governments. The parties (with the percentage of votes cast at the 1998 election) include:

Social Democratic Party Aims to make all citizens equal partners in administering society's productive resources; similar to New Labour in Britain (36.4%).

Moderate Party (formerly Conservative Party) Believes in a market economy, control of public sector expansion, and a

public authority to guarantee social security (22.9%).

Left Party (formerly Communist Party) Strong believer in public ownership (12%).

Christian Democratic Party Promotes pro-family values and environmental responsibility; conservative (11.8%).

Centre Party (formerly Agrarian Party) Based on free enterprise, individual and co-operative ownership (5.1%).

Liberal Party Manifesto built on a socially orientated market economy (4.7%).

Green Party Aspires to a society in ecological balance with the environment (4.5%).

A number of smaller parties received 2.6% of the votes.

separated from the milk through centrifugal force. It is now part of the TetraPak Group, but still a world-leader in its field. Hasselblad, invented by Viktor Hasselblad, is still considered the best camera by all professionals.

Celebrating success

Corporate centennial celebrations have become run-of-the mill, but no company in the world can beat the paper and timber company Stora, which celebrated 700 years in the mid-1980s. In 1998, Stora merged with its Finnish competitor, Enso, and moved its corporate headquarters to Helsinki.

The Swedes are strongly committed to environmental causes. In 1995, more than 1 million metric tons of recycled paper were used in paper production. The percentage of paper consumption that is recycled is among the highest in Europe. Most households separate their waste into tin, glass, paper and kitchen rubbish for collection. Swedish industry takes seriously its environmental responsibility to reduce potentially hazardous emissions and has invested heavily in environmental protection measures. The country is seen as a forerunner in this field and companies export training programmes as well as environmental services.

IKEA has almost single-handedly changed the face of furniture retailing. The founder, Ingvar Kamprad, started out by selling pens by mail order at the age of 17, moved into kitchen chairs in the 1950s, and today controls a company with outlets worldwide.

The car-and-truck manufacturing sector is also strong. Volvo has been at the forefront of automotive safety standards and Sweden is the world's largest exporter of trucks – a remarkable achievement for such a small nation. Volvo might now be in the hands of Ford, but the strength of its brand-name will be its Swedishness, synonymous with safety. Like Volvo, Wallenberg-owned Scania produces trucks and buses sold all over the world.

The defence industry is healthy, which is a curious situation in a country that has not experienced war since the early 1800s. Saab is not only a car manufacturer – its sister company manufactures fighter planes used by many countries; British Aerospace is now a majority shareholder. Bofors, the armaments manufacturer, has lent its name to a world-famous gun.

Global ambitions

The recent concerns over losing the ownership of the industrial crown jewels in the Swedish crown must be seen in the light of Sweden's rush to buy into Europe and the US during the 1970s and 1980s. At one point there were almost daily announcements of buy-outs, takeovers and mergers. Electrolux took over the Italian white goods giant Zanussi, ASEA merged with Switzerland's Brown Boveri, Swedish Match bought Wilkinson Sword, and the UK furniture retailer Habitat was bought by IKEA. The Swedes took pride in conquering the boardrooms of the world. Today, industrial sales and purchases are more evenly balanced.

Singing for Sweden

Inventiveness and talent are the base on which Sweden's astounding success has been built. Talent still provides for Sweden's now greatest export, in revenue terms. The pop group ABBA started it in the early 1970s, and tills have been ringing to their tunes and those of their successors, such as Roxette and The Cardigans, ever since. ❏

LEFT: the Swedes are conscientious about recycling.
RIGHT: manufacturing stainless steel at Nyby Bruk.

THE PEACEMAKERS

Swedish negotiators have increasingly been called in to help resolve
international conflicts. What makes their skills so special?

It may be Sweden's long-held traditions of neutrality and its position as a buffer between the power blocs, but from a population of only 8.8 million it has produced a remarkable number of dedicated peacemakers of international repute. World War II, in which Sweden was relatively untouched, saw the start

of this trend, when in 1939–40 (during the bleak Finnish Winter War against the Soviet Union), many Swedes opened their homes to Finnish children.

After the German attack on Denmark and Norway, a stream of refugees crossed the long border between Sweden and Norway and many Danish Jews were also able to find asylum in the neutral country.

Release of prisoners

From this period, the names of two humanitarians stand out: Count Folke Bernadotte and Raoul Wallenberg. The first of these had high connections and a royal name. He was the

nephew of King Gustav V, and an army officer as well as chairman of the Red Cross. His talent was for negotiation and he was one of the first to recognise that, whatever a country might think of the Nazi regime, it was better to treat with it than to allow its victims to die. Bernadotte's first success was to secure the release of thousands of Scandinavian prisoners, and later prisoners of other nationalities, from the concentration camps.

In 1947, Bernadotte's already proven skills recommended him to the United Nations Security Council, which was seeking someone to mediate in the delicate situation between the Jews and Arabs in Palestine.

Bernadotte moved to Palestine but, although he successfully negotiated a ceasefire, both sides rejected his terms of settlement of the war. He was also faced with many who had a vested interest in making sure that he didn't succeed and were prepared to go to any lengths to continue the struggle.

After a number of threats against his life, his car was ambushed in September 1948 and he was shot down by Jewish extremists.

Escape route

Raoul Wallenberg's aim was also to help the Jews. When in 1944 the United States established the War Refugee Board to save Jews from Nazi persecution, the Board's Stockholm representative called together a group of Swedish Jews to suggest candidates suitable, brave enough, and willing to go on a rescue operation to Budapest.

At this point, the lives of Folke Bernadotte and Raoul Wallenberg came together because Bernadotte was the first choice. When the Hungarian Government would not accept him, Wallenberg was appointed.

The 32-year-old member of the great industrial and banking family became First Secretary of the Swedish Legation in Budapest and began his dangerous mission. His best protection was his authority to deal with anyone he chose and to use diplomatic couriers outside the normal channels. By the time Wallenberg arrived in Budapest, he was too late to save two-thirds of the Jewish population. Already, 400,000 Jews had been transported to the camps, but there were still around 200,000 left in the capital.

Wallenberg's first step was to start to issue protective passports and to open "Swedish Houses" all over the city, where Budapest Jews could take refuge. He used everything from bribery to threats and blackmail, and it is said that as

UNITED NATIONS

The Swedish peacemaker, Dag Hammarskjöld, second secretary general of the United Nations (1953–61), was instrumental in improving the reputation and effectiveness of the UN.

to believe that this brave man died as early as 1947, and his family and voluntary associations are still tireless in their efforts to find out what happened to Raoul Wallenberg.

Keeping the peace

When the United Nations was established after World War II, its first secretary general was a Norwegian, Trygve Lie. He was succeeded in 1953 by another Swedish peacemaker, Dag Hammarskjöld, who became the founder of the UN Peacekeeping Force. Hammarskjöld was

many as 100,000 Jews owe their survival to Raoul Wallenberg.

The saviour could not save himself and his own fate is veiled in mystery. At the end of the war, Wallenberg fell into the hands of the Russians, who seem to have believed that he was a spy. They later declared that Wallenberg had died in captivity and have since refused to re-open the question, though eye witnesses claim that he was alive and still imprisoned as late as the 1970s. Many in Sweden are reluctant

an economist and had been a civil servant and son of a former prime minister of Sweden.

Apart from the establishment of the Peacekeeping Force, Hammarskjöld's other main achievements were to arrange the release of captured American pilots from China. He was also the champion of the small states of the United Nations, and the guardian particularly of the interests of the Third World against the major powers.

Congo mission

Hammarskjöld's stewardship ended when he decided to send UN troops to the Congo after civil war broke out in the area in 1959. As the

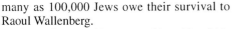

LEFT: Raoul Wallenberg, saviour of Jews.
ABOVE: Dag Hammarskjöld, United Nations leader.
RIGHT: Carl Bildt, peace-negotiator in Bosnia.

political repercussions of Hammarskjöld's actions spread, Russia demanded his resignation, but Hammarskjöld remained. It was in the Congo that this independently-minded man met his death in mysterious circumstances, as so often has been the fate of the peacemaker.

In 1961, when Hammarskjöld was on a peace mission to that war-torn country, his plane crashed, killing all on board. The reasons have never been explained and even today many speculate that this, too, was an assassination.

Sweden's principal woman peacemaker, Alva Myrdal, was also closely connected with the UN and was the first woman to achieve a

position as a top-ranking director within that organisation, when she became head of the Department of Social Affairs.

Demands for disarmament

Myrdal's main contribution to the cause of peace was her tireless effort to promote disarmament and peace during the 1960s when she was involved in the Geneva disarmament talks. Through what must have been a series of dispiriting meetings over a number of years, she held on to her belief that in the end commonsense would prevail. In 1964, she was one of the founders of Stockholm's International Peace Research Institute and its first chair. She

published a number of books and articles. In 1980 she was the first to be awarded the Albert Einstein Peace Prize, and in 1982 the Nobel Peace Prize. She died in 1986 at the age of 84.

That same year, the Swedish peacemaker Olof Palme was gunned down in a Stockholm street as he strolled home from a visit to the cinema with his wife.

Champion of the oppressed

Even before Palme became prime minister in 1969 at the age of 42, he had already begun to acquire an international reputation, mainly in connection with the Vietnam War. For several years, his robust condemnation of American policy in Vietnam led to acrimonious exchanges with the United States administration in Washington and also occasionally with the US Embassy in Stockholm.

In domestic politics Palme's priorities were to combat unemployment and to promote social reforms, building on the work of his predecessors. In foreign policy, however, he broke new ground. He argued constantly against colonialism and the arms race and, during the 1970s and 1980s, he became one of the world's foremost champions of oppressed peoples.

As a member of the Brandt Commission, he helped to formulate proposals for narrowing the gap between North and South, and his own "Palme Commission" presented a concrete plan for reducing armaments and increasing global security. He, too, was involved in the work of the United Nations when he acted as mediator in the Iran-Iraq war at the request of the secretary general.

As prime minister, Swedes had naturally concentrated more on Palme's domestic policies than on his international achievements, but his death and world reaction to it opened their eyes to his international reputation as a peacemaker and statesman. For more than a year, the spot on the pavement where he died was indicated by its tributes of flowers. His grave is marked by a simple stone in a churchyard nearby.

In the 1990s the peacemaking banner was taken up by the conservative politician, Carl Bildt (Prime Minister 1991–4), in efforts to bring an end to the war in Bosnia. ❏

LEFT: Olof Palme, Social Democrat prime minister of Sweden, campaigned internationally for peace and arms reduction. He was assassinated in 1986.

The Non-Aligned Nation

Sweden's King Karl XIV Johan was the first to lay down his country's long-lasting belief in neutrality. In the 1830s he assured both the Russian and British governments that Sweden had abandoned all thoughts of regaining the provinces on the eastern and southern shores of the Baltic lost as a result of the Napoleonic wars. Sweden, he insisted, would not want to do anything that might endanger its existence as a state.

That was the official position – but there were forces within the country which challenged it. The loss of Finland in 1809 to Russia was a blow to Swedish national pride. The aristocracy in both countries had close connections, and Swedish was the official language of Finland. The union with Norway entered into in 1814 could not make up for the loss of Finland. Only a policy of greatest constraint could keep the two countries united and the union was finally dissolved in 1905.

During the years before World War I Sweden, feeling under threat of attack from Russia, moved closer to Germany. It became clear that the Germans were only interested in using a friendship with Sweden as a threat to Russia. A few days after war was declared, Sweden issued an official declaration of neutrality.

Towards the end of that war, neutrality was under strain as civil war broke out in Finland between the Russian-backed Reds and the Whites. Victory for the Reds was a threat to Swedish security, but it was felt that military intervention would entail an even higher risk.

By 1920 Sweden was more favourably placed than ever before. Germany and Russia had lost the war, an independent Finland emerged, German influence over Denmark had disappeared, and none of the other Nordic states was under obligation to a great power. Sweden now concentrated its efforts on limiting the growth of power in other countries through the League of Nations. It adopted unilateral disarmament in 1925.

Sweden stayed out of World War II officially but a number of volunteers from the Swedish forces joined the White Army to fight with the Finns against Russia. At the same time, Sweden

RIGHT: Sweden has remained neutral during two world wars, but retains its own forces for security.

recognised the urgent need to rearm. Denmark and Norway were both occupied by the Germans in 1940 and Sweden was under threat of invasion. Public opinion in Sweden put pressure on the government to take sides.

The coalition government decided to keep Sweden out of the war at almost any cost and reluctantly conceded to German demands to transport troops on leave from Norway through Sweden. This was seen by many as immoral. Others felt that because Sweden stayed out of the war, it was able to make a humanitarian contribution which outweighed any military contribution. After the war, recognising the need for protection, Norway and

Denmark joined NATO, Finland signed a treaty of friendship with the Soviet Union in 1948, but Sweden resolved to maintain its non-alliance in peacetime, leading to neutrality in war time. It has since been very active in the United Nations, promoting peace and disarmament.

Armed neutrality puts Sweden in something of a cleft stick. In order to maintain an up-to-date defence, Sweden has to have an armament industry. An armament industry supplying only Swedish needs would be an intolerable drain on the nation's resources and manufacturers have had to look for customers elsewhere. The peace-promoting Swedes are now among the world's biggest exporters of armaments. ❏

ALFRED NOBEL

*He made a fortune from weapons of war. Then he gave his name to
an international award for peacemakers. Why?*

Some of the most fascinating contradictions of the human character came together inside Alfred Nobel. How, for instance, could one man both found the renowned Nobel Peace Prize, awarded each year to those who have made the greatest contributions to world peace, and at the same time

be the father of Sweden's vigorous armaments industry, which today provides a substantial amount of the weapons held by one half of that same world against the other?

The young inventor

Alfred Nobel was born in 1833 in Sweden, one of three brothers. He clearly inherited his talents as a chemist and inventor from his father, who went bankrupt during Alfred's early childhood. Despite the bankruptcy, Nobel Senior moved the family to Russia where he became a very successful industrialist.

Life in St Petersburg gave Alfred the chance of an international education. He was particularly well tutored in chemistry and, in addition to Swedish, spoke French, Russian, English and German. Nor was he confined to Russia. As a young man he took educational trips all over Europe and to the United States, before joining his father in St Petersburg as a chemist. In 1853, the Nobel family moved back to Sweden, leaving Alfred's two brothers, Robert and Ludwig, to look after their father's business.

An early interest in explosives was also stimulated by Alfred Nobel's father, who in Russia had invented new and efficient land and sea mines which the Russian armed forces used in the Crimean War. Alfred went further and patented many of his own inventions, of which his most famous was dynamite. This revolutionised mining, road building and tunnel blasting because it gave engineers a manageable form of the highly sensitive explosive, nitroglycerine. He also turned his fertile mind to synthetic materials, telecommunications and alarm systems and in his lifetime clocked up the ownership of 355 patents.

International industrialist

Alfred Nobel was more than an inventor. He was a pioneer in the swift industrial exploitation of his discoveries and the founding of multinational companies. His ultimate total was 90 factories and companies in 20 countries, on five continents around the world. At the same time, he did not neglect his Russian interests and entered into partnership with his brothers, who by this time were successfully exploiting the Baku oilfields and became known as the Russian Rockefellers.

The Nobels also had a reputation as benevolent employers who provided social care and welfare benefits for their employees, a foretaste perhaps of the Swedish style of today.

To the world outside, Alfred Nobel was a man with a penetrating mind, shrewd in business and with a sceptical idealism. He was also melancholy, slightly self-deprecating, yet with a good sense of humour. Despite his success, he was not a happy man and wrote of his life as "a miserable half-life, which ought to have been choked to death by a philanthropic physician as, with a howl, it entered life".

Although he had homes in six different countries, his life was that of a vagabond. Paris was close to his heart and so was Bofors in Sweden, where he spent his last years. Today, it is the stronghold of the armaments industry he founded.

Nobel in love

A lonely man, Nobel never married but in later life developed a strong friendship with Bertha von Suttner, an Austrian baroness. Theirs was a close but platonic relationship, as the baroness was not free to marry. Bertha von Suttner was a pioneer in the peace movement and her friendship may well have influenced Nobel's thinking about peace. In any event, she was awarded the Nobel Peace Prize in 1905.

The real love affair of his life was with an Austrian girl, who was 23 years his junior. But even here, his complex mind seemed unable to forget her social and educational inferiority. Despite that, the liaison lasted for 18 years and one hopes he found warmth and affection.

He tried his hand at both poetry and prose and, in his youth, was so strongly influenced by Shelley's pacifist views as to call war "the horror of horrors and the greatest of all crimes". Despite that, Nobel apparently saw no wrong in profiting from the weapons of war and during his lifetime he amassed a huge fortune.

He was not the sort of rich man who prided himself on his frugality, nor did he wait until he was dead to become a philanthropist. His philosophy was always to prefer "to take care of the stomachs of the living rather than the glory of the departed in the form of monuments".

Prize fund

A year before his death in San Remo in Italy, Nobel signed the will which, in less than 300 words, stipulated how to convert his estate into an investment fund. The proceeds were to be used for annual prizes to be awarded to individuals that "shall have conferred the greatest

SPARK OF YOUTH

One of Alfred Nobel's biographers described him in early life as "a prematurely developed, unusually intelligent, but a sickly, dreamy and introspective youth".

benefit on mankind". There were to be five categories: physics, chemistry, physiology or medicine, literature and the well-known Nobel Prize for Peace for "the best work for fraternity between nations, for the abolition or reduction of standing armies and for the holding and promotion of peace congresses".

The first four were to be awarded by Swedish institutions. For the Peace Prize, Nobel went outside Sweden and named a committee appointed by the Norwegian Parliament to make the award.

In 1968, the Central Bank of Sweden added a prize in Economic Sciences to the original categories, in memory of Nobel.

Today, the contradictions of Nobel's complex personality have left a second legacy, quite apart from the Nobel Prizes. Sweden's vigorous armaments industry provides a substantial part of Swedish exports each year, as does the dynamite factory in Karlskoga. In fact, Bofors provides the main employment of the town. Yet it also represents a constant threat to the population – Bofors has cost many lives in accidents. It is as though that strange marriage between peace and war that existed in Alfred Nobel continues in his own country today. ❑

LEFT: the Swedish Royal Family attend a Nobel Prize-giving ceremony in Stockholm.
RIGHT: Alfred Nobel (1833–96), inventor and chemist.

THE SWEDISH MODEL

Close collaboration between employers, employees, the state and trade unions
has created a working relationship that's the envy of many nations

Politicians worldwide have for decades pointed to the Swedish Model, in which socialism and capitalism work hand, in hand as the right way forward. The Americans first latched onto it in the late 1930s with the publication of the book *The Middle Way* by Marquis W. Childs, which outlined the route taken by the Swedish Government to combat unemployment and declining competitiveness.

US politicians held up Sweden as an example at a time when the Americans were experiencing rising unemployment and labour strife. The British Labour Party did the same during the 1960s and 1970s. Ministers travelled to Sweden to look and learn and the two governments developed a close relationship. In the 1980s, Soviet officials looked to their Swedish neighbours across the Baltic to provide the safest method of merging old-fashioned socialism with entrepreneurial capitalism.

It might be easy to dismiss the Swedish Model today. In 1999, the British magazine *The Economist* suggested that the Middle Way had become a cul-de-sac. Amid rising unemployment and some social unrest in Sweden it has certainly lost its lustre, but then times have changed since it was first mooted as a panacea for all social ills.

Rich and poor

The Swedish Model certainly achieved the unachievable. Thanks to close collaboration between business, labour and government, Sweden was transformed from one of Europe's poorer nations into one of its richest. It also helped to create a society that enjoyed a narrowing gap between rich and poor, and where the social welfare system provided security for everyone from cradle to grave.

From 1932 onwards, with only two lost elections in 1976 and in 1991, the Social Democrat Party has ruled and shaped Sweden. The term

socialism is misleading, unless we think of socialism as envisaged by the British prime minister, Tony Blair. Some call it "socialism with a prosperous face", others see it as pure pragmatism. In order to create the wealth that was needed to pay for Sweden's welfare system, the labour force and business were encour-

aged to collaborate and given full support by the government.

The Swedish Social Democrat Party saw co-operation as the only way forward and worked closely with the captains of industry from the day it came to power. Co-operation was made easier by the fact that more than half of Sweden's industry was controlled by a handful of families. The most important was the Wallenberg family, still the powerhouse of Swedish industry, and the Wallenbergs were clever enough to see that close links with the political rulers would benefit them, too.

By working with business the Social Democrat Party set an example for the strong trade

LEFT: markets are a focal point in many towns.
RIGHT: electrical manufacturing is a major source of employment in Sweden.

unions, and co-operation between the employers federation and the trade unions followed the same pattern.

Through the early part of the 1900s, trade unions and management had been locked in bitter combat and strikes were common. The new Social Democrat government recognised the cost of these strikes, both to the economy and to society as a whole, and threatened to intervene by introducing strict labour laws.

The combatants agreed to resolve the issue between themselves. In 1938, at a historic meeting at the Saltsjöbaden Grand Hotel, near Stockholm, the two parties finally agreed on

became the envy of most industrialised nations. It guaranteed the Swedish industrialists peace to build up their factories and invest in the knowledge that they would not suffer costly strikes. The Swedish Model, the Middle Way, was in place. Then World War II intervened.

Generous benefits

The post-war era was one of industrial growth, no doubt helped by the fact that Sweden had remained neutral during the war. With a strong economy, rising exports and no unemployment, the government introduced an ambitious programme of social reforms. Ministers realised

rules for collective bargaining and how to solve industrial disputes. "The Saltsjöbaden Spirit" became synonymous with a new pragmatism, where the benefit for the society was more important than that for individual groups.

Peace pact

Under this peace pact, unions were required to give advance notice of any planned industrial action, which meant a cooling-off period for talks and further negotiations. Wage levels would be agreed upon for the whole labour market by the two confederations representing trade unions and management. The ensuing order and calm of the Swedish labour market

that a profitable private sector would secure jobs, help to expand the economy and, with this in mind, corporate taxes were set at a minimum. Corporate tax levels are still among the lowest in Europe at about 28 percent.

The Social Democrats found other ways to raise money – social security contributions paid by companies for each employee are among the highest in Europe. Staffing has become very expensive, and laying-off staff even more so. This could be one reason why unemployment has risen: employers dare not commit themselves to taking on permanent staff.

The benefits that Swedish employees now have the right to insist upon are numerous.

Each employee has the statutory right of five weeks' paid holiday a year; most have six by contract. Add to that 13 public holidays and the choice of taking double time off instead of overtime. The Swedes also have a system whereby the day before a public holiday counts as a half-day. It is a miracle that any work gets done, but it does and efficiently, too.

Many attribute to this miracle the placid nature of the Swedes. Consensus is important, and political strife on the factory floor or in the boardroom is a rare occurrence. However, during the 1980s, peace in the work-place took a hammering. Corporate mergers changed the

massive increases in taxes," warned the former Swedish prime minister, Carl Bildt, in 1999.

The Social Democrats did not do well in the 1998 election, hanging on to power only by joining forces with the former Communist Party. The government promises more welfare but has so far not explained how it will pay for it. Its new allies want a 30-hour week, which will not bring more revenue for the emptying state coffers.

Adding up the costs

Sweden is the top spender according to the OECD (Organisation for Economic Cooperation

temperature and powerful investors became more interested in the bottom-line than industrial harmony. The beneficial influence of the industrial dynasties waned as their ownership was watered down.

Generations of welfare security has taken its toll on the economy. In the late 1990s, 60 percent of voters depended on the state for work or welfare. Unless there is an unexpected economic up-swing, "six or seven years down the road there will be either massive cutbacks or

LEFT: a comprehensive network of *dagis* (child-care centres) enables parents to take employment.
ABOVE: mothers and children out on an expedition.

TRADE UNION PARTICIPATION

About 90 per cent of all employees are members of a trade union, affiliated to the Trade Union Confederation (LO) for manual workers, the Confederation of Salaried Employees (TCO) for white collar employees, and the Confederation of Professional Associations (SACO) for graduate-level employees. Employers are represented by the Swedish Employers' Confederation (SAF). About 4.3 million people (50 percent) of the population are in the labour force. More than 75 percent of all women between 16 and 64 years are in employment. About 25 percent of the labour force work part-time. A further 3 to 4 percent are on assisted training schemes.

and Development. Almost 60 per cent of its GDP goes on government spending.

Swedes prefer to ignore the gloomy statistics. They enjoy excellent health and social services and top quality subsidised child-care. The streets are clean and the crime rate lower than in most European countries. Pensioners have a decent standard of living and the school system churns out well-educated youngsters. What is there to worry about?

Harmony in the workplace

The Swedish style of management is admired throughout the industrial world. Organisations are flat rather than hierarchical. Top executives have simple offices and often answer their own telephones. Open-plan offices are the norm and directors seldom hide behind closed doors. Pin-striped suits are only for bankers, and instead casual clothing is common – the management team of the furniture retailer IKEA, for instance, has never worn ties. The British entrepreneur Richard Branson would feel at home in a Swedish boardroom.

Power sharing has become just as important as money. During the mid-1970s, the unions insisted on placing employee representatives on the boards of each company with more

SOCIAL WELFARE – FROM CRADLE TO GRAVE

Health Swedes are covered by national health insurance. The patient is charged a fee for medical consultations and any drugs prescribed up to a specified limit. Thereafter, costs are paid by national insurance. If a person is ill or needs to care for a sick child, he or she will receive a taxable daily allowance of 75–85 per cent of lost income.
Parental leave Parents are entitled to 12 months' paid leave when a baby is born. This leave can be shared between the father and the mother to suit them and can be used at any time before the child's eighth birthday.
Housing Low-income families and pensioners are eligible for housing allowances.

Unemployment benefit Unemployment insurance is provided through trade unions. Those who do not belong to a trade union rely on state benefits. There are many state-funded schemes to help the unemployed to find new work.
Pensions A basic old-age pension, financed by both employees and employers, is paid to everyone at the age of 65. The state also pays an income-related supplementary pension financed from employer pay-roll fees and together these two pensions should reach the level of two-thirds of the pensioner's previous earnings. As in other European countries, the government is looking into self-funded pension schemes to reduce the burden on the state.

than 25 staff. Companies complained bitterly at this decision but they have found that a staff which is involved and informed is less likely to take action.

Employees do not suffer from the divisive "them-and-us syndrome". Swedish management wants to be close to its colleagues and endless conferences and team-building exercises are part of strategic planning. Since individuals are highly taxed, conferences and training seminars in exotic loca-

No Secrets

When the Swedes finally joined the European Union in 1995 their first demand was for greater transparency within the Brussels bureaucracy. Their request fell on deaf ears. For the Swedes there is no such thing as secrecy except for national security.

Social Democrats love rich companies but hate rich individuals. This has forced dentists as well as artists to turn themselves into companies to avoid paying the swingeing taxes.

Despite low corporate tax, many larger Swedish companies are contemplating moving their headquarters abroad, following the lead of the paper firm Stora and the telecommunications giant Ericsson (*see page 54*). The reason these companies give is tax, but not

tions have become a way of rewarding employees more tax-efficiently.

Taxing issues

Tax, tax, tax has certainly taken over from sex, sex, sex as the topic for most after-dinner confessionals in Sweden. Personal tax laws are strict, tax rates high and, as in most countries with high tax levels, tax evasion has become an industry in itself. The tax laws favour companies, and it is often said that the

LEFT: working conditions in Swedish offices are generally of a very high standard.
ABOVE: inside Börsen, Stockholm's Stock Exchange.

the corporate tax. It is not the higher salaries in Europe or the United States that are the draw, but rather the lower taxes. Corporate Sweden is experiencing a management brain-drain. Swedish companies are also unable to attract foreign specialists since they can demand a better lifestyle abroad.

The obituary for the Swedish Model does not have to be written yet. Swedes are pragmatists and know how to adapt. The country's record is ample proof of that.

The trade unions have changed and collective wage bargaining has been abolished to the delight of both sides. Certain industrial sectors see it as an advantage to be able to negotiate lower pay rises during cyclical down-turns and the stronger unions can flex their muscles.

At work and play

Swedes have recently learnt the noble art of relaxing. The work ethic was deeply ingrained but now, bolstered by the state, Swedes spend more time with friends and family, and on self-improvement.

Taking a sabbatical is no longer seen as a cop-out, but a healthy break. More than 2½ million Swedes spend their spare time at study circles and others have hobbies ranging from choral singing to weaving. Young men on the

middle rung of their career ladders take time off for paternity leave and it is not seen as odd when high-flyers rush off at 5pm to collect their young children from kindergarten. With so many women working, sharing child-care and domestic chores is a necessity.

Curbing absenteeism

Absenteeism was a common problem among employees. Volvo once complained that only 75 percent of its staff turned up on Mondays and that employees took a staggering 27 days sick-leave a year. When the government introduced a rule that the first day of sickness had to be unpaid sick-leave, absenteeism plummeted. Rising unemployment has also had a salutary effect on absenteeism.

The effect of stress still shows itself in high levels of alcoholism and other stress-related illnesses. Industry has done its utmost to make offices and factories into stress-free zones. Swedish design is at its best in the workplace. Staff have access to facilities for gym and sports, and most canteens would be classified as luxury restaurants in other countries. Larger companies provide crèches for the young children of staff.

Training and personal development is also high on the agenda. Volvo provides all its employees with a computer with its own interactive course for home use and staff are encouraged to take an "IT-licence". Larger companies must by law set aside a percentage of the profits for training.

Most Swedes will admit that Sweden is close to Utopia. Much of the stress and melancholy can be blamed on dark and interminable winters. As one British diplomat said after serving three years in Stockholm, "There are the Winter Swedes and the Summer Swedes and in no way are they related."

The gloomy Winter Swedes turn into fun-loving extroverts as soon as the first pale rays of sunshine are seen, and cafés move their tables out onto the narrow pavements when spring arrives. The people have come to expect the easy living they have admired on holidays in France and Spain. They might not admit it even to themselves, but the Swedes have become Europeans. ❏

LEFT: students in celebratory mood.
RIGHT: time off to unwind in the sauna.

THE SWEDES TODAY

Beneath the cool, reserved exterior, Swedes harbour deep commitments

to their country, to nature... and to schnapps

Most visitors know all about the stereotypical images of Sweden before they have even set foot in the country: blonde blue-eyed beauties, Arctic winters, pop sensation ABBA, reliable cars and seemingly unflappable tennis players. And while all of these images ring true, Sweden today is a country of growing cultural and social diversity; a country in which the traditional mingles with the ultra-modern and in which the political arena has been shaped by a strong democratic tradition that has helped to form the foundation of modern Swedish society.

At first glance, today's Swede may appear something of a paradox: equally as at home in the concrete jungle as on the grassy plains of Skåne, Swedes are a confusing blend of the urban and the provincial. They are sophisticated city-dwellers, yet are never happier than when they can kick off their shoes and go barefoot, swim naked and bond with nature.

Breaking the ice

Swedes may often seem a little cool at first, reserved, even formal. But don't let this fool you. Underneath that composed exterior, beneath that unmistakable aura of self-satisfaction with all things Swedish, and below that tacit conviction that Swedes know best, they are essentially a warm and friendly people – particularly after one or two *schnapps*.

Indeed, there's nothing like *schnapps* for breaking the ice. Like vodka to the Russians or wine to the French, *schnapps* is part of the Swedish cultural tradition. Delicately flavoured with fruits or spices, a bottle of this perennial tipple is as likely to be found on the table at Midsummer as it is at Christmas. Every Swede can name his or her personal favourite.

Strangely, for a nation whose capital was home to some 700 inns by the 18th century

(that's one for every 100 inhabitants at the time) Swedes have a rather uncomfortable relationship with alcohol.

The open and liberal approach to life, which once made them the envy of more conservative societies, makes the prevailing attitude towards drinking (surrounded as it is by taboos and

much moral pontificating) all the more perplexing. Despite EU membership and its initial effects, alcohol remains a contentious issue for modern-day Swedes. Exorbitant prices and an unyielding state monopoly have conspired to create a sense of deprivation and prohibition. It's not so strange then that when the chance to indulge presents itself, Swedes throw themselves into the fray wholeheartedly.

Strict etiquette

The drinking habits of the Swedes may appear excessive to some and perhaps even raise the eyebrows of others, but when it comes to dining, their conduct is beyond reproach. Be it

PRECEDING PAGES: flaunting the national flag; students in university boat race, Uppsala.
LEFT: skipper enjoying the sea air.
RIGHT: hunting for bargains at a flea market.

state banquets or family get-togethers, Swedes are sticklers for etiquette. From arriving punctually to the smallest of glances exchanged with other dinner guests – both before and after a toast is made – the formalities are upheld to the last drop of *schnapps (see page 144)*. Yet Swedes will happily tuck into a crayfish feast, ripping off claws with their hands, clashing beer glasses in a toast, in a fashion oddly reminiscent of their Viking forebears.

National pride

As it did with their ancestors, the travel lust runs deep in the veins of 20th-century Swedes. Although they no longer plunder their southern neighbours, they remain very vocal when abroad. Swedes, like Americans, become intensely patriotic when they are away from the motherland. But national pride has suffered something of a blow in recent years.

Cool wind of recession

Just over a decade ago, Sweden occupied a position in Scandinavia very similar to that enjoyed by England in relation to the rest of the UK, and the US to Canada. Then the Norwegians struck oil. The recession of the early 1990s left Sweden's economy reeling, while

SWEDISH CHARACTERISTICS

The big debate Though naturally inclined to avoid confrontation, nothing gets the ordinarily even-tempered Swede up in arms like a good debate. There is a popular television debating programme for every night of the week in which topical issues are addressed and opposing factions can air their differences in an open forum. In fact, Swedes love to argue. They argue with great gusto, but without the British penchant for circumlocution and without the passionate gesticulating of more Latin temperaments.

Thirst for coffee There is something that is even more Swedish than debating and that is drinking coffee. Coffee shops are as Swedish and as ubiquitous as the Volvo.

Coffee drinking is an intrinsic part of daily life and is, to all intents and purposes, a national pastime. The Swedes even have their own verb for it: "*fika*". After the Finns, Swedes are the biggest group of coffee drinkers in the world. The average Swede drinks four cups of coffee a day. That's 200 litres or about 10 kilos of coffee a year. Meeting for coffee, or *fika*, is a popular way to socialise or celebrate, and rounding off a good meal, either at home or at a restaurant, would not be complete without it.

All in line The Swedes' penchant for queuing is a reflex akin to the herding instinct; they form orderly queues everywhere from the bank to the water fountain.

the Danes, who did not experience as big a slump, recovered comparatively quickly.

Ousted from the position of "big brother" as the largest and formerly most prosperous of the Scandinavian nations, for the Swedes insult was soon added to injury. Riding high on an enviable winning streak, the Norwegians continue to win all the medals in nearly every major winter sports events, leaving the Swedish national ice hockey team, its most successful export on the international sports scene, flying the flag.

boats that crowd the country's lakes and waterways in high summer. But nowhere do you see the national flag more often than fluttering like streamers on the long flagpoles outside the Swedish *stugor*–the small wooden cottages that are dotted all over the countryside.

The little red cottage is perhaps Sweden's most enduring image, and there's almost nothing that Swedes of all ages like better than to take off to their country hideaway for a weekend or for a longer spell during the summer months.

> ### WHAT'S IN A WORD?
>
> *Lagom* is a Swedish word that continues to defy translation but has come to stand for what is essentially the Swedish attitude to life – all things in moderation.

Flag waving

Flags are a common sight, and on national holidays and during the summer it can certainly seem as though there are more Swedish flags flying than there are Swedish people. And the Swedes do not join in the cynical British and American habits of turning their national emblem into cheeky shorts or carrier bags. Everywhere the gold cross on the blue background stands out against the sky: on buses, on buildings, and on the shoals of steamers and

LEFT: taking part in a summer folk festival.
RIGHT: the Swedes enjoy a good barbecue when the weather permits.

Affinity with nature

Swedes long for the often short summer months when they can cast their cares aside and get back to nature – an interest for which is clearly in the genes, for every Swede can name at least 20 of the most common types of trees and berries with uncanny accuracy.

Why this hankering for the great outdoors? It's simple really. Little more than a century ago, Sweden was predominantly an agrarian society. Today this affinity for the land lives on, buried deep inside the Swedish soul. You can take the Swede out of the countryside, but you can't take the countryside out of the Swede.

Ensconced once again in their natural habitat,

Swedes will happily dress up in their national costume at the least excuse to sing and dance to the old tunes. They have even developed their own particular style of country and western music known as *dansband musik*.

Music-making

Although most urbanites cringe at the very idea, *dansband* music enjoys enormous popularity among the rural population. When it comes to more mainstream music the Swedes have, in recent years, taken the international music

scene by storm. Ace of Base, Roxette and The Cardigans are just some of the groups that have turned Sweden into the third largest exporter of music, after America and Britain. It's a pretty impressive record for a country with a population of just under 9 million.

Winter activities

Winters in Sweden are famous for their longevity, Arctic temperatures and the sun's prolonged absence. Swedes eagerly await the spring and the return of sunlight with all the excited anticipation of children at Christmas. Like hibernating animals re-emerging after the long, dark winter, sun-starved Swedes are wont

> **THE MORE IT SNOWS...**
>
> Arctic winters have yet to break the hardy Swedish resolve or bring the country to its knees. Streets are quickly snowploughed, roads salted, and life goes on.

to stand on street corners, at crossings, at traffic lights, and any other spot they can find with a south-facing aspect, soaking up the first warming rays of spring.

But do not think for one minute that winter is entirely abhorrent to the Swedes. For many the lengthy winter is a time for robust, outdoor activity. The Swedish people have learnt how to make the most of their winter, and winter sports are popular with Swedes of all ages: from long walks in the country to skiing in the mountains of Dalarna, from ice-fishing in Jämtland to long-distance ice-skating on Lake Vänern.

Cultural mix

Today's Swede, of course, comes in a variety of creeds and colours. Immigration continues to influence the country's social, cultural and political landscape. The 1990s was a time of change in which Sweden was forced to redefine itself and re-evaluate its global position in the face of new economic challenges and growing questions of social inequality.

The high standard of living once enjoyed by Swedes and their enviable cradle-to-the-grave social welfare system have recently come under increasing pressure in recent years as a consequence of the economic slump that hit Europe in the early 1990s.

For years Swedes championed and supported the causes of others, but their own increasingly precarious position has forced them to abandon, albeit unofficially, their famous policy of neutrality, leave the crusades behind and take closer steps to Europe.

New Europeans

Sweden's entry into the European Union in January 1995 was part of the government's efforts to bring Sweden in line with a changing Europe.

New social and economic policies are gradually helping the country to adapt to an increasingly global economy, while the Swedes themselves are learning to adapt to their new role–as Europeans. ❏

LEFT: hikers in the Sarek mountains of northern Sweden. **RIGHT:** winter is not a time to hide away in Sweden; ice fishing is popular among all age groups.

FAMILY LIFE

*Divorce rates are high and separation is commonplace, yet
the family remains the backbone of Swedish society*

A man sits quietly on a park bench. In one hand he is holding a newspaper, scanning the latest hockey results, the other is gently rocking a child's pushchair in which a toddler is sleeping peacefully. This is not an unfamiliar scene in Sweden today.

It's true that men's attitudes in this country certainly seem to have changed a lot faster than they have elsewhere. For the Swedish father can often be seen pushing a baby round the supermarket in a trolley and is no slacker when it comes to changing junior either. But this was not always the case and his modern approach to family life perhaps owes more to statutory intervention than genuine male enlightenment.

The new-look family

Family life in Sweden has undergone a dramatic change in the past 100 years. Large families were common in the agricultural society of 19th-century Sweden. Male and female roles were, as in many other countries, then and now, more clearly defined. Men were breadwinners and women wives, cooks and homemakers.

The Lutheran church was a dominant influence on family life and the institution of marriage was sacrosanct. It was a time when children born out of wedlock were a shame and disgrace to the mother, and a husband was perfectly within his rights to beat his wife, his children and his servants if he so wished.

Of course nowadays Swedes regard such social mores as prehistoric: now half of all children born in Sweden are born outside wedlock; many couples choose to remain unmarried and divorce rates in Sweden are among the highest in Europe. But this does not mean the end of the family unit. Quite the contrary, in fact.

Separation and divorce

Today, however, the nuclear family takes many forms. Mr and Mrs Svensson with their 2.1

LEFT: Swedes eat outside whenever they can, though they may have to run for shelter between courses.
RIGHT: making the most of a glorious winter day.

children are a thing of the past. Now 14 per cent of families are headed by a single parent and 19 percent of cohabiting couples with children are unmarried. One child in every seven in Sweden currently lives in "mixed" families, in other words, families in which the parent granted custody is living with a new partner.

Couples who live together are known as *sambos*, an informal term derived from the word *samboende*, which means "living together". Cohabitation is something of a social institution and so widespread that it prompted the government to pass the Unmarried Couples Act in 1988. Although such couples are recognised by the law and their rights to property and inheritance are similar to those of married couples, there are still major legal differences that favour married couples.

Divorce rates are high in Sweden: some 45 percent of marriages end in divorce nowadays. Joint custody of children after divorce is automatic unless opposed by one of the parents, providing a framework in which families can continue to function despite the breakdown of the marriage.

This can call for so much contact and co-operation between the former couple, that one wonders why they simply didn't stay together in the first place. However, under Swedish law the parent granted custody of the child(ren) is guaranteed financial aid on a monthly basis which is paid either by the other parent or by the state.

Separation is also common in Sweden. Between 20 and 25 percent of all 17-year-olds in the country today have parents who are sep-

Role reversal

Swedish family policy has been increasingly aimed at enabling both mothers and fathers to combine employment with parenthood. For women the real breakthrough came during the 1960s at the height of the women's movement. With the labour market in short supply, more women sought employment outside the home, which pushed the government to initiate extensive plans for public child care.

Then a series of laws affecting parental leave, which were passed in the early 1970s, began a process in which the concept of the mother being the natural choice to stay at home with

arated; and between 5 and 10 percent of children in this age group have never lived with both their parents.

Having children and parenthood is nonetheless an important part of life in Sweden. Despite the fact that more than 80 percent of Swedish women are in the labour force, birth rates are among the highest in Western Europe. Birth rates fluctuated in the 1990s, but according to recent statistics the Swedish woman, on average, gives birth to 1.7 children.

Studies show that the vast majority of all Swedish women continue to work until the child is born and that an increasing number of them return to work within a year of the birth.

the children became increasingly antiquated. Such steps have been part of a national plan to increase men's participation in the care of children at home and encourage them to take a greater share of parental leave.

In 1996, fathers used around 10 per cent of parental insurance benefits. More recent surveys, however, have shown that more than 50 per cent of fathers use their right to paid parental leave during a child's first year.

Day-care centres

Along with parental insurance and child allowances, good child care amenities are a major cornerstone of Swedish family policy.

As of 1995 it was made incumbent upon local authorities to provide places at day-care centres for all children between the ages of one and six. For many families these day-care centres, or *dagis* as they are known, have become a natural extension of everyday life and they are indispensable for working parents or parents who are both studying. Some parents have even got together to found their own *dagis*: in all such cases the standards are high, the equipment is good and the children are well looked after.

a line of bicycles of all shapes and sizes, many with a child's seat attached to the back. Bicycles are a popular mode of transport for families with young children, particularly in the city, for the daily trip to and from *dagis*.

The rest of the Swedish population lives in houses. The dream of home ownership is very strong in Sweden, and most couples once they start a family want to buy their own home.

Buying a house in Sweden, as in other parts of Europe, is an expensive business, but oppor-

House and home

Just under half of Sweden's population lives in flats. In towns and cities flats are usually rented from local authorities or from housing associations. But living in a flat does not automatically mean poor housing. In fact, many flats have large, comfortable rooms in buildings that are often surrounded by gardens and play areas.

Down in the basement you'll find an immaculate laundry room, with washing machines and dryers for the tenants' use and in the courtyard,

tunities for home ownership are being improved through the simplification of government housing policies and deregulation of the housing market, which will bring down house prices.

Most houses are located on the outskirts of towns and cities, with gardens and plots that back on to woods and meadows beyond. They thus fulfil two fundamental needs of Swedish people: the need for space and the need to be close to nature.

LEFT: almost half Sweden's population lives in rented flats, which often overlook gardens.
ABOVE: a familiar sight, a bicycle made for three.

Caring for the elderly

"*Mitt hem är mitt borg.*" Loosely translated, this means: "my home is my castle", a sentiment that most people (regardless of their nationality) recognise and understand only too well.

The Swedish family home is a place where friends and family are entertained. Swedes love to get together to celebrate the big holidays, such as Christmas, Easter and Midsummer. But unlike many southern European families, for example, one thing you won't find in the average Swedish home is more than two generations living together.

Despite fluctuations in birth rates the number of elderly people in Sweden has continued to rise steadily, as it has in other countries in Europe. Around 18 percent of the total Swedish

population is now more than 65 years old. As in the case of child care, care of the elderly was made the responsibility of the state under Swedish law.

The country's housing policy is aimed at helping pensioners to live in their own homes for as long as possible and there are a number of care and housing options that are available to them when this is no longer feasible. Consequently it is rare to find elderly people living with their families.

However, growing pressure on Sweden's social welfare system means that families are likely to come under increasing pressure to care for their elderly family members in the future.

Children are central

As with most families, whatever the country, family life in Sweden is centred on the children, their needs, daily routines and activities.

The day starts early, with the parents of small children taking them to the day-care centre on the way to work. Children of school age are encouraged to take part in extra-curricular activities, from sports to more cultural pursuits. A recent study showed that 30 per cent of children aged nine to 14 play a musical instrument. Parents it seems are constantly on their way to either *hämta* (pick up) or *lämna* (drop off) their offspring who are engaged in some activity or other. *Hämta-lämna* is almost an activity in its own right and is certainly a way of life for busy Swedish families today.

Children and young people under 18 years of age account for one-fifth of the Swedish population. Swedish children enjoy a good standard of living and most want for nothing. Children in Sweden are protected by a law that has made it a crime to strike, threaten or persecute a child in any way. This law is Sweden's expression of a very fundamental principle: respect for children.

Off to the country

Any summer Saturday you are likely to spot a Swedish family setting out for the day, a small boat atop the Volvo or Saab, with a picnic basket filled with goodies in the back. Or perhaps they are off to spend a weekend out in the country at their cottage. More than 22 percent of Swedish families own a summer home.

When the Swedish family comes together to celebrate Midsummer, for example, despite that stiff wind and the growing threat of rain, they remain united in their collective obstinacy to sit out and dine alfresco. It matters not one iota that they are all forced to rush indoors, taking feast and table with them when the heavens finally open, or that they insist on going out again the minute it stops. All that matters is that they are together.

The Swedish family may take many forms today, but as Sweden moves into the 21st century the family remains the backbone of modern Swedish society. ❏

LEFT: stoking the stove in a Swedish family home.
RIGHT: Samis often put on their traditional costume for special family occasions.

THE QUEST FOR EQUALITY

Class distinctions barely exist and egalitarian policies affect all areas of life,
but the struggle for equality is far from finished

A century ago, Sweden was divided by a rigid class system. "Poverty, overcrowding, starvation and sickness were common," wrote the historian Åke Elmér. "In contrast, there was an upper class, which in magnificence and wealth stood far above the great mass of people." A small intermediate group of propertied farmers, middle-class merchants and white-collar workers "were objects of contempt to the upper class and envy to the working class".

The elite of nobles, senior bureaucrats, military officers and professors were addressed with the respectful *Ni* (you) and a tip of the cap by common folk and they would respond with the more familiar *du*. Railway carriages had three different classes and boats four. Industrial workers normally toiled 12 hours a day, and office workers a leisurely four or five.

Today, foreigners seeing the well-dressed crowds and comfortable homes have difficulty noting any class distinction. Swedes are near the top of the international league of such indicators of living standards as ownership of telephones, television sets and cars. Slums don't exist and the rare cases of individual hardship are widely reported in the newspapers.

Swedes themselves have trouble identifying the class origins of their fellow citizens. Many of the signposts that denote class in Britain, for instance, are absent in Sweden as regional or class accents in speech, as well as the use of *Ni*, have largely disappeared. The uniform high standard of the Swedish press removes the distinction between the readers of quality newspapers and tabloids that exist elsewhere in Europe. Attending university at Uppsala and Lund, Sweden's two oldest learning establishments, does not carry quite the same cachet as being a graduate of Oxford or Cambridge.

Only 25 years ago, most Swedes still identified with the working class; almost everyone now labels themselves middle-class. One indication of this trend is the rapid change in surnames. People are abandoning rural family names – those ending in -son (Ericsson or Carlsson)–and adopting the Latinised surnames (such as Beckérus or Glanzelius) of the 18th-century learned classes, to create the impres-

sion that one's forbears enjoyed a higher social status. Meanwhile, the Swedish nobility prefer to hide their titles rather than flout them. And, although any Stockholmer will tell you that the Östermalm district is upper-class, Norrmalm is middle-class and Söder is working-class, the differences have become increasingly blurred.

Narrowing the gaps

There are two main reasons why Sweden has so few class differences. One is the country's spurt of economic growth – the second fastest in the industrial world in the past century after Japan. And though it is relatively easy to spread the national wealth among a small population of

LEFT: the Swedish dream – a waterside cottage.
RIGHT: Feminists regard Antonia Axelsson-Johnson as a pioneer of women in business.

8.8 million, this has been aided by the policies of the long-ruling Social Democrats.

When the Social Democrats came to power in 1932, they eschewed the traditional socialist doctrine of nationalising industry. Instead, they concentrated on ensuring the even distribution of what is produced in the private sector and promoting equality of opportunity. In the long run the approach seems to have worked: a 1993 UN Development Programme report declared Sweden the world's most equal country.

Class differences have also lessened as gaps in income have narrowed, partly due to the equal pay for equal work policy championed

Housing and education have also received government attention in its push for egalitarian living standards. Before World War II, half of all Swedish urban households lived in tiny quarters with one room and a kitchen. The government embarked on a major construction programme that included rent subsidies to allow low-income families to live in more spacious dwellings. Unfortunately, housing construction has never kept pace with population movements to the cities. Paradoxically, central Stockholm's cramped flats, built a century ago to house the working class, have become highly desirable. For example, Gamla Stan, which 50

by the trade unions. In the 1960s, skilled workers were paid 54 percent more than unskilled labourers. By the mid-1980s, this had narrowed to 25 percent. Differences in income are further reduced by steeply progressive tax rates.

Taxing for equality

Taxes are not only a levelling device but they also pay for Sweden's extensive social welfare system, which guarantees that those such as the elderly, the sick and the disabled will not suffer a fall in living standards. Even the tax system itself is subject to egalitarian principles. Local taxes, which pay for the bulk of social services, do not vary greatly between regions.

years ago was a working-class slum, is today one of the city's most chic addresses.

The Social Democrats also felt that the education system they inherited maintained class barriers since it streamed pupils into "ability" groups. An American-style comprehensive school system was gradually introduced, making it easier for the children of working-class families to gain admission to university. Sweden now has the highest proportion of working-class youth in Western Europe at university.

By the late 1960s, with progress made in achieving economic equality, the government turned its attention to promoting sexual equality. A change in the tax rules, to require husbands and wives to file separate tax returns, encouraged the entry of women into the workforce since it penalised one-income households. Today, some 78 per cent of Swedish women are in the workforce, and of these 45 per cent are in full-time work.

Not there yet

"We have come a long way in equality between men and women in Sweden. But this is not enough. Every political decision must be permeated with an equality perspective." This was the

---

UPHOLDING FAIR PLAY

The principles of gender equality in Sweden are enshrined in the Swedish Constitution and upheld by the Office of the Equal Opportunities Ombudsman.

---

ment in all areas, including the armed forces. Collective agreements on gender equality have protected women's rights to equal pay for the same jobs undertaken by men. Women's position in the workforce has been helped by government training programmes and projects to support women starting their own businesses. However, women, on average, still earn less than men, and the majority do relatively low-paid "women's" jobs, such as nursing and secretarial work.

The problem women face in securing influ-

view expressed by the Social Democratic Party in its 1998 election manifesto. The political arena, it seems, leads the way in promoting gender equality in Sweden. By March 1996 both the Swedish parliament and cabinet consisted of an equal number of men and women, making it the world's most equal parliament.

The good news doesn't end there. Pay differences between the sexes are much smaller in Sweden than in many other countries. By law, Swedish women have the right to employ-

ential positions underlines the fact that Sweden has by no means achieved the perfect egalitarian society. The country's sizeable immigrant population also has difficulties in achieving the same standards of living as native Swedes despite government attempts to assimilate them into society. And while income distribution is relatively even, the distribution of wealth is not, with Swedish industry controlled by an oligarchy of family dynasties, such as the great banking family, the Wallenbergs.

As the distinction between male and female roles becomes fuzzier, one thing is clear: that even in a country as progressive as Sweden, the struggle for equality is not over. ❑

LEFT: the start of feminism – a women's sewing co-operative in the early 20th century. **ABOVE:** women weaving at a modern community centre.

THE IMMIGRANT DILEMMA

Sweden is no stranger to immigration, but growing cultural diversity and new economic realities raise the spectre of racism

Immigration – and its natural counterpart, emigration – have been a vital part of Swedish history for centuries. Not only have people from a host of nations made Sweden their temporary or permanent home over the ages, but hordes of Swedes left their homeland during the second half of the 19th century and the early 20th century, choosing to start over, most often in America. Virtually every Swede has at least one distant relative who emigrated to the New World.

During the 1990s ex-ABBA members Benny Andersson and Björn Ulvaeus wrote *Kristina från Duvemåla*, a new musical based on a Swedish novel-series, *Utvandrarna (The Emigrants)*. The story behind this internationally acclaimed musical is well known to most Swedes: the trials and tribulations of Kristina and her family as they emigrated from southern Sweden to Minnesota in the United States. It is interesting that as the 20th century closes, this beloved Swedish tale has been revived for the stage while the subject of immigration has provoked very mixed emotions within political and social arenas. From being a topic of historical and genealogical interest, immigration has become a hot issue linked with unemployment, crime and urban problems.

Historical upheavals

Although there were colonies of German merchants and craftsmen in Sweden as early as the 13th and 14th centuries, major immigration started from neighbouring Finland in the 16th century. The first non-Nordic wave of foreign immigration can be traced to the arrival of Dutch merchants and Walloon smiths during the 17th and 18th centuries. Their numbers were few by present standards, but even today there are villages, settled by Walloons, where the colouring is darker than average, though their descendants have long since been inte-

grated into the ethnically homogenous Swedish society that existed until recently.

The first wave of modern immigration during the 1930s didn't affect Sweden's homogenous nature as they were mostly ethnic Swedes who returned to escape the Depression in the United States. Also during the 1930s, immigrants out-

numbered emigrants for the first time. In only two years since then, 1972 and 1973, has the outflow been larger than the inflow.

In 1950, foreign nationals in Sweden totalled only 1.8 percent of the population, which was then a little over 6.9 million. Between 1944 and 1980, immigration accounted for nearly 45 percent of Sweden's total population growth and one of every four children born was of foreign extraction. By 1975, the number of foreign immigrants jumped to 5 percent of the population, which had increased to nearly 7.8 million.

The latest figures show that more than one million out of a total population of 8.8 million are foreign-born or the first generation children

---

LEFT: dressed for the Midsummer celebrations.
RIGHT: some Swedish schools have pupils from as many as 20 different races and 100 nations.

The Finn Connection

No two nations are more inextricably linked in past and present than Sweden and Finland. At any given time, there are probably more Finnish immigrants in Sweden than there are ethnic Swedish-speaking Finns living in Finland. The Finns have been emigrating to (and emigrating from) Sweden since the 16th century. As a result, the Finns now constitute the largest foreign national group in Sweden, totalling over 320,000. Of these, 190,000 hold Swedish citizenship.

Their life-line is the ferry traffic dominated by

the Viking and Silja Lines with the main routes operating from Stockholm to Helsinki and Turku in Finland. These ferries across the Baltic carry more than eight million passengers a year between the two countries, mostly Finns on visits to relatives and friends in Sweden or Finland. Recent traffic growth has turned the ferry into a floating luxury hotel, with berths in cabins for 2,000-plus passengers, and a choice of restaurants, nightclubs and bars to idle away the time.

Finnish domination among Sweden's immigrant population can be traced back to the historical relations between the two nations and, more recently, to the common labour market that allow citizens of the Nordic countries to cross borders without the need of a passport or work permit. But the ratio between immigration and emigration for Finns in Sweden is now almost even, with as many people returning each year as arriving; this is because Finland's economy is at least as strong as Sweden's.

For more than 500 years, Finland was a part of Sweden, and the Finns were more often than not the foot-soldiers for Swedish generals. The 16th- and 17th-century immigrants were usually retired soldiers who helped to settle wilderness areas in central and northern Sweden. Succeeding waves of Finnish immigrants worked in Sweden's mines and forests, then in its factories and hospitals.

Although the two nations have a distinctly interrelated history, their differences are quite significant. This is evident from the three Finnish groups that live in Sweden: Finns with Finnish as a mother tongue (Finn-Finns); Finns with Swedish as a mother tongue (Finn-Swedes); and Swedes with Finnish as a mother tongue (Swede-Finns).

Finn-Finns, the largest immigrant group, are the ones most likely to return to Finland after a while. They usually cross the Baltic Sea in the first place because Sweden is where the jobs are. Even if they establish roots there, they never forget that Finland is at most a 10 to 12-hour boat ride away.

Finn-Swedes, on the other hand, are likely to stay for a long time. Their Swedish mother tongue is often a hangover from the time when Swedish was the offical language in Finland and used for all bureaucratic purposes. Today, they are a minority in their own country, accounting for less than 10 percent of Finland's total population, and they often have family ties to Sweden.

The Swede-Finns – the smallest group – usually live along the northern border between the two countries and strictly speaking cannot be counted as immigrants.

Despite these differences, all Finns living in Sweden unite in common cause at least once every year. They all shout for Finland during the two-day annual track and field meet, held alternately in Stockholm or Helsinki, that pits a Swedish national team against a Finnish national team. More often than not, the Finnish teams, both men and women, come out on top – which is no small achievement since Sweden has almost twice the population of Finland. It is a sweet victory for all Finns, who have had to put up with a "poor cousin" relationship with the Swedes. ❏

LEFT: Swedes and Finns get together on their shared northern border to celebrate Midsummer.

of a foreign parent. The foreign-born alone total more than 900,000, of whom about half have become Swedish citizens. Immigration's record year was 1970, when arrivals peaked at 77,300.

During and immediately after World War II, a different type of immigrant arrived, refugees from the war and suppression in the Baltic states and central Europe. They included 122,000 refugees from the other Nordic countries, including 60,000 Finnish children. Those who stayed in Sweden after the war have mostly

PEOPLE AND JOBS

In 1986 the number of non-European immigrants exceeded the European immigrants for the first time. Assimilation was made harder by rising unemployment.

market, which does not require work permits.

With changing economic conditions in the 1970s, Sweden sought to stem the tide of economic immigrants, but still took in humanitarian immigration and political refugees – including Chileans, other Latin Americans and Kurds. In 1979, a large wave came from Iran, including many Kurds. In the 1980s and 1990s came Palestinian refugees from war or terror in Lebanon, Iraqis, Africans from Somalia, Ethiopia and Kenya, and refugees from war in the Balkans.

become Swedish citizens. The post-war wave of the 1950s and 1960s were mostly "guest workers" invited by Sweden to work in its factories and help expand industrialisation. They came principally from Italy, the United Kingdom and West Germany.

The 1950s and 1960s also brought immigrants from Hungary, Czechoslovakia, Greece, Poland, Turkey and Yugoslavia. Many other Nordic country nationals, especially Finns, also moved to Sweden in the late 1960s – a trend facilitated by the common Nordic labour

ABOVE: dark heads and fair heads at the Rinkeby Immigrant Festival, near Stockholm.

Racism rears its head

The later arrivals from the Middle East are not as welcome as the earlier immigrants. To the Swedes, they appear both too different and too many, and liberal Sweden, long the conscience of the world, now has its share of skinheads and other racists. In the past, immigrant groups most often came from Europe, and within a couple of generations they assimilated into Swedish society. Today, the sheer numbers needing refuge, plus the wide disparity between Sweden's culture and those of Asia and Africa, makes assimilation more difficult.

The problem of racism – and its by-product, discrimination – has surely been compounded by social and economic problems unknown to post-war Swedes until the late 1980s. Earlier in the 20th century, unemployment was virtually zero and immigration was essential because there were not enough Swedes to do all the work. By the mid-1990s, unemployment was over 10 percent, with immigrants making up a large number of those out of work. This problem was both caused and exacerbated by the global downturn in the economy and the critical situation of the Swedish national debt. Cutbacks were increasingly widespread as a result of both. The amount of money spent on social relief programmes regularly came under

attack. The mix of economic troubles, increasing populations of immigrants, and the need to alter cradle-to-grave social welfare has been central to problems of racism in Sweden.

Unemployment – the number one problem facing immigrants – and discrimination are clearly interconnected. Language is the primary obstacle facing most newcomers. And in a country where foreign names are easily detected, and where unemployment now vexes all sections of society, getting shortlisted for a job is extremely difficult. The government has tried a variety of remedies, including temporary job projects *(praktik)* aimed at helping to introduce immigrants into the working com-

munity and to get the obligatory *betyg* (certificate or reference received from all educational and employment endeavours).

Integrating new arrivals

Today's Sweden has some suburban housing projects where the immigrant population far outnumbers the ethnic Swedes. There are also schools with students from up to 100 different nations and day-care centres with almost as many nationalities as there are children.

Creating ghettos is not the intention, and Swedish authorities have made many successful attempts to integrate the new arrivals into Swedish society, including free Swedish lessons which may be taken with full pay during working hours.

Paradoxically, many of the more recent immigrants, who often come from small villages in Turkey, Syria or Iran, tend to live together because of language difficulties and for economic reasons.

Many municipalities are concerned about isolated immigrant communities and are creating programmes to encourage integration and reduce unemployment. In Kronogården, an immigrant-rich neighbourhood of Trollhättan, south of Lake Vänern, an EU-funded project began in the mid-1990s with the aim of reducing unemployment among immigrants. Language classes, for example, have been set up at a playgroup where mums with small children can study Swedish while their children play.

Even if they are not naturalised, immigrants have some say in how their lives are run, with a right to vote in municipal and county council elections but not in national elections, provided they have been residents for three consecutive years. All the political parties try to woo the immigrant vote, which can be decisive.

The percentage exercising the right, however, is far below the national average. This may be because some immigrants have never before participated in a democratic process, they do not understand the differences between the numerous political parties, they do not feel that the political parties are addressing their interests, or perhaps they hope that their stay in Sweden is not permanent. ❑

LEFT: boys at the Rinkeby Immigrant Festival.
RIGHT: the emergence of a black community in Sweden is comparatively recent.

THE SAMI

For as long as anyone knows, the Sami have lived in the wilderness of
Lapland, dependent on the seasons and their reindeer

They call themselves "the people of the eight seasons". They are the Sami (once known as the Lapps), who live in Sweden's most northerly province of Lapland – a vast wilderness where nature and the reindeer set the course of the year.

In the eighth century a Lombardian monk, Paulus Diaconus, described the reindeer as a strong and hardy little animal that was "not unlike a stag". But that was not the first written reference to the Sami and their country. Both the Roman historian Tacitus and the later Procopius had already mentioned Scandinavia. It is unlikely that Tacitus or Procopius visited the far north, but perhaps Paulus Diaconus found his way there: he describes the snow-covered mountains, the dress of the Sami and the skill with which they managed to move along. His writings were also the first to mention the Midnight Sun and the winter solstice.

Hard times

The eight seasons of Lapland start with springwinter in April, when there is still heavy snow cover over the plains. The reindeer must dig deep through the snow to find their most important food, the lichens – reindeer lichen, beard lichen which hangs heavily from the branches of the trees, and the tangled horsehair lichen, with its comic name of "nervous wreck".Life is bleak for the reindeer. It is also a hardworking time for the Sami who breed the reindeer and keep the herds in order.

But spring is in the air and soon they will be trekking up the high mountains. The stags have sloughed off their horns and the does are carrying their young in their swollen stomachs. The sun arrives at the beginning of May. It is the second season and the doe is ready to calve.

Before long the spring-summer is here. The mountains blossom with Sami heather, globe flowers, cloudberries and countless species,

offering a feast for the eye. The region is botanically rich, and the life of its people provides a rare insight into a unique culture.

Modern methods

The reindeer keeper of today is very different from his ancestors. In the past, even up until

the early decades of the 20th century, the whole family accompanied the reindeer up into the mountains, the draught-reindeer loaded with all the paraphernalia required for the summer, not least the *kåta* or cone-shaped hut to provide shelter. There the family would live out the summer, making the most of the endless daylight, storing up for the long nights of winter.

Today, the families live in towns and villages and only the men care for the animals and follow the herd. To assist them, they have acquired helicopters and scooters, mobile phones and all the modern-day equipment that makes communication easy. But, despite modern life, the reindeer must stay up on the high mountains

PRECEDING PAGES: herding reindeer.
LEFT: Sami in traditional costume at Jokkmokk fair.
RIGHT: the mountains blossom in the short summer.

where the pasture is rich and a fresh wind blows, in contrast to the birch woods below where the heat is too oppressive for the animals and the insects sting ferociously.

After the spring-summer comes the summer proper, to bring the grazing land that the Sami dream about during the winter. Fresh and clean, the small streams babble and the lakes are rich in trout, Arctic char, and whitefish. Up here, there is not a single tree or bush to be seen.

Reindeer herding is not easy. The men must mark all the new-born calves with their own distinctive criss-cross sign and herd the deer, throwing their lassoes with a skill and accuracy

soon shed its leaves but first it goes through a kaleidoscope of yellow, orange, red and brown, turning the mountains into a stunning sight.

Ritual slaughter

The slaughter begins and the ancient scene is like a feast from some primeval rite, full of the strong odours of sweat, blood and dung. The meat that the men do not sell fresh is frozen to become a delicacy – such as thin slices of reindeer fried with onions, mushrooms and cream.

Now it is autumn-winter, the northern lights are blazing and the aurora carries frost in its colours. The days grow perceptibly shorter and,

that they learned in their childhood games. Today, the lasso is made of nylon and, once the calf is caught, the men make a small incision in its ear with a sharp knife and thread the small pieces of flesh cut out on to a string or sinew. That way, all the men know how many calves are in the herd and which belong to each man.

All too soon the summer is gone and the men must drive their reindeer herds back down the mountains into the folds where they will be separated from each other before slaughter.

In the autumn-summer, the reindeer are fat from the fine pastures. The flies and mosquitoes are gone but heavy storms rage over the mountains and the plains. The knotty dwarf birch will

when mist and storms cover the stars, the nights are black. On the moors, the reindeer huddle together to keep warm along the edges of the birchwoods where the snow is loose and the lichens are still moist and full of nourishment.

Today, beasts of prey are little danger to the Sami. The wolf is almost extinct in Sweden, the bear hibernates, and the wolverine no longer lies in wait to lap the reindeers' fresh blood.

Traditional market fairs

In every way, the life of the Sami has changed in modern times. It is only for festivals and ceremonial occasions that they put on the knee-length costume, trimmed with handwoven ribbons in red and yellow. But the tradition of handicrafts continues strongly and the best place to see it is at one of the big market fairs at Jokkmokk. The Sami make use of any natural materials from tree bark to reindeer horn.

Visitors come not just from Sweden but from all parts of the world to meet the Sami at this traditional fair. The Jokkmokk fair is unique in that it has only genuine Sami handicrafts such as the beautifully designed knives, the bowls and baskets plaited from the thinnest root fibres, pieces of

A SCATTERED PEOPLE

Today, the fascinating Sami people are a scattered remnant numbering around 85,000. They are divided between Finland, Norway, Russia and Sweden.

August and February, but all over Lapland there are delicacies to taste and Sami handicrafts to buy and to view in museums.

In 1732, the botanist Carl von Linné made an expedition to Lapland, and some years later a copper engraving was made of him in Sami dress, with the frock, bottle-nosed boots, and the typical Sami accessories. In his hand he holds a drum with mythical signs, now considered one of the most precious possessions for any Sami. But the mythical signs are another

carved wood, and ribbons and woven fabrics. (*see pages 306–7*).

Reindeer delicacies

In Jokkmokk, you can also taste all the delicacies associated with the reindeer – the pure Lapland *lappkok*, a casserole made of marrow bones and shredded liver to form a substantial and tasty broth; or *renklämma,* a thin slice of unleavened bread shaped into a cone and filled with slices of smoked reindeer. The fairs are in

story – a tale from ancient times, from the special religion that belongs to the Sami.

Finding a stronger voice

Independence has always been important for the Sami, and since 1986 they have had their own national anthem and national flag. In 1993, they also acquired their own democratically elected parliament based in Kiruna, where about 10 political parties are represented. Its influence is limited and it acts as an administrative authority under the control of the Swedish government. All the same, the Sami have certainly acquired a stronger voice in regional government. ❑

FAR LEFT: travelling hopefully in Arctic Sweden.
LEFT: lasso-throwing is a skill learned in childhood.
ABOVE: inside a Sami cone-shaped tent or *kåta*.

ART IN SWEDEN

From medieval times Sweden has embraced artistic and architectural styles from the continent – and made them distinctly its own

The rich and varied history of Swedish art is highly indebted to the royal and aristocratic patronage that fostered many of the most significant developments. Artistic styles brought from the continent were adapted to Swedish taste and climate, giving them a distinct Swedish quality.

Picture stones

Artistic production in Sweden reaches back to the magnificent rock carvings of the Bronze Age (1500 BC–500 BC). These carvings, known as *hällristningar,* are to be found throughout the southern coastal areas of Sweden, but the richest concentration can be seen in the province of Bohuslän, on the west coast. Featuring images of ships, battles, hunting, fishing and farming scenes, and mating couples, these simple, curvilinear carvings convey a wealth of information about daily living as well as religious beliefs.

Picture stones, images carved with a figural and circular-ornament style on to raised stones (as opposed to the rocky coastlines where the *hällristningar* are found), are the most prominent artefacts remaining from the Iron Age. The majority of surviving picture stones (nearly 400) are on the island of Gotland.

By the 5th century, Scandinavian art is principally defined by the animal-ornament style, a flowing, interlacing abstract design featuring fantastic animal heads and other body parts. Examples are found on ship carvings and portable metal objects, such as brooches and other pieces of jewellery, which constitute most of the art objects remaining from this period.

Ecclesiastical architecture

After the baptism of King Olof Skötkonung, c.AD 1000, Christianity became widespread in Sweden. This date also marks the start of the

medieval period in Sweden (1000–1520), a time in which, not surprisingly, ecclesiastical art dominated – from the church buildings themselves, to the carvings on them and the sculptural items common to most churches (such as fonts and triumphal crucifixes). Stylistically, most of the art and architecture of this

PRECEDING PAGES: the unmistakable *Dalahäst* (Dala horse), handpainted at Nusnäs.
LEFT: nude in a landscape – *Bather* by Anders Zorn.
RIGHT: runic stone with carved inscription, Uppsala.

period is an adaptation of styles imported from England, France and Germany. Many fine examples of works, especially church murals, remain from this period thanks to the lack of iconoclasts within the Lutheran Reformation.

The first cathedral in Sweden was built in 1103 in Lund, Skåne (which was in Danish hands until 1658). It is a Romanesque structure clearly influenced by German and Lombardic architecture.

Swedish Gothic architecture, as seen in the cathedrals in Uppsala and on Gotland, is not as flamboyant and ornate as that found in France. This is partly due to problems inherent with

Royal portraiture, often produced by foreign artists, dominated Swedish painting from the 16th to the 18th centuries, with many of the finest examples kept at the National Portrait Gallery, in Gripsholms Slott (castle).

Swedish baroque

During the Thirty Years' War (1618–48) Sweden experienced a lengthy period of prosperity. Queen Kristina (1644–54), a tremendous patron of the arts, commissioned numerous building projects and imported several artists from abroad; it was during Kristina's reign, for example, that work began on Riddarhuset (the

Sweden's prevailing weather. Another unusual feature, again compared with France, is the conspicuous use of brick for building churches.

Court patronage

Beginning with the court of Gustav Vasa (1523–60), the first king to consolidate the Swedish monarchy, art in Sweden experienced a period of dynamic development. The increased power within the Swedish court coincided with the Renaissance, a time throughout Europe where secular art began to supplant religious art. In Sweden, the most notable artistic production consisted of building castles (Gripsholm, Vadstena, Kalmar) and decorating them.

House of Nobility), in central Stockholm, which is one of the finest structures in the city.

The father-and-son team of Tessin the Elder and the Younger were two of the most gifted architects of the 17th and 18th centuries, and Drottningholm Palace was one of their most important undertakings. The structure as a whole remains the finest example of Swedish baroque art.

French influences

King Gustav III (1771–92) was an avid francophile and a devoted supporter of the arts. Not surprisingly, French culture and style heavily influenced Sweden in the 1700s. Nonetheless, even the most elaborate Rococo-inspired Swedish art is tempered in comparison with its French and Italian counterparts. The lack of exuberance is undoubtedly due, in part, to the Lutheran background, which contributed to a starker aesthetic than that of the Catholic southern countries of Europe. The somewhat austere aesthetics of Protestant Germany and Holland also had a restraining influence.

French art continued to inspire Swedish painters during the 19th century. In the early

MASTER PAINTER

Portrait painter Alexander Roslin (1718–93), admired for his skilled rendition of textiles as well as facial expressions, is one of Sweden's most celebrated artists.

A touch of romanticism

Upon returning to Sweden in the last decade of the 19th century, many artists embraced Swedish themes. This period is usually defined as National Romanticism. Back in Sweden, Carl Larsson's style changed in favour of much more defined and curvilinear lines and strong, dark contours. Anders Zorn arrived later in Paris and became one of the leading portrait painters for the wealthy in France, Britain and the United States for a time. When not painting portraits,

1880s, several Scandinavian artists – including Carl Larsson, Karl Nordström and Richard Bergh – travelled to France, spending their summers at Grèz-sur-Loing, not far from Fontainebleau, where they practised *plein-air* painting. While few Swedish artists really took up Impressionism *per se*, some of the techniques of the genres – such as using a looser brushstroke, asymmetrical composition and a brighter palette – found their way into a number of the artists' works.

LEFT: Drottningholms Palace, a baroque masterpiece.
ABOVE: characteristic interior by Carl Larsson, who still exerts a strong influence on Swedish design.

AT HOME WITH THE ARTISTS

The homes of Carl and Karin Larsson at Sundborn, and Anders Zorn in Mora, both in Dalarna, are open to the public. The picturesque house at Sundborn is a showcase of the talents of Larsson and his wife Karin. She inherited the house in 1888 and together they created the simply furnished family home that inspired so much of 20th-century Swedish design. The preserved rooms, featuring Carl's artwork and Karin's textiles, are easily recognisable from his paintings. Zorn's 19th-century home is very different – larger and more richly decorated. It houses his collection of art and applied art, and there is a museum of his own work in the grounds.

he often painted scenes from his native Dalarna and female nudes in landscapes.

Colourists of the 20th century

In the 20th century, many Swedish artists were proponents of the various "isms" imported from the continent. They included Isaac Grunewald and Sigrid Hjertén (Fauvism), Otto Sköld (Cubism), and the Halmstad Group (Surrealism). During the 1930s, a number of artists based on the west coast painted with brilliant colours inspired by those used in both Fauvism and Expressionism; and although they were never a real school, they became known as the

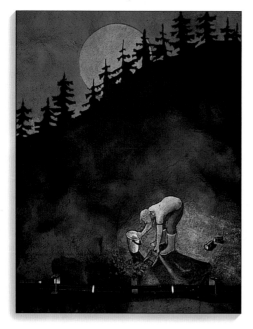

Göteborgkolorister (Göteborg Colourists).

Following World War II, Olle Bonniér and Olle Baertling were among the adherents of Geometric Abstraction. Oyvind Fahlström, influenced and stimulated by European and American Neo-Realism of the 1950s and 1960s, developed a highly unique style, and his art has gained new interest in Sweden.

Though Sweden was not a spawning ground for any very influential art movements of the 20th century, Stockholm became an important player in the international art scene following the opening of the Moderna Museet in 1958.

The contemporary art scene in Sweden has plenty of participants (if not many venues for presentation), and the work of women artists, including Charlotte Gyllenhammar, Annika von Hausswolff and Lena Mattsson, is becoming increasingly prominent. Journals and Internet web sites follow and analyse the latest trends.

Touring the museums

Nationalmuseum: The National Museum of Fine Arts is Sweden's largest art museum. It is beautifully situated on the water in Stockholm in a building modelled on Florentine and Venetian architectural design. The museum grew from private royal collections, starting with the works gathered by King Gustav Vasa at Gripsholm Castle in the 16th century. Today, the collection includes paintings, sculpture, decorative arts, drawings and prints from the Middle Ages to the 20th century.

Works by artists such as Rembrandt, Goya, Degas and Gauguin are on display. In addition to the strong holdings of Swedish 18th- and 19th-century painting, there are fine examples of Dutch 17th-century art and French 18th-century art. Objects from the decorative arts departments span five centuries, and here you will find Scandinavia's largest collection of china, glass, Swedish silver and furniture.

Some of the finer works to be seen here are Rembrandt's *The Conspiracy of the Batavians under Claudius Civilis* (1661–62), as well as Swedish works including Alexander Roslin's *The Lady with the Veil* (1768) and Anders Zorn's *Midsummer Dance* (1897).

Frescoes by Carl Larsson also flank the main staircases in the museum's entrance hall, and his large painting, *Midvinterblot* (*Sacrifice at the Winter Solstice*, 1914–15), and Gustav Vasa's *Intåg i Stockholm* (*Entry into Stockholm*, 1908) are prominently displayed at the top of the stairs.

Moderna Museet: The Modern Museum opened in 1958 and, under the guidance of director Pontus Hultén, soon became an important site for exhibitions and artistic exchange. A new building designed by Rafael Moneo opened in 1998, giving the museum the opportunity to expand, both physically and functionally, and perhaps become, once again, a major force on the art scene.

The permanent collection is strong in American 1960s art, and includes many fine pieces of early modern art. Acquisitions of more recent works have a more marked Scandinavian accent. Works of particular note include Rauschenberg's *Monogram* (1955–59) and *Mud Muse* (1971), as well as Picasso's *La Source* (1921) and Ulf Rollof's *Kylrock* (*Cold Mantle*, 1989).

Magasin 3 (Konsthall, Stockholm): This slightly out-of-the-way, privately funded exhibition space opened in 1987 in an old warehouse in Stockholm's Frihamn (Free Port). Exhibitions feature contemporary art, and the art centre has its own permanent collection of more than 400 works.

Waldemarsudde: On the island of Djurgården in central Stockholm, the former home and are of Scandinavian art from the end of the 19th century and were donated by Pontus and Göthilda Furstenberg. The Hasselblad Centre for photography forms part of the museum.

Rooseum (Malmö): This museum acquired its name and permanent collection from its founder, Fredrik Roos (1951–91), a financier and avid collector of contemporary art. After amassing a vast collection, he needed a site to display it. Housed in the former quarters of the Malmö Electricity Company, Rooseum is an ideal-sized museum that has earned a well-deserved and widespread reputation for its shows of international contemporary art. ❑

studio of Prince Eugen is now a museum featuring art that he both created and collected, mostly from the latter half of the 19th century. The waterside setting and gardens are attractive and inviting.

Konstmuseum (Göteborg): The collection at Göteborg Museum of Art (founded 1861) owes its existence entirely to the donations of private citizens rather than to royal patronage. Some of the most important works in the collection

---

LEFT: more than 70 artists have contributed to the decoration of Stockholm's underground railway stations (*see page 186*). **ABOVE:** *Monogram* by Robert Rauschenberg in the newly housed Moderna Museet.

ART AND CRAFT TRADTIONS

Swedish glass-making is world renowned. The centre of this 250-year-old tradition is the Växjö areain southern Sweden, where artists continue to produce glass of the very finest quality. When travelling outside the major cities, the art most often encountered – in craft shows and *hemslöjd* (craft) shops – is handicrafts ranging from wooden cheese boards, butter knives and serving trays, to handwoven textiles, straw decorations, hand-smithed candlesticks and the distinctive *Dalahäst* (Dala horse). In many of the crafts simplicity of design is combined with high quality materials. The same aesthetic principles inspire most of the contemporary furniture production.

TRADITIONAL SWEDISH INTERIORS

Recent years have seen a revival of interest in traditional Swedish style, with its emphasis on simplicity, light and natural materials

The very restraint of Swedish interior design which makes it so appealing to modern tastes was born from the restrictions imposed by the country's climate and economy. Since sunshine is scarce during the winter, the Swedes have generally sought to maximise light in their rooms, for example by choosing pale colours for the walls.

Since so much of the country is forested, wood prevails in Swedish interiors rather than marble and stone. Similarly, the rich tradition of painted decoration has traditionally provided a cheap substitute in poorer homes for costly wallpapers and multi-coloured, patterned fabrics.

Swedish interiors have been subject to fluctuations of fashion and the income of their owners, but there seem to be certain constant features of Swedish style – a lack of clutter and a love of symmetry and clean lines. Perhaps the purest embodiment of these principles can be seen in the interiors dating from the short reign of Gustav III (1771–92). Gustavian style was really a pared-down form of Neoclassicism, in which gilt was replaced by a more restricted palette dominated by greys, blues, creams and yellows. The simple elegance of that period continues to inspire decorators today, particularly those many people who are buying and restoring traditional country cottages.

▷ **UNCLUTTERED DESIGN**
Several firms make excellent reproduction antique furniture. This chest of drawers by IKEA displays the clean lines of more traditional pieces.

▷ **RESTORING THE PAST**
Many people are painstakingly restoring old homes: the bedrooms in this 17th-century hunting lodge have walls hung with the original handpainted wallpaper.

△ **TILED STOVES**
An essential feature of the traditional Swedish room, the tall tiled stove, kept occupants warm during the bitter winter months.

▽ **CLEAR COLOURS**
The woodwork in this country kitchen has been painted in the fresh colours traditional in rural cottages in Sweden.

▷ **STENCILLING**
Stencilling has been a popular method of decoration since the Middle Ages. This pattern was stencilled directly onto a wooden wall.

CARL LARSSON AT HOME

The artist Carl Larsson (1853–1919) and his wife Karin were instrumental in reviving interest in traditional Swedish decoration and crafts at the turn of the 20th century. They and their eight children lived in a wooden farmhouse in the province of Dalarna, where they created the series of exceptional interiors that Carl recorded in his watercolours (detail above).

His illustrated books *Ett Hem* (*At Home*, 1899) and *At Solsiden* (*On the Sunny Side*, 1910), which were hugely popular in Sweden and elsewhere, promoted a traditional style that was given a modern, idiosyncratic twist by the Larssons' absorption of the ideas of the English Arts and Crafts movement and of country crafts. While the emphasis was placed on simplicity, embellishment was added in the form of embroidery, folklore-inspired textiles and hand-painted friezes or panels. Some of the fine 18th-century furniture the Larssons had inherited was painted in bright colours inspired by rural houses rather than using the original, more muted palette.

The Larssons' home at Sundborn is now a museum (*see page 277*).

> **REINTERPRETING TRADITION**
At Sundborn, Carl and Karin Larsson combined the old and the new. In the studio, for example, Gustavian chairs were painted bright red.

WORDS, MUSIC AND CELLULOID

*Strindberg, Bergman, Garbo... Sweden occupies a central place in Europe's
cultural life, and continues to champion press freedom*

For a small country in the distant north of Europe, Sweden has given the world an impressive legacy in literature, film, theatre, music and the media. From Sweden emerged the imposing literary figures of Selma Lagerlöf and August Strindberg; beloved children's author Astrid Lindgren; world-famous film director, Ingmar Bergman; luminous female movie stars like Greta Garbo and Ingrid Bergman; and the celebrated pop group ABBA.

Less well known is that Sweden, in 1766, was the first country to establish freedom of the press, and the nation has continued zealously to protect the public's right to information and the role of journalist as watchdog. This is particularly appreciated by Swedes, who are among the world's most avid newspaper buyers.

The government generously subsidises the arts, so ticket prices are reasonable. The Royal Opera, the Royal Dramatic Theatre, the Swedish National Touring Theatre and the Royal Philharmonic Orchestra are entirely publicly funded; private sponsorship of the arts is rare.

The legacy of the Theatre King

King Gustav III, "the Theatre King", set up the Swedish national theatres in Stockholm in the late 18th century to provide venues for the performance of dramatic arts in Swedish. Until then, opera and drama were performed at the court theatre in their original languages, Italian and French. Kungliga Teatern (The Royal Theatre, now known as the Kungliga Opera, or the Royal Opera) was founded in 1773. In 1788, Kungliga Dramatiska Teatern (the Royal Dramatic Theatre or Dramaten), opened its doors.

Today, Ingmar Bergman still directs productions of Strindberg and other classics at Dramaten, although Lars Norén has taken over Bergman's former position as Sweden's national dramatist. A poet and prose writer in the 1960s, Norén cemented his reputation as director with the 1980 trilogy, *Modet att Döda*

(*The Courage to Kill*), a claustrophobic middle-class drama reminiscent of Chekhov.

In 1842 the crown's theatre monopoly in Stockholm was abolished and new theatres raised their curtains. Several municipal theatres opened in the 1920s and 1930s, followed by the advent of regional theatres in the 1960s and

1970s. Today, there are three national and 27 regional/municipal theatres in the country. With economic cutbacks, growing commercialism, and competition from electronic media and other leisure activities, theatre in Sweden is less prominent than it has been, but still vibrant.

Performances, however, are nearly always in Swedish. For a taste of the Swedish dramatic scene, you could try the internationally respected Folk Operan (Swedish Folk Opera) or the Drottningholm Theatre productions of late baroque plays and ballet. The theatre is part of the royal family's permanent residence, on an island in Lake Mälaren, which itself is well worth a visit.

LEFT: folk festival in Falun, Dalarna.
RIGHT: accordion player at a folk festival.

In 1994, Göteborg Opera opened in its new home by the harbour, giving Sweden another major house for classical productions, including many by Swedish composers, such as Wilhelm Peterson-Berger's *Arnljot* and Ingvar Lidholm's *A Dream Play*, first presented in 1992.

Musical heritage

As with the visual arts, royal patronage and generous appropriation from the continent were crucial to the history of music in Sweden. The country's best loved poet, composer and musician is probably Carl Michael Bellman, whose witty lyrics immortalised 18th-century life in

Stockholm. Like so many successful Swedish artists, he found his greatest patron in Gustav III. His songs are still very much alive today.

National holidays and folk festivals provide opportunities to enjoy Swedish folk dancing and music. The violin is the most common folk instrument, with fiddlers providing the rhythm for the polka, waltz, *schottishe* or *polkette*.

Sweden hosts several music festivals. At Musik vid Siljan (Music by Lake Siljan), held in summer, music ranges from organ concerts to jazz. International jazz festivals, such as those in Umeå (October) and Sandviken (summer), draw many of the biggest names in jazz. There are numerous choirs throughout the country.

Major international musicals often arrive in Sweden shortly after premiering in London and New York, and some, such as the 1990s hit *Kristina from Duvemåla*, written by ex-ABBA members Benny Andersson and Björn Ulvaeus, are even exported by Sweden. Following in ABBA's footsteps, other successful exports of the 1980s and '90s have included Roxette, Ace of Base and The Cardigans.

Great film-makers

In around 1920, during the silent film era, Sweden was among the leading cinematic nations of the world. Directors Victor Sjöström and Mauritz Stiller made several films which were regarded as masterpieces at the time and are now considered classics. Some are based on books by Selma Lagerlöf, such as *Körkarlen* (*The Phantom Carriage*) and *Herr Arnes Pengar* (*Sir Arne's Treasure*).

This age of greatness was brief. Sjöström and Stiller went to Hollywood and took with them a rising star named Greta Garbo. When talking pictures arrived in the 1930s, Swedish films took a rather provincial turn. During World War II, directors such as Alf Sjöberg and Hasse Ekman created more serious, artistic work. Following the war, the modern festival system heightened demand for artistic and prestigious theatre. Documentary film-maker Arne Sucksdorff won international praise; Sjöberg won a 1951 prize at Cannes for his production of Strindberg's classic, *Fröken Julie* (*Miss Julie*). Finally, with Ingmar Bergman's acclaim for *Sommernattens leende* (*Smiles of a Summer Night*), Sweden was once again the subject of global cinematic interest.

Bergman's star continued to rise over the decades, but otherwise, Swedish cinema has not made international headlines. Swedish cinemas offer a primarily American selection; Swedish films account for only 20 percent of box-office revenues. Part of the revenue from box office sales, video hires, and Swedish television goes to the Svenska Filminstitutet (Swedish Film Institute) under a government plan to promote "high-quality Swedish films".

Swedes bridle at the term "Schwedenfilm", the German phrase that in the 1970s described the daringly erotic Swedish films being made at

LEFT: rising star, Greta Garbo.
RIGHT: Ingmar Bergman directs *Fanny and Alexander*.

the time, which are said to have paved the way for cinematic pornography, but Sweden itself has not contributed much to this genre.

The star quotient

Sweden's female movie glamour queens are perhaps most associated with the country's cinematic history. The greatest was Greta Garbo, who made silent films in Sweden before going to Hollywood. The "divine" Miss Garbo came to exemplify the idea of movie star for decades, with such films as *Anna Karenina*

ORIGINAL FILM STUDIO

Kristianstad is the birthplace of the Swedish film industry, c.1910. The original studio is now a museum where you can watch some of the old movies on video.

(1927 and 1935), *A Woman of Affair* (1929), *Queen Christina* (1934) and *Camille* (1937).

Another Swedish-born movie goddess was Ingrid Bergman. She went to Hollywood in 1939 to play opposite Leslie Howard in an American version of the Swedish film *Intermezzo*, which made her a star. In Hollywood she shared top billing with Humphrey Bogart in *Casablanca*, Gary Cooper in *For Whom The Bell Tolls* and Gregory Peck in *Spellbound*.

Other Swedish film stars of somewhat lesser

INGMAR BERGMAN

Born in 1918 as the son of a clergyman, Ingmar Bergman has throughout his career been associated with the Swedish film industry. He first came to public attention with the script he wrote for *Torment* (1944). His own productions, made with a small company of devoted actors, including Liv Ullman, Bibi Andersson and Eva Fröhling, are often concerned with questions of faith and belief. They include *Smiles of a Summer Night* (1955); *Seventh Seal* (1956); *Wild Strawberries* (1957); *Persona* (1966); *Shame* (1968); *Cries and Whispers* (1971); *Scenes From A Marriage* (1973); *Face to Face* (1976); *Autumn Sonata* (1978); and *Fanny and Alexander* (1981), his last feature-length motion picture.

Bergman remains active, writing film scripts and directing productions at Stockholm's Royal Dramatic Theatre. He has written an autobiography, *The Magic Lantern*, followed by *My Life in Film*, and *Good Intentions*, a depiction of his parents' love affair, marriage, and life together until Bergman's birth. The film version, directed by Bille August, won the 1992 Golden Palm Award in Cannes. A year later Bergman's son Daniel directed *Sunday's Child*, a film that portrays "young Ingmar's" relationship to his father, taking up the theme of childhood and family where *Good Intentions* left off. Bergman's work offers a very personal perspective on what is Swedish, and yet universal.

brilliance have come and gone over the years; they include Lena Olin, Max von Sydow, and Stellan Skarsgård.

The annual Swedish International Film Festival has helped to restore the country's reputation as an important cinematic centre, actively promoting original artistic work by today's generation of film-makers.

The literary century

The 20th century was the defining period of Swedish literature, with the transition from poor, agrarian society to industrialised country. Literature through these tumultuous decades varied with the public, political and private moods of the day, from folk romanticism and expressionism to social criticism and surrealistic poetry. Prevailing themes in society, from the collapse of the welfare state to the fragility of the individual, have been expressed in a variety of voices.

Two great figures dominated Swedish literature at the turn of the 20th century: Selma Lagerlöf (1858-1940) and August Strindberg (1849-1912). Their influence on literature and drama has been felt ever since. Strindberg's *Röda Rummet* (*The Red Room*), 1879, and Lagerlöf's *Gösta Berlings Saga*, 1891, are con-

AUGUST STRINDBERG (1849–1912)

The son of a serving woman and a bankrupted ex-gentleman, Strindberg knew poverty and misery from childhood. Later, he was variously employed as a journalist, a tutor, and an assistant at the Royal Library. His first significant play was *Master Olaf* (1874). It was followed by *Lucky Per's Travels* (1880), reminiscent of Ibsen's *Peer Gynt*, and *Sir Bengt's Wife* (1882), an answer to Ibsen's *A Doll's House*, which Strindberg hated. His satirical novel *The Red Room* (1879) is considered the first example of modern Swedish realism. For the satirical, bitter stories in *Married* (1884–86), he was prosecuted for blasphemy. Strindberg's life was characterised by periods of mental crisis and marital breakdowns. The work of his realistic-naturalistic period centres on the duel between the sexes. In *Miss Julie* (1888), he depicts both sexual antagonism and class conflict in the figure of the aristocratic girl who seduces her father's footman. After Strindberg's brush with madness in 1896 he wrote the haunting, surrealistic "dream plays" that became the forerunners of modern expressionism. Strindberg's collected writings – plays, fairy tales, poems, short stories, prose sketches, essays, autobiographical writings, novels, fill 55 volumes. His autobiographical works include *The Son of a Servant* (1886), *A Fool's Defence* (1893) and *Alone* (1903).

sidered to be the first modern Swedish novels. Symbolism was fashionable during this period, best illustrated by Strindberg's *Ett Drömspel* (*A Dream Play*), 1902, which contains one of his most famous lines: "Humanity is to be pitied." Disillusioned sophistication was skilfully captured by Hjalmar Söderberg, whose novel *Den Allvarsamma Leken* (*The Serious Game*), 1912, is the most widely read of the classic Swedish romance novels.

In the first decade of the 20th century, writers often turned to social issues. Hjalmar Bergman (1883–1931) was one of the best storytellers of Swedish literature, with his 1919 novel about small-town life, *Markurells i Wadköping* (*God's Orchid*). Modernist poets like Pär Lagerkvist and Birger Sjöberg emerged in the 1920s and 1930s, along with writers with working-class roots, such as Vilhelm Moberg, whose four novels about 19th-century Swedish emigration to America, *Utvandrarna* (*The Emigrants*) became a film as well as a literary classic.

Pessimism, anxiety and guilt were recurrent themes in Swedish literature, often expressed in experimental forms. Lars Ahlin (1915–97) came to represent the rebellion against realism, in his 1946 novel *Om* (*If*). Another genius of this generation was Stig Dagerman, author of symbolist and grotesque novels such as *Ormen* (*The Snake*) and *De Dömdas Ö* (*The Island of the Doomed*). Internationally respected poet Tomas Tranströmer made his debut in 1954, with *17 dikter* (*17 Poems*). Socially aware literature emerged in the 1960s, with Jan Myrdal's *Rapport Från Kinesisk By* (*Report from a Chinese Village*) and Per Wästberg, who became involved in the struggle against racial oppression in Rhodesia and South Africa.

In the 1970s, the broad epic novel became prominent. Kerstin Ekman, whose importance continues to grow, wrote a series of novels about working-class women in a small Swedish town. *Jack,* the best-selling novel by Ulf Lundell, became associated with "the young Seventies". In the spirit of the Beat generation, Lundell wrote novels that portray contemporary life and are self-reflective. In the post-

modern 1980s and the 1990s, no other writers have quite taken his place. Today's writers show a desire to return to social realism and documentary storytelling, as in the dark psychological novels of Robert Kangas.

Children's books

Sweden is forever identified with pioneering children's literature, thanks to Astrid Lindgren. Her 80 books have been translated into 76 languages and sold 80 million copies. Her best-known characters, such

AWARD-WINNERS

Swedish Nobel Laureates in Literature: Selma Lagerlöf (1909); Verner von Heidenstam (1916); Erik Axel Karlfeldt (1931); Pär Lagerkvist (1951), and Eyvind Johnson/Harry Martinsson (1974).

as the eponymous heroine of *Pippi Longstocking* (written in 1945), are independent and unconventional. Lindgren defended the right of children to be treated like human beings without being oppressed: if children are given love, good behaviour will look after itself, she wrote. Lindgren broke conventional literary codes with her novel *The Brothers Lionheart*, in which she dealt with death and reincarnation. She has never won the Nobel Prize for Literature, to the dismay of her fans.

The media scene

Swedes are serious about their newspapers. About 170 newspapers are published daily in

LEFT: Ulla Jacobson, Swedish star of the 1950s.
RIGHT: August Strindberg, great Swedish writer.

Sweden, as well as 5,000 other papers and magazines. And people read them keenly. On average they spend 30 minutes every day reading daily papers and another 20 minutes reading weeklies and magazines. A Swede requires a morning daily on the breakfast table, along with the requisite cup of strong black coffee.

Traditionally, newspapers have tended to sympathise with and even actively advocate political party programmes and ideologies. The publishers' political preferences, however, have rarely been reflective of voters' preferences.

Sweden provides extensive subsidies to the daily press. Concerned that newspaper clo-

sures would leave the daily press less equipped to do its job in a democratic system, the government instituted subsidies in 1969. While this practice may seem to the outsider to support an artificial democracy, the majority of Swedes defend it vigorously. Without government support, Sweden, for instance, would only have one daily newspaper, *Dagens Nyheter*. The other, *Svenska Dagbladet*, is heavily subsidised in accordance with the policy of government funding for the national daily with the lowest circulation.

Several attempts were made in the 1980s to launch new daily papers. Only one succeeded, a business daily, *Dagens Industri*, founded in 1982. In 1995, *Metro* was launched, a newspaper distributed five days a week and free of charge on the Stockholm underground. Now local editions of *Metro* are being exported to other cities in Europe. Stockholm has two tabloids, *Aftonbladet* and *Expressen,* but the tabloid market declined sharply in the 1990s.

Television and radio

Satellite-borne television in the mid-1980s paved the way for increasing commercialism of Swedish television and radio. In 1991, TV4, Sweden's first commercially financed television broadcasting company was launched. Two years later, commercial radio was introduced. Yet many Swedes remain loyal to public radio and television, despite the choice offered by cable and satellite programming. As in other countries, home video viewing along with TV has encroached on the popularity of the cinema. Since the mid-1950s, the number of cinema visits has dropped from 80 million to 16 million a year.

With the legacy of its literature, film and theatre, and the values of democracy consistently voiced by the press through the decades, Sweden occupies a central position in the cultural life of Europe.

One need only look at the emergence of Greta Garbo from the Söder city quarter of Stockholm to later become the world's most celebrated film star to realise that the creative and the unexpected are synonymous with Swedish cultural life. ❑

SELMA LAGERLÖF (1858–1940)

Selma Lagerlöf, novelist and short-story writer, is a major figure in 20th-century Swedish literature. Uncomfortable with the literary realism current in her day, Selma Lagerlöf returned to the past for her stories and wrote in a romantic, imaginative manner. Her best-known works are the novels *Gösta Berlings Saga* and *Jerusalem. The Wonderful Adventures of Nils,* 1906–7), a much-loved children's book which serves as a playful introduction to Sweden's geography as it tells the story of a young boy's adventures when he travels all over the country on the back of a wild goose. This was followed by *Further Adventures of Nils* (1911).

LEFT: the poet Tomas Tranströmer.
RIGHT: free entertainment in Stockholm park – an open-air production of Strindberg's *Hemsöborna.*.

THE GREAT OUTDOORS

With its richly varied landscapes and its wealth of sporting activities,
Sweden offers something for everyone who loves the open air

Sweden is one of the world's most sporting nations, with nearly half the population engaged in some form of sport or outdoor recreation. On any given day, you can find them walking, hiking, cycling, sailing, rafting, skiing, skating, golfing, rock climbing, ballooning, hang gliding, and even dog-sledging. All of these activities beckon to the visitor as well, in a splendid variety of landscapes, from deep forest and high mountains to gentle meadows and the vast archipelago.

One of the least densely populated countries in Europe, Sweden has room to breathe, and when they get the chance many Swedes love to step outside their front doors, draw a deep breath of fresh air and wander off into the great outdoors. Not surprisingly, walking is a popular pastime, but a day's walk is rarely sufficient to satisfy anyone's desire to commune with nature, and there is always an urge to take part in much longer treks.

Nature trails

Throughout the country, there's an excellent network of waymarked footpaths. Close to Stockholm is the 850-km (530-mile) Sörmlandsleden (Sörmland Route), starting at the Björkhagen underground station. Carefully laid out, the trail offers hikers constantly changing vistas of deep forest, historic sites, lookout points and lakes. It passes several camps where you can eat, rest and buy supplies, with shelters at regular intervals. Sörmlandsleden is an easy hike, but it offers plenty of excitement. You rarely meet another soul, particularly in spring, autumn and winter, but you will spot deer, elk, capercaillie, hawks and grouse. The area is full of mushrooms and berries to pick.

For the most exotic views, however, head for the Kungsleden (Royal Route) which runs for more than 500 km (300 miles) from Abisko to Hemavan. Waymarked footpaths are found in

the more scenically outstanding areas like the national parks. These areas are often well away from towns and villages, and as a result many of them have a chain of mountain stations set a comfortable day's walk from one another along the footpaths, providing shelter for walkers. Most of the mountain stations are equipped

with cooking facilities, a shop and comfortable beds. Some even have a self-service restaurant and a sauna. They are not hotels but simple accommodation designed to provide a haven at the end of the day for tired walkers.

Camping out

Not all areas, though, are so well off for comfort and a tent becomes a necessity. With a sleeping bag, cooker and food, it can mean a walker has to carry 18 kg (40 lb) of gear, or more. There are no camp sites in the Swedish wilderness, but camping out is never a problem, thanks first of all to a plentiful supply of fresh water from the many lakes and streams,

PRECEDING PAGES: canoeing on the River Ljusnan.
LEFT: waterskiing on one of Sweden's 100,000 lakes.
RIGHT: golf at midnight under the Midnight Sun.

and secondly to *Allemansrätten* or Everyman's Right. This is an old custom that permits you to camp anywhere for a night, or to walk, ski or paddle a canoe anywhere, as long as the area is not fenced in or too close to a private home.

While the forests, particularly in northern Sweden, are home to bears, wolves, lynx and elk, it is rare that hikers would glimpse these shy animals, aside from the occasional elk. However, there is one beast that walkers fears, a beast that will attack the ill-prepared walker in large numbers and leave him or her a quivering wreck: the mosquito. The forests are full of mosquitoes in the summer, and all that walk-

ers can do to combat them is plaster themselves with liberal quantities of insect repellent.

On your bike

Cycling and, in recent years, mountain biking, is another popular outdoor sport for Swedes, and there are many well-designed and well-lit cycle routes all over the country. You could spend a week touring the island of Gotland on a bike. Keen cyclists also head for Östergötland, particularly along the banks of the Göta Kanal where the towpaths make ideal cycling tracks. You can hire bikes at several places, and the most popular route for cyclists is between

A BIRDWATCHER'S PARADISE

In Sweden, with its many lakes, wetlands and forests, birdwatchers can spot species that they would not see in Continental Europe, such as the great grey owl, the great black woodpecker and the three-toed woodpecker. Several wetland species are also special to Sweden: the ruff, the godwit, the curlew and the whimbrel, for example. Sweden has some 50,000 birdwatchers and some 20 bird stations. The tradition of birdwatching dates back to Carl von Linné (*see page 40*), the father of modern botany and Sweden's first avid birder. He named most of Europe's bird species.

The best places in Sweden to birdwatch are the Ottenby bird station in southern Öland, with its nature and science

centre; Falsterbo and Skanör Ljung in Skåne, and Lake Hornborgasjön in Västergötland. The lake is famous for the thousands of cranes which rest there for a while during their migration to nesting grounds in the north of Sweden. They perform a sort of slow-motion ballet in their mating rituals, and thousands of birdwatchers from all over Europe make the pilgrimage to Hornborgasjön each spring to watch this spectacle. Finally, Tysslingen Lake near Örebro, where 7,000 whooper swans migrate each April, and Getterön near Varberg are also worth a visit.

For more information, see the Swedish Ornithological Society's home page at www.sofnet.org.

Berg and Borensberg. For the truly ambitious, there is the Sweden Bicycle Route/Sverigeleden, from Stockholm to Göteborg – a distance of 2,576 km (1,610 miles).

Play golf at midnight

For golfers, Sweden offers some exciting landscapes, including golfing under the Midnight Sun in the north and winter golfing at Arvidsjaur near Jukkasjärvi and its Ice Hotel. Sweden offers the most beautiful coastal locations for golfing, especially in Bohuslän, Halland and Skåne, which has the longest season. Around Lake Vänern, there are boat excursions for golfers to try different waterfront courses. The number of golfers in Sweden grows apace, particularly among women, perhaps inspired by top women's golfer Annika Sörenstam.

Up and away

Other outdoor sports that can be enjoyed in Sweden are hang gliding and hot-air ballooning. Horseback riding is not an exclusive sport, and most towns have either stables or a riding school. Experienced riders can enjoy a pony-trekking safari in the Kebnekaise mountains.

Skis and skates

When the snows come – and in the north that can be as early as October – walking becomes more difficult and much less of a pleasure. Away, then, go the walking boots and out come the skis and the skates.

Swedes get used to the idea of skiing from an early age. Even before they can walk, they're towed behind their skiing parents in a kind of pram-sledge, and once they've mastered the art of walking it isn't long before they start to get to grips with skis of their own. Almost everyone in Sweden owns a pair of cross-country skis.

Frankly, it makes getting about in winter so much easier. But it also opens up further opportunities to enjoy the countryside, or even city parks. Winter doesn't mean a shut-down of the great outdoors. It just requires a different approach.

In fact, one of the most unusual ways to tour the Stockholm archipelago in winter is to don a a pair of long-distance skates, in which relatively long distances can be covered with very

> **SWEDISH SAFARI**
>
> Thanks to Sweden's rich wildlife and varied landscape you can drift on a canoe and watch elk calmly grazing or follow reindeer as they migrate over the mountains.

LEFT: redshank – birdlife is plentiful and protected.
ABOVE: skiing at Åre, one of Sweden's best ski areas.

Tennis, anyone?

I t has all the makings of a Hollywood movie. Lone-wolf schoolboy from the frozen backwoods of northern Europe beats a tennis ball against a garage door from morning until night, battles his way to Wimbledon, sweeps to victory against all odds, and retires at the age of 26 to become a multi-millionaire in Monte Carlo.

Recognise it? Of course you do: it's the Björn Borg story. And for tennis fans the world over, Borg's astonishing career still represents a golden era for the sport that will probably never be

repeated. For, since 1983, when the quiet, willowy Swede with the steely eyes, the long, blond locks and devastating two-handed backhand abruptly disappeared from the world's centre courts, there has never been anyone quite like him. And even stories about his failure to build in later life on his early success have not dimmed the memories of those triumphs.

"It was obvious right from the start that Björn was something special," recalls Christer Hjärpe of the Swedish Tennis Association. "He was simply one of a kind. I doubt if there will ever be anyone to take his place."

But what about today's Superswedes of tennis – the Edbergs, the Larssons, the Gustafssons, et

al? Admittedly, they may lack something of Borg's famous charisma – the icy cool, the sexy stride, the hair and the headband (very chic, back then), the three-day stubble (now even more chic), not to mention the Rolls-Royce, the bodyguards and the hordes of female admirers.

But let's be fair. Stroke for stroke, Sweden's current top players have got what it takes. With incredible regularity (some would say monotony) they dominate most international tournaments and win many Grand Prix titles and Davis Cup victories. Sweden is still one of the world's most successful tennis nations.

After Borg won his first Wimbledon title in 1976, (he won it five times in a row) the Swedish tennis scene erupted. The game that had been widely dismissed as a "snob sport" suddenly shot to the top of the popularity polls, second only to ice-hockey.

Tennis was "in". And just about everyone wanted to have a go. To cope with the surge in demand for facilities, sports associations, local authorities, and clubs up and down the country began pumping money into the game. The national tennis association beefed up its operations. Individual club membership soared and a string of new tournaments got under way.

Sweden also began to provide heavily-subsidised training schemes for the thousands of youngsters who were queuing up. Now virtually every community in the country boasts a modern tennis centre with indoor and outdoor courts.

But perhaps the best illustration of "the Borg effect" is the rise and rise of the Donald Duck Cup, which is the biggest junior tournament in the country for kids aged from 11 to 15. It was Borg's first trophy. He won it at the age of 14 against a field number of 1,000. Since then the number of competitors has leapt to 8,000. The Donald Duck Cup is held in Båstad, an attractive holiday resort on Sweden's southwest coast. And here, on finals day, the atmosphere is almost as charged as at a Grand Prix contest.

The main events of the year – the Stockholm Open (a Grand Prix tournament in the autumn) – and the Båstad Open – (an international round-robin in late summer) – are immensely popular and draw huge crowds.

Even if Sweden isn't banking on the birth of another Borg, it is certainly determined to cultivate an everlasting crop of élite players. ❑

LEFT: Björn Borg, whose astonishing career still inspires Sweden's young tennis players.

little effort. The reward is the chance to enjoy a fantastic Arctic landscape where you seldom encounter another soul.

Red cross routes

Whereas in summer the wilderness trails attract walkers, in winter they are covered by the parallel lines of skiers. Of course, the paths themselves are not visible, but to make sure people don't get lost, the paths are marked by red crosses mounted on poles. And to make sure one cross can be seen from another in the height of a blizzard, they are spaced fairly closely together. On a clear day they make a

country in the spotlight these days. As a result, Swedish downhill resorts such as Åre and Björkliden attract skiers from all over Europe. Sälen is the largest ski-resort in Sweden with various Alpine and cross-country skiing facilities. World Cup Ski Championships are held in Åre, so there are hundreds of top-class, superbly groomed pistes served by high-speed lifts and cabins. Half-pipes and snow parks are available for snowboarding fanatics.

Dog-sledging

To enjoy the wintry wilderness in an entirely different way, try dog-sledging, which is

strange sight, hundreds of crosses disappearing across a huge white expanse to the horizon.

Superb pistes

Downhill skiing in Sweden attracts a growing number of visitors thanks to the more reliable snowfall, the reduced risk of avalanches, when compared to the Alpine resorts, and the variety of slopes. And while slalom champion Ingemar Stenmark put Sweden on the international skiing map, it is Pernilla Wiberg, the World and Olympic champion skier, who is keeping the

ABOVE: heading north on the Kungsleden (Royal Route), a waymarked path with outstanding views.

offered by many firms up north, including in Åre and Kiruna. Drive the dog-sledge yourself in or sit back in the vast silence of the mountains and be driven by a team of huskies. Your guide will tell you how to take care of a sledge dog and share bits of trivia, like the fact that in the Inniut language there are 18 different words for snow. Dog-sledging, common in Greenland, is now well established in Sweden.

Climb a frozen waterfall

With such long winters, Swedes have added to their *smörgåsbord* of winter recreation with tobogganing, reindeer sleigh rides and lake fishing through the ice (*pimpling*), common on most lakes and rivers. You can even go ice climbing. Many resorts have access to frozen waterfalls and equipment with guides to hire.

Water sports

A country that has some 100,000 lakes and countless miles of rivers is bound to be in favour with canoeists. There are canoeing centres all over Sweden, though the district of Värmland offers canoeing waters that are hard to beat: there are so many lakes with interconnecting rivers and creeks that you can work out a circular route avoiding the need to portage. Because it is ideal for tours of the waterways,

the open Canadian canoe is by far the most common. It's a stable craft capable of carrying two people, and, just as important, it will take all the equipment needed for a week-long trip.

Some people can keep their equipment down to the minimum – some food, a couple of pots, matches to light a fire for cooking, a sleeping bag, and a shelter provided by their upturned canoe. Most though, prefer a few more home comforts, and perhaps a tent for shelter.

More popular than the canoe these days is the kayak, the enclosed type of canoe preferred for white water canoeing. Kayaks require a great deal of skill in handling, particularly over rapids, but they are also used on the coast. A

favourite area for sea kayaking is around the Stockholm archipelago.

These days white water isn't only the domain of kayaks. Rubber dinghies add to the excitement of white-water rafting. Suitably clad in waterproofs and life-jackets, crews of half-a-dozen people or more descend raging torrents in large inflatable rubber dinghies. It can be a very bumpy ride, but isn't really dangerous.

Down on the Klarälven River, though, there is a much more sedate form of rafting. Herean enterprising company, Vildmark i Värmland (Wilderness in Värmland), hit on the idea of charging people to build rafts out of logs and spend a few days on board drifting down river. Until 1991, the Klarälven was the only river in Sweden where logs were still floated down the forests to the sawmills. At the end of the rafting journey, the rafts were dismantled and the logs sent down the river to the sawmills at Skoghall, to be turned into pulp for paper. Nowadays, the logs for the mill are transported by truck, and the logs used to make the rafts are picked up at the journey's end by the tour operator to be used again.

It takes a couple of people several hours to build a raft, using ready-cut logs lashed together in three layers. One or two layers isn't enough because the logs don't have sufficient buoyancy to support the crew and equipment they need. When all is complete, camping equipment and provisions are placed on board and the crew paddle out to mid-stream to pick up the current. It's not a strenuous task because the current provides most of the power.

Drifting down river

Then follow five days of idyllic unwinding. The raft drifts along at a languid two kilometres an hour; its passengers relax on deck, fish or watch for shy beavers nosing through the water. The slightest sound and the beavers slap their broad tails and dive for cover beneath the surface. Occasionally, a little effort is called for, to paddle the raft out of the lazy gyrations of a small whirlpool, or to reach the shore to tie up for the night. The 100-km (60-mile) stretch of river you travel is Sweden's longest stretch of river without encountering factories, power plants, or other obstacles. Just pure nature. ❑

LEFT: white-water rafting – a bumpy ride.
RIGHT: canoes negotiate a lock on the Göta Kanal.

CATCH OF THE DAY

No matter where you are in Sweden, you will always be close to superb fishing waters, even in the heart of the capital

Anglers are beginning to appreciate the wealth of excellent fishing that Sweden provides. The travel trade, too, is bringing Sweden's fishing potential to a wider international public by making it easy to book packages which combine accommodation with fishing permits for a particular area.

One of the most remarkable and most accessible places to fish is right in the centre of Stockholm, in the fast-moving Strömmen channel which links the fresh water of Lake Mälaren with the Baltic Sea. At one time the water here was badly polluted but now a clean-up programme has brought salmon and sea trout back to the very heart of the capital. What is more, the fishing here is completely free of charge.

But big salmon and sea trout can also be caught almost anywhere in Sweden – in world-famous waters like the Mörrum river in southern Sweden and, above all, in the large and wild rivers of northern Sweden, as well as along the coast when the fish are on their migration.

The salmon season varies between rivers, but it usually starts during the summer and continues well into the autumn. The sea trout tend to arrive a little later. Both spinning and fly-fishing can produce good salmon catches, but sturdy tackle is advised.

Trolling for large salmon and sea trout is also popular in Sweden, and every year fish in the 15–30 kg (33–66 lb) bracket are caught. Lake Vättern, for instance, is popular for trolling enthusiasts with its unusual stock of fast-growing non-migratory salmon.

Pike, perch and zander (sometimes known as the pike-perch, although it is a distinct species, not a hybrid) are regarded abroad as coarse fish which are not worth eating. But they are frequent and highly prized catches in Sweden and are all regarded as fair game for the table. Perch tend to be rather bony for some tastes, but the zander is a delicious fish.

An unusual aspect about pike, perch and zander in Sweden is that they are caught not only in freshwater lakes and rivers but also in the brackish sea water of the Baltic, including the Stockholm archipelago. Västervik on the east coast, for example, has recently produced record pike of 16.5 kg (36.3 lb) or perch of 2.1 kg (4.6 lb), not to mention salmon of up to

18.7 kg (41.1 lb). Elsewhere, zander of up to 14.2 kg (31.2 lb) have been caught.

Game fishing

More conventional game fishing can be had in virtually all of Sweden's 96,000 lakes, as well as its countless streams and rivers. Apart from the migratory salmon, sea trout and whitefish (a little-known member of the salmon family), there are wild stocks of brown trout, grayling and char, an attractive fish which some gourmets rate even more highly than salmon.

There are also plenty of so-called "put and take" lakes with introduced stocks of rainbow trout and sometimes brown trout, too. All these

LEFT: angling is one of the most popular sports in Sweden. **RIGHT:** a fine catch.

game species are usually caught on light spinning tackle or fly, but in the winter they can also be caught by ice-fishing on frozen lakes with "jigging" or "angeldon" equipment. But restrictions on ice-fishing apply in some areas, so check locally before you start fishing.

Coarse fishing

Many visiting anglers, particularly from Britain, head for Sweden's coarse-fishing waters which provide some excellent sport, particularly in northern and central Sweden. Tench, bream, roach and common carp are just some of the species which can be tempted by a

maggot, corn or other bait. Float-fishing is the most common method but legering can also produce good results.

Sea fishing

Sea fishing is highly popular along Sweden's 8,000 km (5,000 miles) of coastline, from the Norwegian border in the west to the Finnish border high up in the Gulf of Bothnia.

The west coast produces plenty of cod, haddock, ling, coalfish and mackerel, but there is also excellent fishing for garfish and migrating sea trout close inshore. A relatively new species to Swedish waters is the grey mullet, which has been attracted by the warm-water outlets from power stations in the south.

The fishing season on the west coast lasts the whole year. Fishing for cod here is usually best in the spring and autumn, though large fish are caught in the Öresund strait in winter: in fact, the world's biggest sea-fishing contest – the Cod Festival – is held in this area every January.

A good way to enjoy a day's deep-sea fishing on the west coast is to go out on one of the many tour boats, whose experienced skippers will make sure that you attract some big fish to your hook. Tackle is often provided, or it can be hired for the day.

On the east coast the sea becomes less salty the further north you go, so you are more likely to catch freshwater species like pike, zander and whitefish. (See page 315 for more information on fishing in the far north.)

Making plans

If you are planning a fishing holiday, a good starting point is to contact Sportfiskeförbundet (the Swedish Angling Federation), also known as "Sportfiskarna", Box 2, SE-163 21 Spånga, Sweden (tel 46-8-795 33 50, fax 46-8-795 96 73, e-mail: hk@sportfiskarna.se).

Top 10 Fishing publishes an annual brochure (in English) in co-operation with the Swedish Travel & Tourism Council. This lists some of the best waters, with information on accommodation, packages and fishing guides. It can be obtained from Tourism Council offices or from Top 10 Fishing Sweden, SE-566 93 Brandstorp, Sweden (tel 46-502-502 00, fax 46-502 502 02, e-mail: top10fishing.se). ❏

FISHING RIGHTS

You can fish in the sea with rod and line free of charge around the Swedish coastline. Fishing is also free from the shores of the five largest lakes: Vänern, Vättern, Mälaren, Hjälmaren and Storsjön. In other lakes, rivers and streams the fishing rights are privately owned and a permit is required. Special conditions may apply, covering permitted equipment, close seasons, minimum size and catch limits. Close seasons may also apply to salmon and sea trout fishing along the coast. Trolling and similar fishing which requires the use of a boat is free only on public waters. Permits are available through local tourist information offices. Poaching is severely punished.

LEFT: women enjoy fishing almost as much as men.
RIGHT: enough fish to feed an army.

NATURE AND CONSERVATION

The Swedes combine a healthy appetite for the fruits of nature
with a passionate concern for conservation

Love of the land and their country is deeply rooted in Swedes. Even the national hymn *Du gamla du fria* does not concentrate on glory, honour or warfare, but on a land of high mountains, silence and joyfulness.

From the air, you get a picture of virgin territory with miles and miles of woods, forests (covering 70 percent of the country), and the twinkling eyes of many lakes – almost 100,000, great and small. Everywhere, it is a diverse landscape, from the fertile areas of Skåne to the tundra on the mountains of Lapland, known as Europe's Last Wilderness. In between is a land of small hills and valleys, rolling fields, small farms and clusters of red wooden cottages.

There are 8,000 kilometres (5,000 miles) of coastline, offering clean, if often chilly, water to swim in, and rocks to sun on (but few sandy beaches). The most spectacular seascape is the Stockholm archipelago, with its 24,000 islands, but nearly as thrilling are the waves crashing on the rocks of Bohuslän's archipelago.

A right to roam

"Everyman's Right" (*Allemansrätten*) is an ancient Swedish custom designed to guarantee every person the right to enjoy nature without undue restriction of access. You may pass over any grounds, fields or woods, as long as you respect the owner's privacy by not camping too close to a private home, walking in a fenced-in area, or crossing cultivated farmland. You may also travel by boat over any water, and gather wild flowers, berries and mushrooms.

There are 26 national parks in Sweden, all owned by the State. The aim is that selected areas of superior natural value and beauty should be protected from exploitation, both in the interests of the natural environment and because of their value in human terms.

Padjelanta is the biggest national park in Europe. The name comes from a Sami word

that means "the higher mountain", and it is one of Sweden's most beautiful mountain areas, with rolling plains, gently rounded mountain massifs, and huge lakes, such as Vastenjaure and the beautiful Virihaure. Almost the entire park is above the tree line. There are many small streams, which the Lapps call *jok*, and it has

always been an important pasture for their reindeer herds. Here, it is safe to drink the stream water and to enjoy its own special, clean taste.

At the opposite end of the country and on a very different scale is Norra Kvill, a uniquely well-preserved virgin forest in the highlands of Småland in southern Sweden. The forest has not been felled for over 150 years and some pines are more than 350 years old. The flora are surprisingly varied, and this park is an El Dorado for the lover of mosses and lichens.

Rich birdlife

If you want to study the herbaceous flora and listen to the birdsong, Dalby Söderskog near

PRECEDING PAGES: summer in Härjedalen.
LEFT: Fagertärn Lake at Tiveden National Park.
RIGHT: a rich cranberry harvest in Dalarna.

Lund in Skåne is at its best in the spring, while Store Mosse in Småland, the biggest national park south of Lapland, is worth a detour for birdwatchers: there are whooper swan, marsh harriers, cranes and many more rare species.

Countryside pursuits

The greatest proportion of Sweden is virgin country and for anyone from a densely populated and polluted area, from north to south the whole country seems like a "green lung" – a place where you can breathe. In this untouched countryside, you can stroll for miles along tracks without seeing another human being, or drive a car on serpentine gravel roads and never have to pass another vehicle, or cycle through untouched land on the special bicycle trails.

The Swedes are dedicated to the countryside. Many families save for years in order to buy a *stuga* (cottage) in the country or on the coast. Others are lucky enough to have inherited their little spot in a meadow. Most Swedes are only a generation or two away from rural life and many have relatives who still live in their original home districts.

The Swedes do not just enjoy the countryside and its fruits, they make use of them. At the first sign of spring nettles, the Swede rushes out,

NEW NATIONAL PARK IN A RIVER LANDSCAPE

Sweden's latest national park, opened by King Carl Gustaf in autumn 1998, is Färnebofjärden, a river landscape with many threatened species. A rich selection of flora and fauna, more than 160 species on the Swedish endangered list, has been recorded at the park. Bird life is most intense in the spring. The unique river archipelago with more than 200 islands and rocky islets is an ideal habitat for owls and woodpeckers as well as many threatened species of lichen, moss, and beetles. The park is located about 200 km (125 miles) north of Stockholm by the lower part of the river Dalälven, on the border to Norrland, and comprises 10,000 hectares (25,000 acres) of water and land. The landscape is extremely beautiful and unusual, with its damp meadows, woods, open water, islands, and rapids. More than 100 bird species breed regularly in the park, including all seven species of Swedish woodpeckers and several species of owl. Notably, grey-headed woodpeckers and lesser spotted woodpeckers and around 25 pairs of Ural owl, perhaps the biggest number in Sweden, are found here. There are plenty of elk, roe deer, hares and pine martens. Lynx breed in the park, bear have been observed, and there is a thriving beaver population.

Two other areas are next in line to be designated national parks: Söderåsen in Skåne and Fulufjället in Dalarna.

gloves on hands, with a pair of scissors and a paper bag to collect the nettles. For, despite their stings, nettle broth is a fine start to a meal even at a first-class restaurant, and nothing beats the first nettle broth of spring, made from nettles picked with your own hands.

After·that come sweet gale, and the tiny leaves of blackcurrant which Swedes use to spice the Christmas aquavit. Then comes the summer harvest: raspberries, cloudberries, wild strawberries, blueberries and, towards autumn, lingonberries, rose hips and blackberries.

To traditional Swedish families, no cultivated fruit can ever hope to compare with the wild ones they have picked themselves, even if they have had to fight off the mosquitoes to do so; and it is positively fashionable to appear in Stockholm on a Monday morning with the stain of berries still dark on your fingers.

The mushroom season begins with turban-tops – now slightly suspect – followed by baskets of chanterelles, ceps, edible agarica, ringed boletuses and all the rest of the mushroom family which the nature-conscious Swede can find. Swedes take their fungi very seriously: there are organised excursions to look for mushrooms and berries, and classes to tell people what they can and cannot eat.

Conservation matters

It is no wonder that the Swedes are worried about dangers to the environment such as acid rain, which has already killed off some plants and over-encouraged others, and also damaged many of the fishing lakes. Particularly in the west, the lakes lie there, clear, beautiful, and totally empty of any water life, except for a strange white lichen-type plant on the bottom. Many fishing societies have taken an active part in trying to save these "dead" lakes and, with government co-operation, have organised programmes of liming the water. However, this is no more than a palliative which they have to repeat at regular intervals.

Millions of Swedes fish in their spare time, and all along the coasts and in the big lakes fishing is free from land or boat, with rod and line, though amateurs are expected not to disturb the activities of the professional fishermen.

LEFT: the end of a day's berry picking.
RIGHT: the islands of the Swedish archipelago are rich in widlife, and fox are particularly common.

Strict laws protect the rarer mammals such as the bear, wolf, wolverine, lynx, musk-ox (a late immigrant from Norway), Arctic fox, otter or whale. In any case, they are rarely seen. But other animals are very common – roe deer live in the forest and only in Scandinavia will you see the traffic sign which means "Danger, Elk". This is no joke: traffic accidents involving animals have increased as the number of cars has grown, especially at dusk and dawn when the elks are crossing the roads between the forests.

The Swedes are dedicated to protecting birds, particularly the more endangered species. Rescue operations have been enacted to save the

white-tailed eagle, the white-backed woodpecker, peregrine falcons, the gyr falcon, and the Caspian tern, and there has been great success in saving the population of eagle owls. The biggest threat to birds and other animals is the continuing destruction of wetlands due to intense agriculture and over-use of pesticides.

The very variety of the countryside offers suitable habitats for many rare plants, from the alpines of the high mountains to the rich orchid flora of the limestone areas. The months of May and June in particular bring out an army of botanists – but always just to look, never to touch. For Sweden began to protect its plants as early as the beginning of the 20th century. ❑

EATING AND DRINKING

*Sweden has won international recognition for its cuisine, based
on an abundance of fresh fish, wild berries and succulent mountain meat*

Perhaps the best testimonial to the high standards of Swedish cuisine is the sight of all those healthy looking tanned Swedes you see in the summer, who certainly do not appear to have succumbed yet to the junk-food culture, although inevitably most towns have their fair share of fast-food outlets.

Sweden may not have the great international gastronomic reputation of, say, France or Italy, but you can certainly expect to eat very well. In fact, Sweden's chefs have been achieving a good deal of acclaim over the past few years. A Swedish team won the European culinary championships in 1995 and 1998, came second in the unofficial world championships – the "Bocuse d'Or" – in 1995 and first in 1997. The future looks bright, too, because Sweden's junior team had an outright victory in the culinary Olympic Games in Berlin in 1996.

The secret of Sweden's increasing prominence on the gastronomic scene is probably that its chefs make the most of their natural resources. Gathering mushrooms and wild berries is a national preoccupation in the autumn, while favourite meat dishes include reindeer, venison or elk from the mountains and forests. Above all, the Swedes are great eaters of fish, from both the sea and from the many rivers and 96,000-plus lakes. And freshwater fish like pike and zander, usually thrown back by British anglers, are much-prized items on restaurant menus.

Smörgåsbord delicacies

Sweden is probably best known abroad for its *smörgåsbord*. Translated literally, a *smörgås* is simply a slice of bread and *bord* is a table, but it is definitely a misnomer to describe it as a "bread and butter table".

Going back 200 years, an "aquavit buffet" was the prelude to a festive meal in Sweden and it was laid out on a separate table in the

dining room. Guests could indulge in a modest snack of herrings, sprats and cheese before getting down to the serious business – accompanied, naturally enough, by a few aquavit (schnapps) sharpeners.

This buffet became more and more lavish over the years as hosts and hostesses vied with

each other to provide the best spread, culminating in the giant *smörgåsbord*, which had its heyday in the 19th century and even then was still regarded only as the prelude to a "proper" meal. Nowadays, the Swedes are gourmets rather than gourmands, so the *smörgåsbord* is a meal in itself; but the groaning table can still present a daunting picture to the foreign visitor.

The secret of *smörgåsbordmanship* is to take things gradually and not to overload one's plate. Start with a few slices of herring prepared in all kinds of mouth-watering ways – in a mustard or horseradish sauce, maybe – accompanied by a hot boiled potato. If you're lucky, you may encounter *gravad lax*, thinly-sliced salmon

LEFT: the first toast (*skål*) of many during a summer boat party on the Bohuslän coast.
RIGHT: prawns, a favourite seafood dish in Sweden.

An Education in the Skål of Life

The British and the Germans are mocked for their stuffy formality, but they have nothing on the Swedes when it comes to the rigorous protocol which surrounds social entertaining and, particularly, the drinking of toasts (*skåling*).

A visitor is more likely to be asked to a Swedish home for a casual meal than invited to a very formal dinner party, but, even then, there are quite a few social rules to be borne in mind. First, it's

necessary to look at the etiquette for a formal party because it provides the basis for the more informal occasions.

To start with, arrive on time – punctuality is the norm in methodical, organised Sweden. Take some flowers or a box of chocolates for your hostess and, if there are a number of other guests, introduce yourself to them.

Once seated, you may find that a glass of schnapps or wine is already poured out. But on no account take a sip till the host has raised his glass for the first "*skål*" to welcome the guests. This first toast can also be a kind of communal *skål* in which you exchange greetings with your fellow guests, particularly those seated close to you.

The most important part of *skåling*, whether formal or casual, is that you must establish eye contact, glass raised, with the other party or parties not only before you take your sip but also immediately after.

On a formal occasion, each male will *skål* the ladies, starting with the one on his right, then the one on his left. Men will also *skål* fellow guests at random throughout the meal, but if there are more than eight guests at the table it is considered polite not to *skål* your host or hostess, on the basis that an input of schnapps on that scale might well have dire consequences. Incidentally, the normal routine is to *skål* with schnapps, but not with wine.

The rules are naturally much less rigid if you are invited for an informal meal with Swedish friends. But again *the first* rule holds good: wait for your host to "*skål*".

The *skåling* tradition does not seem to have been especially affected by Sweden's tough laws against drinking and driving. Most people attending an evening party either take a taxi or one partner (guess which one) "volunteers" to stick to the mineral water and drives home.

When the meal is over, and before you retire to the drawing room for coffee and liqueurs, you must do what every Swedish child is taught to do at an early age and say to your hostess: "*Tack för maten*" ("Thanks for the food", literally). At some stage your hostess will probably disappear into the kitchen and re-emerge with a tray of tea or beer, snacks and sandwiches. This is a tactful signal that the evening is coming to an end – although by the time you've quaffed your beer another hour will probably have passed all too rapidly.

Someone will eventually make the first move to depart, sparking off the ritual exclamations of "Is it that late?"

There then starts a round of farewells in which each guest shakes hands with the host and hostess and says "*Tack för i kväll*" ("Thanks for this evening"). All the guests will likewise shake hands with each other with mutters of "*Tack för trevligt sällskap*" ("Thanks for your pleasant company") or "*Det var trevligt att träffas*" ("It was nice to meet you").

If all this sounds rather daunting, just remember to say "*skål*" and "*tack*" in the right places and you won't go far wrong. ❑

LEFT: aquavit (schnapps) is served chilled in small glasses – purists drink it with herring.

cured in dill, a delicacy which is now well-known outside Sweden.

For the main course (or courses), you graduate to a bewildering choice of cold meats or fish and salad, or a typical hot dish like Swedish meatballs or "Jansson's Temptation" (a popular concoction of potatoes, onions and anchovies) before rounding off the meal with fruit salad or cheese.

The *smörgåsbord* is not such a dominant trend in Swedish cooking these days as it once was, but it still prevails in the south in Skåne,

CHOICE CHEESES

Sweden has a wide selection of cheeses, including strong ripened products like *Västerbotten* and *Lagrad Svecia* and spiced cheeses such as *Kryddost*.

uitous *Wasabröd* crisp-bread). Sometimes you may even find some scrambled eggs and sausages or bacon on the hot-plate.

Dish of the day

You can certainly stoke up for the day with a hearty Swedish breakfast – which could be a pity because the best-value eating out is to be had at lunchtime rather than in the evening. Particularly in the cities, you'll find many restaurants offering an inexpensive *dagens rätt* ("dish of the day"), which includes a main course,

where the good-living tradition is maintained most faithfully. You can also still find hotels that make a speciality of a lunchtime *smörgåsbord*, particularly on Sundays.

Breakfast feast

Perhaps the best value for visitors is the breakfast served in most Swedish hotels, which is really a mini-*smörgåsbord* in its own right. You will usually find several kinds of cereal, cheeses, herrings, boiled eggs, jams, fruit, milk and different types of bread (including the ubiq-

ABOVE: eating outdoors, preferably near water, is an essential ingredient of summer life.

salad, soft drink and coffee, and helpings are usually generous. Desserts or cheese are not often included on menus of this kind, although it could be worth paying a bit extra to sample some of Sweden's delicious wild berries such as the whortleberry, cloudberry or bilberry, served with a lavish portion of cream.

Dining out

Eating out in the evening is generally more expensive, although not necessarily prohibitive, so check prices before you venture into a restaurant. The price of wine in restaurants is high, so you may prefer to stick to mineral water (*Ramlösa* is the best-known local brand).

The budget-conscious will find plenty of cafés and cafeterias in the larger cities, as well as fast-food outlets such as McDonald's. For something more typically Swedish, try the *korvkiosk*, the nearest equivalent to Britain's "chippy"; it specialises in fast-food items like grilled chicken, hot dogs or sausage with French fries.

Foreign flavours

Cuisine in the larger cities is increasingly international with Swedish overtones, and many of the up-and-coming chefs have been influenced by immigrant owners. In a cosmopolitan city like Stockholm, for example, you can enjoy

meals based on many different culinary traditions – Chinese, Japanese, Korean, Thai, German, Italian, Yugoslavian, in addition to the home-grown Swedish product.

Home-cooking

It's better to head for the rural regions if you want to experience the more typical Swedish home cooking known as *husmanskost*, which produces strange combinations like pea soup with pancakes, traditionally eaten on Thursdays. The drink to accompany this is the lethal and deceptively sweet alcoholic *punsch*. Another favourite dish is *pytt i panna* (literally, "Put in the Pan"), a gigantic fry-up which is a good way of coping with left-overs.

If you are in Sweden in August, you may be lucky enough to be invited to a *kräftor* (crayfish) party. These delicious freshwater shellfish are boiled in water, dill, salt and sugar and left to cool overnight and are then served with hot buttered toast and caraway cheese, accompanied by schnapps and beer.

What to drink

The Swedes themselves will admit that the most negative aspect of their gastronomy is the high cost of beer and spirits resulting from punitive taxes and excise duties.

Beer comes in three grades – Class I (light beer), Class II (ordinary beer) and Class III (export). The best-known brand is probably Pripps, which is an acceptable enough drink, even if many drinkers think it isn't up to Carlsberg or Tuborg standards.

Lower excise duties usually apply to wine, which can be bought in the State-controlled *Systembolaget* at prices which are generally quite reasonable. But, as elsewhere, a threefold mark-up will push up the price of wine if you're having a restaurant meal.

It's worth splashing out on the odd aquavit, if only to assess which type is worth buying to take home. Skåne is the best-selling brand, but many connoisseurs prefer O.P. Anderson, which is flavoured with caraway, aniseed and fennel seed and goes well with herring dishes. Devotees of vodka will probably prefer to stick to Absolut, a 100-year-old brand now sold all over the world. ❑

REGIONAL SPECIALITIES

Every region of Sweden has its own specialities. Skåne, in the far south, is a favourite region for gourmets with its eel feasts in the early autumn and goose dinners later on. Skåne is also the home of *spettkaka*, a tower-shaped confectionery of sugar, eggs and potato flour baked over an open fire. The west coast is ideal for seafood, particularly in Göteborg, where you can eat fish landed that very morning. On the island of Gotland smoked flatfish is a popular speciality, while other dishes include smoked lamb and stuffed pike with horseradish sauce. In the far north, you can enjoy Sami specialities such as smoked reindeer meat.

LEFT: a mouthwatering Swedish dessert.
RIGHT: coffee prepared alfresco.

which is so influenced by the whims of the sun and the long dark winters.

Midsummer festivities

Midsummer Day is a slightly movable feast because it was decided in the 1950s that the celebrations should be on the weekend nearest to 24 June, the Feast of St John the Baptist, but in many areas people still observe the festival on 23 June.

On Midsummer Eve Swedes decorate their homes and churches with garlands of flowers and branches, and the dancing round the maypole goes on right through the night. Like Maundy Thursday, Midsummer has all kinds of supernatural connotations. Young Swedes traditionally used to pick flowers and place them under their pillow in the hope of dreaming about their future bride or bridegroom.

After Midsummer, Sweden tends to pack up for a couple of months as people head off to the countryside or the coast for the summer, and there are no more public holidays until All Saints' Day at the beginning of November. This is when families lay flowers on the graves of their loved one, and it can be a moving sight to see the graveyards at dusk glowing with candles and lanterns.

Christmas lights

December rounds off the year with a bout of festivities, starting on Advent Sunday, when houses and streets are decorated with trees, garlands and lights for the Christmas season.

St Lucia's Day – the Festival of Light – is celebrated on 13 December, a throwback to the days when it was mistakenly regarded as the longest night of the year. In the present-day Lucia celebrations, a young girl dressed in a white gown and wearing a crown of lighted candles brings in a tray of coffee, ginger biscuits and mulled wine (*glögg*) for the guests, accompanied by girl attendants also dressed in white and boys wearing tall conical paper hats and carrying stars. As they process, the youngsters sing "Santa Lucia" and traditional carols.

Christmas is generally celebrated in Swedish homes on Christmas Eve rather than on the day itself. The festivities resemble Christmas elsewhere in Europe, with the traditional tree and the giving of presents, but after dinner there is a visit from the *tomte* or Christmas gnome, a benevolent sprite who was supposed to live under the barn and look after the livestock in bygone days. The *tomte* comes into the house loaded down with a sack of presents as a kind of substitute Santa Claus.

New Year's Day is a lower-key affair, but families tend to have a lavish meal on Twelfth Night (Epiphany), a public holiday. The last fling is one week after Twelfth Night, "Knut's Day", when the decorations are removed from the Christmas tree. The year's festivities may be over, but Shrove Tuesday is not far away. ❑

LOCAL FESTIVALS

Apart from the traditional seasonal events, a bewildering variety of local festivals are organised all over Sweden throughout the year, and particularly during the summer. Many have a musical theme, like the annual "Music on Siljan" festival in Dalarna, and there are also plenty of events for folk-dancers, fiddlers and accordion players. More offbeat happenings include an annual medieval week at Visby on Gotland, a sausage festival in Falun (Dalarna) and a potato festival in Alingsås (Västergötland). Winter sees events like the cod-fishing festival at Helsingborg in Skåne, and the famous *Vasaloppet* cross-country skiing race between Sälen and Mora in Dalarna.

LEFT: dancing round the Midsummer maypole.
RIGHT: the start of the crayfish season in August.

PLACES

*A detailed guide to the entire country, with principal sites
clearly cross-referenced by number to the maps*

If you could pivot the whole of Sweden on the southernmost city of Malmö, it would stretch as far as Rome. This long, narrow country is both the largest and most prosperous in Scandinavia, but its population of only 8.8 million makes it one of the least crowded countries in Europe.

To fly over Sweden is to discover a land of forest where lakes glint among the trees. Even Stockholm, which covers a much wider area than you might expect for its 1½ million population, is a city of sea, lake and open spaces, and never far from the thousands of islands that form its archipelago, reaching out towards the Baltic. If you arrive by boat from Western Europe, the magnificent west-coast harbour of Göteborg (Gothenburg) is the first view. This is Sweden's second city, noted for its wide avenues and canals. The third main city, Malmö, in the far south, is also a port; the gateway to Denmark is just half an hour or so away across narrow straits and from the year 2000 will be accessible for the first time by bridge and tunnel.

As well as these three principal cities, there are the two university towns, Lund, near Malmö, and Uppsala, north of Stockholm; the latter was the ancient capital of Uppland, the cradle of Sweden and the home of the old pagan ways.

Outside the main centres, Sweden has miles and miles of road through endless forest, a coastline spiked with rock and smoothed by beaches, and unspoilt northern mountains ideal for summer walking and winter sports. The southern provinces of Skåne, Blekinge, Halland (plus Bohuslän on the west coast) were for centuries part of Denmark and even today in Skåne the accent is faintly Danish. Much of south central Sweden is dominated by the great lakes, Lakes Vänern and Vättern, the heart of a network of waterways that make it possible to cross this widest part of Sweden by boat along the Göta Kanal, which links Stockholm to Göteborg.

Further north, the geographical centre of Sweden holds Dalarna, often called the Folklore province, where old customs linger. At the end of the long road or rail route north are the mountains, many with a covering of snow all the year round. This is the land of the Midnight Sun. It is also the home of Scandinavia's second race, the Sami, whose wanderings with their reindeer herds take little account of national boundaries.   ❑

PRECEDING PAGES: reindeer cool their feet in July; the fields of Skåne; summer retreat – holiday cottages dot the islands and coastline.
LEFT: Läckö Slott on Lake Vänern, built in the 17th century in baroque style.

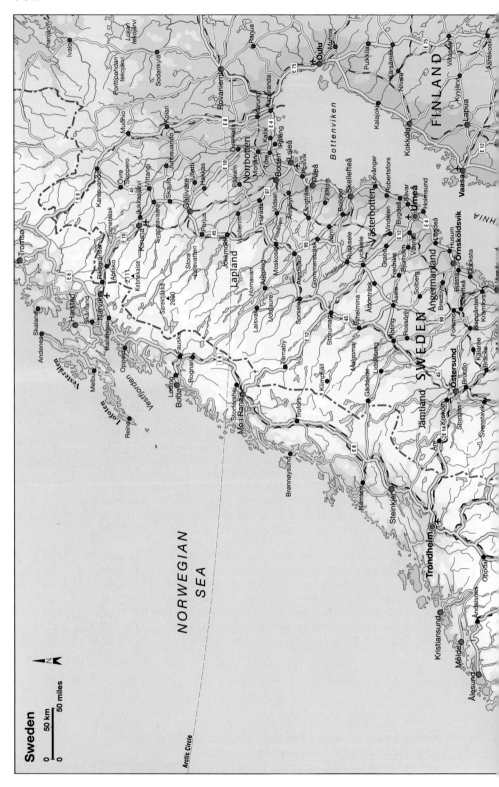

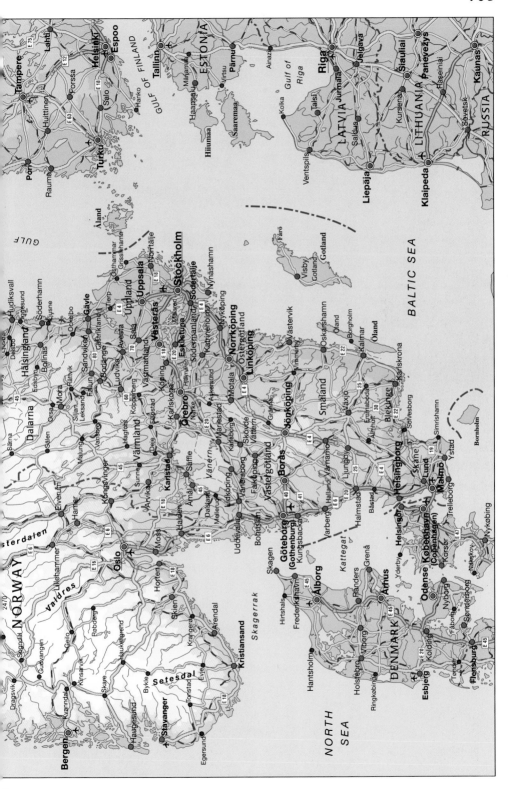

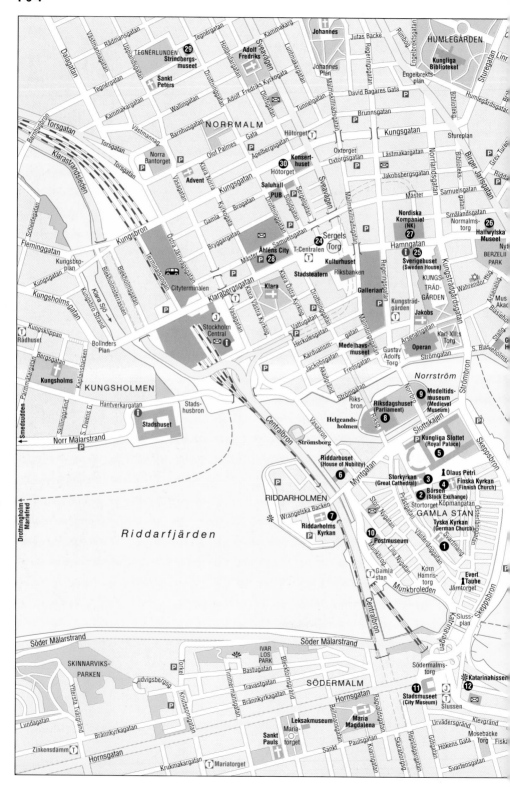

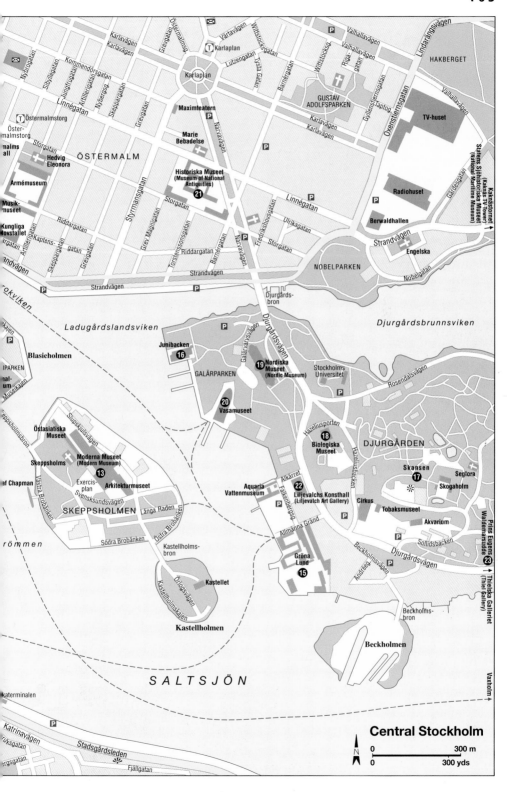

Central Stockholm

STOCKHOLM

*Sweden's capital is a city of islands, where glorious palaces
and waterfront hideaways line the shores and where cobbled
streets lead to chic shops and cosmopolitan restaurants*

Map
on pages
164–5

The novelist Selma Lagerlöf called Stockholm "the city that floats on water".
Nowhere do you see this more clearly than from the dizzy observation
platform on top of the **Kaknästornet** (Kaknäs Television Tower),
Ladugårdsgärdet, which rises 155 metres (508 ft). Below, Stockholm spreads out
in a glinting panorama of blue water and the red of old buildings against the
stark white and glass of the new, cut through by green swathes of trees and
grass in a country where space is abundant (open May–Aug: 9am–10pm;
Sep–Apr: 10am–9pm; tel: 08-789 24 35). For the ultimate in high-altitude sightseeing, however, why not drift over the city in a hot-air balloon? Stockholm is
the only capital city in the world that allows balloon trips within the city limits.

In winter, a white blanket lies over the city, fading the colours to pastel, and
the summer ferries and pleasure boats are held fast in the solid ice of bays that
cut deep into the heart of Stockholm. At that dark time of the year, only the
icebreakers keep the more open stretches free of ice around the wharfs where
ships for Finland and Denmark are docked.

Treasure islands

To the east are the thousands of islands of the archipelago, estimated at 24,000.
The hundreds of small boats along the edge of the
inlets and islands indicate the passion of every
Stockholm family to own and sail a boat.

Fresh and salt water are separated by the island of
Gamla Stan (Old Town) and the great lock gates of
Slussen at the southern end. This island barrier is
where Stockholm started some time before the 13th
century. Today, half the city is on Lake Mälaren, the
other on Saltsjön (Salt Lake), which leads out to the
archipelago and the Baltic Sea, and the city continues to grow. From its small beginnings as a trading
post and fort, Stockholm had no more than 75,000
inhabitants by the 18th century. Then came the late
industrial revolution at the end of the 19th century,
bringing Swedes by the thousands into the cities from
the land. By 1900, Stockholm had 300,000 city
dwellers. Now the population of the city has more
than doubled at over 700,000, and the Greater Stockholm region has more than 1½ million.

The whole area is the powerhouse of Sweden, and
accounts for more than one-fifth of the country's
employment and a quarter of its total production. In
many countries this would make Stockholm a noisy,
industrial city, but Sweden's wide countryside means
that the area covers some 6,500 sq km (2,500 sq miles)
and has space enough for everyone and more.

From Kaknäs, it is easy to understand why the
Swedes were a seafaring people, and why the Swedish

PRECEDING PAGES:
Riddarholmen and
the yacht-hotel
Mälardrottningen.
LEFT: Royal Guard.
BELOW: Stockholm
by balloon.

Vikings went east over the sheltered sea to Russia and down the great rivers to Constantinople rather than face the more perilous routes to the west, and this high vantage point reveals something about modern Stockholm, too. In this city life is still focused on the water and, though nowadays Swedes may sail for pleasure rather than plunder, the affinity is as strong as ever.

Today, Stockholm is also considered a modern and sophisticated metropolis, famous for Scandinavian design in furniture, textiles and interiors and host to a flora of international festivals. Once considered a place of *husmanskost* ("homely fare"), the city features some of the top chefs and most exciting cuisine in Europe. Stockholm's nightlife has exploded into an array of young, hip clubs and older, more sedate nightspots offering music and ambience for every taste. Infusing the old with the new is a speciality of today's vibrant Stockholm, as quick to seize on a new trend as Milan or Paris.

There is no shortage of restaurants in Stockholm. In the 18th century there were 700 inns – one for every 100 people. Today, around 1,500 places serve everything from elk and reindeer to hamburgers.

Gamla Stan

Stockholm's history starts in **Gamla Stan (Old Town)**, which still has the character of a medieval city. Its narrow lanes follow the same curves along which the seamen of former times carried their goods. No one restores a house or hotel in Gamla Stan without revealing the remains of an old fortified wall or an early workshop. Traces of even earlier times remain. At the corner between Prästgatan and Kåkbrinken, some bygone workman has casually repaired the wall with a Viking runestone, probably the first stone that came to his hand.

These early years are shadowy, as is much early Swedish history, perhaps because the Vikings were too busy raiding and plundering to spend time writing more than the runes that decorate their memorials. As long ago as pre-

BELOW: filling the city with music.

history, this small stony islet between Lake Mälaren and Saltsjön was used by fishermen and hunters, but in the 12th century it became a base for German merchants from Lübeck who had begun to trade in iron, and an early king built a primitive watch tower.

Map on pages 164–5

The first mention of Stockholm is in 1252 when Birger Jarl, one of the regents in an age when kings died young and left infant heirs, built strong city walls and enlarged the original tower, which became the Tre Kronor because of the three golden crowns (still a national symbol) above the central tower. The present Royal Palace stands on the same site.

Stockholm was never a Hanseatic town, though one of the landmarks today is the graceful copper-clad spire and the bells of the **Tyska Kyrkan (German Church) ❶**, which at four-hourly intervals during the day alternate two hymn tunes. Other reminders of the Germans are Tyska Brinken (German Slope) and Tyska Skolgränd (German School Lane).

Today, Gamla Stan covers the original island of Stadsholmen, Riddarholmen (the island of the knights and nobles), Helgeandsholmen, occupied by the Riksdag (Parliament) and the tiny blob of Strömsborg, all so close that it is sometimes difficult to realise you have crossed from one to another. The best place to start a tour is **Stortorget**, the centre of the original city, from which narrow streets fan out in all directions.

See more and pay less with the Stockholm Card. It offers free admission to museums and sights, free travel, discounts and a guidebook.

Medieval traders

Today, Stortorget is a peaceful square. In medieval times, it was a crowded, noisy place of trade, where German merchants, stallholders, craftsmen, and young servant girls and boys jostled and shouted. Along one side is **Börsen ❷**,

BELOW: Gamla Stan, the old town.

the old Stock Exchange building, and the modern Stock Exchange still occupies the ground floor. On the floor above, chandeliers that once looked down on the glittering royal splendour of the New Year balls, now preside over the Swedish Academy's weekly meetings. The Academy also meets here to elect the winners of the Nobel Prize for Literature.

In the cobbled square, people laze on benches or sit at one of the outdoor cafés, and it is hard to visualise that in 1520 the cobbles ran with blood during the Stockholm Bloodbath. Despite a guarantee of safety, the Danish King, Kristian II, known as The Tyrant, murdered 82 people, not only nobles but innocent civilians unlucky enough to have a shop or a business nearby. This gory incident triggered the demise of the Kalmar Union, which had united Sweden with Denmark and Norway. The following year, Sweden's first heroic king, Gustav Vasa, put an end to the union and made Stockholm his capital.

More peaceful memories greet you if you follow **Köpmangatan** at the eastern corner of the square to number 11. Open the small door to the surprise of a gentle courtyard created in 1930 in what had been a dirty huddle of overcrowded buildings. The work was carried out as an example of successful restoration and renewal by the St Erik Association, which has done so much to preserve Gamla Stan.

Back in the square, take the opposite Trångsund opening and you come to **Storkyrkan (Cathedral) ❸**, which is both the parish church and the scene of many royal occasions and coronations (at least until 1907, when Gustav V, the great-grandfather of the present king, decided against a formal coronation). This awesome Gothic cathedral is the oldest building in Gamla Stan, in part dating to the 12th century. It has high vaulted arches and sturdy pillars stripped back

BELOW: Stadshuset, the City Hall, on Lake Mälaren.

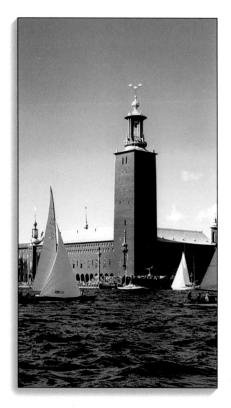

A CITY AND ITS SYMBOL

From any part of Stockholm that lies south of Lake Mälaren, Stadshuset (City Hall) dominates the skyline. On the water's edge of Riddarfjärden, this is the masterwork of architect, Ragnar Östberg. A massive square tower rises from one corner of the elegant central building, made of decorated brickwork with an open-fronted portico facing the lake. The building is topped with spires, domes and minarets, and the roofs are clad in a delicate green copper. Above it gleam the Tre Kronor, the three golden crowns that symbolise the city.

Östberg began work in 1911 and devoted the next 12 years of his life to the City Hall. He used 8 million bricks and 19 million gilded mosaic tiles, the latter mostly in the famous Golden Hall. The effect is stunning. The gardens of the southern terrace hold a statue of the 15th-century Swedish patriot, Engelbrekt, who championed the cause of the peasants in his native Dalarna. The tower is around 105 metres (450 ft) tall.

A procession of St George and the Dragon emerges twice a day as the bells play a medieval tune. Guided tours are available Oct–May: 10am, noon; Jun–Aug: 10am, 11am, noon, 2pm; Sep: 10am, noon, 2pm; entrance fee; tel: 08-508 290 59).

to their original red brick, and a magnificent organ. On a Saturday lunch-time, you can enjoy a recital, and then examine the church itself (open Sep–Apr: daily 9am–4pm; May–Aug: 9am–6pm; free; tel: 08-723 30 16).

Storkyrkan's most famous statue is St George and the Dragon, the largest medieval monument in Scandinavia, a wooden sculpture carved by Bernt Notke in 1489, which somehow has retained its original colouring. Don't overlook the candelabra of various ages from the 17th century, or the plaque to the three generations of the Tessin family, who built the Royal Palace.

Outside the cathedral, overlooking Slottsbacken and the front of the Royal Palace is a **statue of Olaus Petri**, the father of the Swedish Reformation. He was at one time sentenced to death for an alleged plot against Gustav Vasa but was reprieved to become Sweden's first celebrated writer. He looks like a man whom it would be dangerous to cross.

If you feel like a rest between church and palace, cross over to the **Finska Kyrkan (Finnish Church)** ❹ opposite the palace gate. Behind it is Bollhus-täppan (Ball Court Garden). This little courtyard has flowers, a small fountain and benches to welcome the weary sightseer and, most unexpectedly, Stock-holm's smallest statue, a seated figure of a boy only a few inches high.

Standing guard at the Royal Palace.

Three generations

The present **Kungliga Slottet (Royal Palace)** ❺ was built on the site of the Tre Kronor Palace, which burnt down in 1697, some say not without the help of Nicodemus Tessin the Younger, who had already built a new northern wing and who obviously relished the glory of rebuilding the palace to his Renaissance designs. His father, Nicodemus the Elder, had been architect to the old Tre

BELOW: Golden Hall of the Stadshuset, decorated with gilded mosaic tiles.

Kronor palace, and the grandson Carl Gustaf was responsible for supervising the completion of the new palace many years later. The palace comprises 608 rooms. Various suites are open to the public and the oldest interiors from the 1660s are in the north wing (open Sep–Apr: daily noon–3pm; May–Aug: 10am–4pm; entrance fee; tel: 08 402 6130; www.royalcourt.se).

The palace is famous for its tapestries, both Gobelin and of Swedish design, but the most evocative room is Oskar II's Writing Room in the Bernadotte Apartments. This has been kept exactly as the king left it when he died in 1907; even his desk is untouched. It is a comfortable, homely room, full of 19th-century clutter and family photographs.

In the old vaults (Skattkammaren) underneath the palace are the Crown Jewels, including 12 royal crowns, orbs and sceptres and other pieces of jewellery. They are immensely valuable and brilliantly lit so that they glow in the dim light of the vaults. Also below ground is the **Livrustkammaren** (Royal Armoury), including the stuffed remains of the horse of Gustav II Adolf, who extended the Swedish domain as far south as Poland until his death on the battlefield of Lützen in Germany in 1632. It's easy to see from his armour what a big man he was. At noon each day in summer, the Royal Guard marches across the bridge from Norrmalm to change the guard in the palace yard, and two young sentries stand outside the main gate, trying to ignore attack by camera.

A noble island

To reach **Riddarholmen**, go west from Storkyrkan and then along Storkyrkobrinken through Riddarhustorget. Here you will find **Riddarhuset (House of Nobility)** ❻, once one of four parliamentary estates (open Mon–Fri 11.30am–12.30pm; entrance fee; tel: 08-723 39 90). It is arguably the most beautiful building in Gamla Stan, with two pavilions looking out across the water. Inside, the erstwhile power of the nobles is matched by the grandeur of the Main Chamber, where the nobles deliberated, watched from the ceiling by a painting of Mother Svea, who symbolises Sweden.

Riddarholmen is the silent island. Few live here and most of the fine buildings are now government offices. As you cross the bridge, straight ahead is **Riddarholms Kyrkan (Riddarholm Church)** ❼ with its latticework spire and mellow red brick. Hard to imagine that in the days of the Franciscans who built it, the walls were painted bright red. Although the church is now used only on special occasions, its interior is as noble as the name of the island because it holds almost all the graves of Swedish royalty since Gustav II Adolf (open May–Aug: daily 10am–4pm; Sep: Sat–Sun noon–3pm; entrance fee).

On a summer evening, Riddarholmen is a pleasant place to stroll, past the quayside with a few pleasure boats and the graceful yacht, *Mälardrottningen*, once the luxury yacht of the American millionairess Barbara Hutton, now a waterborne hotel, with the only restaurant on the island. There are no cafés or shops here, just slanting sun against the old buildings.

The idea of constructing the **Riksdagshuset (Parliament)** ❽, on an island called "The Holy

Reconstruction of the old salmon runs, as well as salmon-stocking programmes, have increased the number of salmon and sea trout in the heart of the city. This is a fisherman's paradise.

BELOW: Sergels Torg, at the centre of Stockholm's modern business district.

Spirit" (Helgeandsholmen), has a piquant charm. Do they speak with tongues on the chamber floor? The Riksdag and the old **Riksbank** (State Bank), now part of the Parliament buildings, cover almost the whole of the island, with the Parliamentary extension, a copper-clad, semi-circular structure attached at the second level and following the curves at one side of the old building. Parts of the Parliament buildings are open to the public, and there is a public gallery open year-round; tel: 08-786 40 00).

Map on pages 164–5

Archaeological discovery

The refurbishment of the Riksdag led to a remarkable archaeological find and a new museum. When the builders started to excavate the Riksdag terrace to form an underground car park, they discovered layer upon layer of the past, including part of the medieval wall and the cellars of an apothecary shop. As good conservationist Swedes, the parliamentarians immediately foreswore their claim to a car park. Stockholm's **Medeltidsmuseum (Medieval Museum)** **⊙**, on Strömparterren, Norrbro, incorporates the old wall and other treasures dug up during the excavations. It also includes the town gallows. The museum is open July–Aug: Tues–Thurs 11am–4pm, Fri–Mon 11am–4pm; Sep–June: Tues–Sun 11am–4pm, Wed 11am–6pm; entrance fee; tel: 08-508 318 00; www.medeltidsmuseet.kif.stockholm.se).

Detail from the roof of the Riddarhuset (House of the Nobility), one of the former parliamentary estates of Sweden.

Gamla Stan is an ideal place for browsers and strollers. It always reveals something you have not seen before in the criss-cross of small lanes, hidden courtyards and unexpected nooks and crannies, and along the two favourite shopping streets, **Österlånggatan** and **Västerlånggatan**, which lie just outside the line of the first city walls. The old town is very much alive and working, and

BELOW: the Royal Palace, jewel of Gamla Stan.

Crowning glory – a performer in the annual Stockholm Water Festival.

Stockholmers fight for the privilege of living in one of the tall houses that line the old district's narrow streets.

Don't miss **Mårten Trotzigs Gränd**, the narrowest street in Gamla Stan at the southern end of Västerlånggatan. It is more a stairway than a lane, less than a metre wide, which you can clamber up to reach **Prästgatan**, a route that more than any follows the lie of the island.

Only a step or two from Mårten Trotzigs Gränd, in **Järntorget**, is a statue not to miss. Evert Taube was a popular musician in the robust tradition of the Swedish troubadour, who died in 1976 much-loved and in his 80s. The statue is so alive that, at first glance, the unpretentious figure almost seems to be Taube himself, ready to burst into song.

One of Gamla Stan's few museums is the **Postmuseum (Postal Museum)** Lilla Nygatan 6. The Postal Service has owned the gracious old building since 1720, and the collection includes the world's first stamp from 6 May 1840, as well as an early mail coach, a train sorting office, and postal boat, which all indicate the rigours postmen endured in getting mail to Sweden's far-flung communities (open May–Aug: Tues–Sun 11am–4pm; Sep–Apr: also open Wed 11am–7pm; free; tel: 08-781 1755; www.posten.se/museum).

How Stockholm grew

From the southern end of Gamla Stan it is worth making a detour to **Slussen** where the lake is divided from the salt-water harbour by big lock gates, in order to visit Stockholm's **Stadsmuseet (City Museum)** , on Ryssgården. While Stockholm received virtually no mention until the 13th century, the museum makes it clear that this strategic spot had been inhabited for many centuries

before, and now archaeologists are working against the clock to save many treasures before modern building techniques destroy them. Just as interesting are the exhibits which illustrate the more recent past and life down the recorded centuries and also the collection of early 20th-century photographs of the city as it was (open Jun–Aug: Tues–Wed, Fri–Sun 11am–5pm, Thurs 11am–7pm; Sep–May: Tues–Wed, Fri–Sun 11am–5pm, Thurs 11am–9pm; entrance fee; tel: 08-508 31 600).

Map
on pages
164–5

After the museum, it would be a pity not to make a quick trip up **Katarinahissen** ⑫, an old 19th-century lift rebuilt in 1935 that takes you to the heights of **Södermalm**, the next island south (open Mon–Sat 7.30am–10pm, Sun 10am–10pm; entrance fee). At the top, you look down to one of Stockholm's outdoor markets, bright with the colour of fruit, vegetables and flowers which Swedes love, to counteract the darkness of their long winters.

Those footsore from discovering the hidden treasures of Gamla Stan should not forget that the old town has an abundant selection of restaurants, jazz pubs, and cafés. Many are in the same cellars where the merchants of old stored exotic imports. As you walk down the stone steps to a cellar restaurant or sit at one of the many courtyard tables, history is still strongly in evidence.

On Mariaberget Hill, on the western shore of Södermalm, most of the buildings are 18th-century. Stroll down Bellmansgatan, named after the Swedish troubadour Carl Bellman.

Stockholm's playground

From Gamla Stan, it is just 10 minutes by boat across the harbour to the island of **Djurgården**, past the wharves where the big ferries leave for the Baltic, and Kastellholmen, now a military base. Once a royal deer park, much of Djurgården is still in its natural state, with paths and woods where you may spot an old hunting lodge or pavilion through the trees. There is fine birdwatching in the

BELOW: view along Strandvägen.

Restaurants often offer a good-value "dagens" lunch (dish of the day), which usually includes a soft drink and coffee.

BELOW: sailing ship *af Chapman*, now a youth hostel.

marshes and wetlands, and the forest reveals small creatures, both everyday and rare, such as hares and the occasional deer. A good way to get around is to hire a bike at the bridge which forms the road entrance.

Between Djurgården and Gamla Stan lies **Skeppsholmen**. The sleek schooner moored off the island is the 100-year-old *af Chapman*, now used as a youth hostel. Also on the island is is the spectacular new building of the **Moderna Museet (Modern Museum)** , designed by Spanish architect Rafael Moneo, with a collection of 20th-century art that is considered one of the finest in the world, with works by Dali, Picasso and Magritte among others (*see page 110*). Its large restaurant-café offers a beautiful panorama of the city skyline (open Tues–Thurs 11am–10pm; Fri–Sun 11am–6pm; entrance fee; free first Tuesday of every month, 6pm–10pm; tel: 08 519 552 82; www.modernamuseet.se).

Musical evenings

Heading northwest from Skeppsholmen is the waterfront of **Blasieholmen**, where the big sumptuous building is one of Scandinavia's most famous hotels, the **Grand**. Nearby, on Södra Blasieholmshamnen, is the **Nationalmuseum (National Museum of Fine Arts)** , featuring Sweden's national collection of art, with most of the great masters from 1500–1900. Rembrandt is particularly well represented (*see page 110*). In summer, the National Museum holds concerts in the evening, a lovely setting for music (open Tues 11am–8pm, Wed–Sun 11am–5pm; entrance fee; tel: 08-519 544 10; www.nationalmuseum.se).

As the ferry slides into the Djurgården quay, there is no mistaking that this is an island devoted to enjoyment. On the right past the quayside is **Gröna Lund** , an amusement park with its roots in the 18th century (open May–mid-Sep: Mon–Wed 3pm–11pm, Thurs–Fri 3pm–midnight, Sat 12pm–noon, Sun noon–8pm; entrance fee; tel: 08-587 501 00; www.gronalund.com). Its thrill rides and ghost trains are strictly up to date and its new ride, Fritt Fall (Free Fall), is Europe's highest at 80 metres (262 ft). Like a bungee jump, only without a bungee rope, riders travel about 100 km (62 miles) per hour before the magnetic brakes bring them back to safety. Yes, it's as terrifying as it sounds.

Fans of Astrid Lindgren's children books should not miss **Junibacken** , a new museum dedicated to her life's work. An electrically operated indoor tram, with narration in English, allows the rider to experience *Astrid's World*, floating over miniature scenes from her books with moving figures, lights, and sound, as familiar figures pop suddenly out of corners. After this fanciful journey, children can play in a replica of Junibacken, the house of the character Madiken. It also has exhibits, a computer games room, a well-stocked book and toy store, and a waterfront café (open Jan–May: Wed–Sun 10am–5pm; Jun–Aug: Mon–Sun 9am–6pm, Sep–Dec: Wed–Sun 10am–5pm; entrance fee; tel: 08-587 230 00).

Another way of life

Heading south on Djurgården, where the island rises in steps to a hilltop, is **Skansen** , the oldest open-air museum in the world (open Jan–Apr: 10am–4pm

May: 10am–8pm; Jun–Aug: 10am–10pm; Sep–Dec: 10am–4pm; entrance fee; tel: 08-578 900 05; www.skansen.se). In 1891, long before such things became fashionable, Artur Hazelius, who believed in practical education, decided to preserve the then familiar Swedish way of life, fast disappearing under a wave of Industrial Revolution that came late but fast to Scandinavia. He began to collect traditional buildings from different areas and today there are some 150, including an 18th-century church which is still in use for regular services and a popular place for weddings.

Many of the houses and workshops are grouped together to form the town quarter along a steep cobbled street. They include authentic workshops where tradesmen once practised their craft. During the summer, many of the buildings revive their traditional use, when Skansen employs craftworkers to carry on the old skills. In the shoe-maker's house, where shoes have been made for more than 100 years, they still stitch and cut, and the glass-blowing workshop and the pottery demonstrate and sell their products. In the village shop, you can buy the old handmade sweets that few stores stock today. Tempting smells draw you into the bakery, where Stockholmers queue up for their Sunday bread and tasty *bullar* (cinnamon buns).

Wildlife park

Skansen is not just a museum of life past; it also tries to give a picture of the Swedish countryside and wildlife today, so that you get a clearer view of an elk than you can hope for from a car, as the creature slips carefully back into the forest at dusk or dawn. This area, which is largely too informal and the surroundings too natural to be called a zoo, also holds a few more exotic beasts. Some

There are more than 100 allotment garden areas in central Stockholm, with 8,000 small kitchen gardens, cultivated by residents who rent them cheaply from the city.

BELOW: traditional shop at Skansen open-air museum.

TIP

Stockholm is a city of festivals: which celebrate water, Strindberg, jazz and tango among other things. Check www.stoinfo.se for details.

BELOW: celebrating Bellman's Day in honour of the troubadour Carl Bellman.

are species once native but now extinct in Sweden, others such as monkeys and elephants are there to please children, and there is also **Lill-Skansen**, where children are allowed to handle and stroke small creatures.

About 300 metres (330 yds) north from the main entrance to Skansen is the **Biologiska Museet (Museum of Biology)** ⓲, the first of its kind in the world, where Nordic animals are depicted against dioramas to create an illusion of their natural habitat. All these dioramas were reproduced from works of one of Sweden's most distinguished nature painters, Bruno Liljefors (open April–Sep 10am–4pm; Sep–April: Tues–Sun 10am–3pm; entrance fee; tel: 08-442 8215).

Djurgården has music of many kinds, everything from chamber music in the old Skogaholm Manor at the heart of the island and nightly entertainment on the Main Stage at Gröna Lund, to rock concerts in the open air and folk-dancing and special celebrations for Midsummer and other festivals. Against the green of the hill, the traditional costumes look as though they belong.

Bridal crowns

If you choose bus instead of boat and enter the island over Djurgårdsbron from Strandvägen, the first museum you come to is the ornate building that houses the **Nordiska Museet (Nordic Museum)** ⓳, which depicts Nordic life from the 16th century. It has peasant costumes, a special collection of bridal gowns and the traditional silver and gold crowns worn by Swedish brides, Lapland culture, folk art, and more, to show how Swedes live and lived (open Mon 3pm–9pm; Tues–Sun 10am–9pm; entrance fee; tel: 08-519 560 00; www.nordm.se). The **Children's Playhouse** on the first floor is a fun place to dress up and experience life in the olden days.

Marine treasure

To the west of the Nordiska Museet on the waterfront is the huge, oddly shaped building **Vasa Museet (Vasa Museum)** ㉔, Gälarvarvet, which houses the *Vasa* warship, inaugurated in 1990 (open late-Aug–early-Jun: 10am–5pm Wed 10am–8pm; early-Jun–late-Aug: 9.30am–5pm; entrance fee; tel: 08-519 548 00; www.vasamuseet.se).

Map on pages 164–5

The warship was built in the 1620s for the Thirty Years' War, on the orders of Sweden's warrior king, Gustav II Adolf, in honour of the founder of his dynasty, Gustav Vasa. She was a magnificent ship, gold leaf on her poop and bow, guns of bronze, and decorated with 700 sculptures and carvings. In 1628, she set off from Stockholm harbour on her maiden voyage, watched by king, court and people. With her gun ports open for the royal salute, she was 1,300 tons of too, too solid oak. A sudden gust caught her, water flooded in through the gun ports, the ship heeled over and sank, drowning most of those on board.

An ornate emblem from 17th-century warship Vasa, *which was raised from the sea bed in 1961.*

There she lay until 1956, when a Swedish marine archaeologist, Anders Franzén, found her and spent the next years planning her recovery. In 1961, the hulk of the great ship broke the surface again, and the long process of restoration began. More than 24,000 objects have been salvaged from the sea bed, including skeletons, sails, cannon, clothing, tools, coins, butter, rum and many everyday utensils. The marine archaeologists also found thousands of missing fragments large and small of the vessel herself, which were numbered and their positions recorded.

Over the past 25 years, working inside her protective shell, the ship has been pieced together like a giant three-dimensional jigsaw, and now Vasa has regained her early splendour. The fact that the *Vasa* sank so swiftly without fire or explo-

BELOW: the *Vasa*, a remarkable work of restoration.

sion meant that most objects were recovered and this valuable collection reveals a lot about the life of a 17th-century ship. To most people, these simple utensils that speak of everyday life are as fascinating as the structure and statuary – a sailor's *kista* (chest) which contains his pipe, his shoe-making kit and all the other necessities of a long voyage, as well as the admiral's cabin where 12 officers slept in no great comfort.

The *Vasa* project is part of the **Statens Sjöhistoriska Museet (National Maritime Museum)**, north of Djurgården on the southeastern shore of Östermalm at Djurgårdsbrunnsvägen 24, which has two other interesting vessels moored at piers not far from the *Vasa*. The *Sankt Erik* (1915) was Sweden's first large icebreaker and transformed winter trading in and out of the Baltic. The other is one of Sweden's last lightships, the *Finngrundet*, which dates from 1903 (open 10am–5pm; Tues through late May: 10am–8.30pm; entrance fee; tel: 08-519 549 00). The Sjöhistoriska Museet covers shipbuilding and merchant shipping as well as naval history. At the Children's Museum, young visitors can climb onto boats and explore, and on Sundays from noon–4pm in the workshop they can make their own boats in the traditional way.

Heading west, along Djurgårdsbrunnsvägen and Linnégatan, you'll come to the **Historiska Museet (Museum of National Antiquities) ㉑**, Narvavägen 24. This museum is dedicated to Sweden's first and best known sailors, the Vikings. A real Viking house shows the simple household implements which the Vikings used each day. Don't miss the new, spectacular Gold Room, an underground vault designed for maximum security for the more than 3,000 prehistoric gold and silver artefacts (open Tues–Sun 11am–5pm; winter, Gold Room, Thurs 5–8pm; entrance fee; tel: 08-519 556 00; www.sshm.se).

BELOW: Ulf Rollof's
Kylrock, 1989,
Moderna Museet.

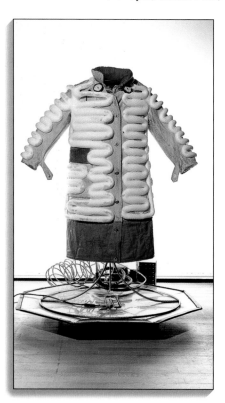

Djurgarden's art galleries

About 400 metres (440 yds) south from the Nordiska Museet is **Liljevalchs Konsthall (Liljevalch Art Gallery) ㉒**, at Djurgårdsvägen 60. It is devoted largely to contemporary work, and the Spring Exhibition is a must for aspiring artists (open Tues 11am–8pm, Wed, Fri–Sun 11am–5pm; Thurs 11am–8pm, guided tours Tues–Sun 2pm; entrance fee; tel. 08-508 313 30). The gallery's **Blå Porten** restaurant and café offers fresh food and delicious baked goods in a garden oasis.

About 1.5 km/1 mile southeast of Liljevalchs (a 15-minute walk, or accessible on bus 47) is what many describe as the most beautiful gallery in the city – **Prins Eugens Waldemarsudde ㉓** (Prins Eugens väg 6; open Jun–Aug: Tues–Wed, Fri–Sun 11am–5pm. Thurs 11am–8pm; guided tours Tues–Fri 2pm; Sep–June: Tues–Fri 11am–4pm, Thurs also 5–8pm; entrance fee; tel: 08-545 837 00; www.waldemarsudde.com). It is the former home of Prince Eugen, the "painter prince" and brother to the late King Gustav V. When he died in 1947, the prince left his lovely home and garden as well as his collection, which includes many of his own impressive landscape paintings, to the nation. This gem of a gallery, looking south over Saltsjön, is not to be missed.

Another 2.5 km (1½ miles) southeast, on the bus 69

or by foot, is **Thielska Galleriet** (Thiel Gallery), at Sjötullsbacken 6, designed by a popular architect of the time to house the collection of the banker Ernst Thiel. The marvellous range of pictures includes the work of Norwegian Edvard Munch, and Sweden's Anders Zorn, Carl Larsson, Gustav Fjaestad and Bruno Liljefors, all close friends and part of the National Romantic Movement of the late 19th and early 20th centuries. The gallery even has some pictures by the playwright August Strindberg. In the early decades of the century, Thielska Galleriet became a meeting place for artists, poets, and writers. When Thiel went bankrupt in the 1920s, the city bought the gallery (open Mon–Sat noon–4pm, Sun 1–4pm ; entrance fee; tel: 08–662 58 84).

Strolling and shopping

It's anyone's guess what John Tobias Sergel might have thought of the huge illuminated obelisk, modern fountain and square that bear his name, and of the modern city around it. He was a neo-classical sculptor, famed in Rome, who returned to the cultured court of Gustav III. Sergel sculpted many statues for Gustav, including one of the king himself and another, *Oxenstierna and History*, to commemorate the early statesman Axel Oxenstierna.

The heart of this modern business and commercial area is not large, but it sits somewhat uneasily with the rest. From **Sergels Torg ㉔** it is hard to miss the five towering office blocks on **Sveavägen**, which cast their shadow over the other buildings. In fact, they are visible from almost every part of the city.

In the 1960s, Stockholm City Council, like so many others, succumbed heavily to the temptation to knock things down and build concrete and glass highrise buildings, which are concentrated on Norrmalm's business area and around

Map on pages 164–5

Stockholm is a relatively safe city. But beware of pickpockets.

BELOW: enjoying the green lungs of the capital.

STOCKHOLM'S EKOPARKEN

Ekoparken is the world's first national city park, a huge set of green lungs which stretch out in a 12-km (7-mile) arch from Ulriksdals Slott (Ulriksdal Palace) in the north to the archipelago islands of Fjäderholmarna in the south. This greenland is so large that you need a full day of serious hiking to explore it, by foot during the warmer months or on skis or long-distance skates in winter. The inexpensive Brunnsviken Runt (Around Brunnsviken) boat trip is an excellent way to tour the Ekopark, including three royal parks, Djurgården, Haga, and Ulriksdal, and the palaces of Ulriksdals Slott, Gustav III's Paviljong, Haga, and Rosendals Slott. Visit the tropical Fjärilhuset (Butterfly House) where colourful species land lightly upon your waiting palm, the Bergianska Botanical Gardens and the Naturhistoriska Rikmuseet (Museum of Natural History). For a pleasant retreat on northern Djurgården you'll find Rosendalsträdgård (Garden), Rosendalsterrassen 12, with greenhouses, a café serving excellent homemade food, and garden shops. Wander through orchards, flower gardens and lush vegetable patches. For many Stockholmers, this has become the ideal retreat after a day of play on Djurgården. For information on Ekopark's attractions, call Stockholm Information Service, tel: 08-789 24 90.

Central Station, where most of the big hotels stand today. The destruction of many fine old buildings continued until it threatened **Kungsträdgården (King's Garden)** with a famous statue of Karl XII on its southern side.

At this point the Stockholmers had had enough. Normally placid and biddable, they mustered at the King's Garden, climbed the trees that were in danger of the axe, and swore that if the trees went so did the people. The City Fathers retreated and Kungsträdgården survives to soften the edges of the new buildings and harmonise with the older buildings that are left. This is the place to stroll or sit beside the fountains on a summer day and enjoy a coffee at its outdoor café. In August every year it forms part of the main fairgrounds of the Stockholm Water Festival. In winter, part of Kungsträdgården is flooded with water and becomes a popular ice rink, and the restaurant moves indoors.

At Hamngatan 27 is **Sverigehuset (Sweden House)** , with Stockholm's main **tourist information centre** on the ground floor (open Oct–Apr: Mon–Fri 9am–6pm, Sat–Sun 10am–3pm, May–Sep: Mon–Fri 9am–6pm, Sat–Sun 9am–3pm; Jun–Aug: Mon–Fri 8am–7pm, Sat–Sun 9am–5pm; tel: 08-789 24 90). The centre can advise and book tours and other entertainment, sells the *Stockholmskortet* (Stockholm Card), which provides free travel and entrance to many museums, and is the place to go for help. It has a well-stocked bookshop and is the starting point for some city bus tours.

A short stroll east is the early 20th-century private palace of one of Stockholm's most unusual museums, the **Hallwylska Museet (Hallwyl Collection)** ㉖, at Hamngatan 4, a magpie collection of one person, Countess von Hallwyl, from her ornate piano, to china, beautiful furniture and personal knick-knacks (open mid-Jun–mid-Aug: guided tours Mon–Fri hourly between 11am–4pm, and 6pm Wed;

TIP

Sverigehuset (Sweden House) at Hamnagatan 27 houses the city's main tourist information centre and is open daily all year round. See the main text, oppposite for details.

BELOW: *Humour* by K. Bejemark, in Hamngatan.

mid-Aug–mid-Jun: tours Tues–Sun hourly noon–3pm, and 6pm Wed; year-round, guided tour in English, Sun 1pm; entrance fee; tel: 08-519 555 99; www.lsh.se/hallwyl).

On the southern side of Sergels Torg, **Kulturhuset** (Culture House) is a popular meeting place and venue for lectures and entertainment (open Tues–Thurs 11am–7pm, Fri 11am–6pm, Sat 11am–5pm, Sun noon–5pm).

On the next block east on Hamngatan is **Gallerian**, a huge covered shopping arcade that stretches from Hamngatan to Jakobsgatan. At the north end of Gallerian is the oldest auction house in the world, **Stockholms Auktionsverket** (Stockholm Auction House), Jakobsgatan 10, which has been in business since 1674 (open Mon–Fri 9.30am–6pm, Saturday 10am–4pm; tel: 08-453 67 10; www.auktionsverk.se). Everything from china to Chagall and furniture from the 7th to 20th century is crammed into the storerooms. Many items are small enough to carry, and make unusual Stockholm mementoes.

To buy is easy: you just leave a bid in advance for the Tuesday and Wednesday auctions, or you can take part in the auction yourself, no Swedish required. Even if you don't care to bid, browsing among the showrooms sheds light on Swedish homes, the way Swedes live, and what they keep or discard.

Sweden's equivalent of Harrods is **Nordiska Kompaniet (NK)** ㉗, on Hamngatan (just opposite Sweden House), whose rooftop illuminated sign, constantly turning, is visible from far and wide in the city. NK sells everything from shoes to sporting equipment, men's and women's clothing to glass, pottery and silver, jewellery and perfume; its services range from optician to post office and travel agency, and you can get your sightseeing shoes soled and heeled when you come to collect the high-speed prints of your latest roll of film.

> **Map on pages 164–5**

Silk mill Almgrens Sidenväveri (at Repslargagartan 15, Södermalm) wove fine silken goods and ribbons from 1833 until 1974. It has now re-opened as a working museum (tel: 08-642 56 16).

BELOW: an invitation to try the Swedish delicacies, in Östermalmshallen.

The World's Longest Art Gallery

It's hard to understand what inspired Swedish engineering designers to cover the walls of Stockholm's underground railway with paintings at a time when every other country was lining its undergrounds with shiny, cream tiles. But it has made Stockholm's underground, the Tunnelbanan, into much more than a mere transport system. Down the escalators is a world of caverns full of colour, texture, and shape, giving Stockholm the world's longest art gallery. Booking halls, ceilings, platforms and track walls offer an endless variety of styles and colours – all for the price of a ticket. Half of the 99 stations have paintings, sculptures, mosaics or engravings. More than 70 artists have contributed.

T-Centralen, the hub of the network, became home to the first embellishments in 1957: Egon Möller-Nielsen constructed terrazzo sofas on the upper platform; track walls were decorated by other artists with white clinkers and figures in ceramic material, and glass prisms in varying colours and patterns. A year later, Tom Möller's tile decoration, *Goat*, appeared in Hammerbyhöjden (line 19).

Stockholmers argue about which is the best line for paintings, but the route out to Akalla (line 11) is a strong contender. The train leaves from T-Centralen's lower platform and to go down the second escalator is to enter a deep mysterious cave. The platform and tracks have been tunnelled out of natural stone, left in its rough-hewn form, and covered with huge blue leaf fronds on a white and blue background.

As you pass the various stations, also look at Västra Skogen with a 18-metre (60-ft) human profile in terrazzo, tile patterns and cobblestones. But the high spot on this line must be Solna Centrum, which deserves a special stop. It has green hills and forests behind the rail tracks, silhouetted against red. The scene shows a man playing an accordion, and, the longer you look at the work, the more you find. This environmental theme, *Sweden in the 70s*, was completed in 1975 by Karl-Olov Björk and Anders Åberg.

On the other arm of this line (10), is Tensta, one of the larger immigrant communities with some 30 different nationalities represented. The paintings show a *Tribute to the Immigrants*. But many think the most interesting station on this line is Kungs-trädgården, which has two beautiful entrances. Other more unusual exhibits are the *Green Bird* sculpture at Rågsved (line 19), the scientific, engineering, and mathematical symbols of Tekniska Högskolan (Royal Insitute of Technology, lines 15 and 24), and the fantasy beetles in glass cases at Gärdet (lines 13 and 14). The theme *Women's Lib, The Peace, and Environment Movement* at Östermalmstorget (lines 13, 14, 15, 24) shows how early the Swedes were interested in equality for women. At Vällingby (lines 17 and 18) Casimir Djuric has turned the platform pillars into giant trees.

What direction will the Tunnelbanan decorations will take in the 21st century? ❏

LEFT: artists have gone to town decorating Stockholm's underground stations.

Find a bargain

Shopping in Sweden is rarely cheap, but it is always good value. For a bargain, the words to look out for are *rea*, which means sale, and *extrapris*, which does not mean extra, but special low price.

Åhléns City ㉘ is on the corner of Sergels Torg and Drottninggatan. It has a similar range and quality to NK ,and a visit to its supermarket food department is a sightseeing tour in itself. The third of this trio of stores is **PUB**, on Drottninggatan at Hötorget, which is a galleria featuring a variety of Swedish and international-brand shops.

Drottninggatan (Queen's Street), an old street which leads directly through the Riksdagshuset and over the bridge from the Royal Palace, is one of Stockholm's main pedestrian ways, with multi-coloured flags strung between the buildings. In summer, it is full of casual crowds strolling in T-shirts and shorts or sitting at one of the outdoor cafés. Immigrants sell their wares on blankets spread out on the pavement. This area is a haven for pickpockets, so be careful.

Strindberg's Blue Tower

Not to be missed is **Strindbergsmuseet (Strindberg Museum)** ㉙, at Drottninggatan 85, housed in the top-storey flat of the Blåtornet (Blue Tower) where Sweden's greatest playwright spent his last years and wrote his last epic play, *The Great Highway* (1908). It is open Sep–May: Tues 11am–7pm; Wed–Fri 11am–4pm, Sat–Sun noon–4pm; June–Aug: daily 11am–4pm; entrance fee; tel: 08-411 53 54; www.strindbergsmuseet.se.

August Strindberg's taste in room furnishing followed his ideas for stage sets, and the rooms in his flat are full of bright green, yellow and red. Even at the end of his life, Strindberg was astonishingly prolific, and he produced some 20 books in his four years in the Blue Tower.

His study is just as he left it. The wreath beside a photograph of his daughter Anne-Marie was presented to Strindberg on the first anniversary of the theatre he founded, Intiman (the Intimate Theatre). The Strindberg Festival held each year in late summer features plays, concerts, lectures and other events.

Fruit and finery

Walking south along Drottninggatan to Kungsgatan, on your left you'll find **Hötorget** ㉚, with its open-air food stalls and indoor market. This is where Swedes shop for food. Here you can find Swedish delicacies such as elk steak and reindeer and the many varieties of Scandinavian cured herring.

Swedish design is world-renowned not just in beautiful objects but also in designer clothes for men and women. Wherever you go, either in the city centre or in Gamla Stan, you will never be far from shops selling crystal, china, pottery and fur and the fashions of well-known designers such as Pia, Wallén, Filippa K and Anna Holtblad.

In addition to exploring Gamla Stan's antique shops, you might like to take the underground railway (Tunnelbanan) south to Slussen station on **Södermalm**, once the great working class area of the city;

Map on pages 164–5

The "smörgåsbord" (sandwich table) evolved from the 18th century "brännvin" (herring) table. Today, this buffet of hot and cold dishes is enjoyed at formal dinners, Christmas and Easter (see pages 143–4).

BELOW: markets are popular with Stockholmers.

BELOW: ferries ply between the many thousand islands.

the journey takes just 5–10 minutes. Nowadays, this district is a popular place for artists to live and work. It has become a trendy place to hang out, and new cafés, restaurants and boutiques seem to open daily.

The steep slope of **Hornsgatan** has a cluster of galleries. If you start at the Galleri Origo, they will tell you about the past and present of Söder and suggest where and what you might buy.

Islands by the thousand

It is a rare city that has 24,000 islands on its doorstep and 100 km (60 miles) of lake at its heart, but this is Stockholm's eternal good fortune. Until the building of the Tunnelbanan, boats were often the only way of getting around these great expanses of water, and boats are still part of Stockholm life.

To maintain contact within the archipelago, Stockholm County Council's own shipping company, Waxholmsbolaget, subsidises boat transport to all the inhabited islands – thereby providing a valuable service for visitors who want to explore, as well as to the islanders themselves. The largest private company, **Strömma Kanalbolaget** (www.strommakanalbolaget.com), specialises mostly in transporting passengers across Lake Mälaren, and there are various other touring vessels that ply lake and sea. Between them, they provide a variety of craft, from beautiful old coal-fired steamers to modern ferries. Excursions vary from brief introductory tours to day-long excursions and evening cruises with dinner. The latter almost invariably involve music, allowing you to dance your way gently through the islands. (*See also pages 196–7*).

Mälaren stretches for more than 100 km (60 miles) to the west, a lake of narrow straits, vast sweeping bays, with beaches and rocky shores. You sail out

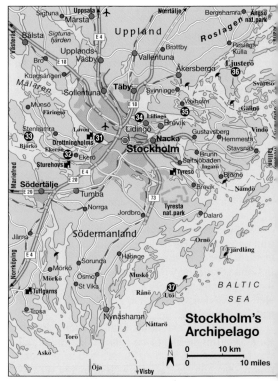

Stockholm's Archipelago

past the modern buildings on **Norrmälarstrand**, but once the boat passes under the high arch of **Västerbron**, the shores change. On the left is the island of **Långholmen** and to the right, a bathing beach, **Smedsudden**, one of 15 such beaches within the city limits. At the weekend and in the evenings, the lake is dotted with the sails of small boats.

Map on page 188

Drottningholms Slott: home of royals

The most popular place to visit in the archipelago is **Drottningholms Slott (Drottningholms Palace)** ❸ on Lovön. It is now the main home of the Royal Family, who moved from Gamla Stan to provide their young family with a garden. In this they have certainly succeeded. Drottningholms, a smaller version of Versailles, looks out on to formal gardens of fountains, statues, flower beds, box hedges and small dark trees, pointing upwards like green standing stones. The palace was built by the energetic Tessin family headed by Nicodemus the Elder, and the gardens laid out by Nicodemus the Younger. Although the Royal Family live there, much of the palace is open to the public (open May–Aug: 10am–4.30pm; Sep: noon–3.30pm; tel: 08-402 62 80). The 17th-, 18th-, and 19th-century interiors are magnificent.

In the parkland stands the Swedish version of Grand Trianon, the exotic pagoda roofs and ornamental balconies of the **Kina Slott (Chinese Pavilion)** (open Apr–Oct: 1–3.30pm; May–Aug: 11am–4.30pm; Sep: noon–3.30pm, guided tours Jun–Aug: 11am, 2pm; entrance fee; tel: 08-402 62 70; café serves coffee and waffles). At the end of the 18th century, the courtiers of King Gustav III sunned themselves in the pavilion's gardens and played at rural life. The silkworms introduced to Kanton, a small village built next to the Kina Slott,

August is the time for a "kräftskiva" (crayfish party). Under the glow of paper lanterns, Swedes enjoy this beloved shellfish, once plentiful in freshwater lakes but now imported.

BELOW: Stockholm's archipelago – a summer playgound.

fared less well. The worms were no match for the frozen depths of a Swedish winter, thwarting the court's attempts to produce cheap silk.

Drottningholms Theatre

The island's greatest treasure is undoubtedly the 18th-century **Drottningholms Slottsteater** (Drottningholm Court Theatre), which opened in 1766 for Queen Louisa Ulrika, mother of Gustav III (open May: noon–4.30pm, June–Aug: 11am–4.30pm, Sep: 1–3.30pm; entrance fee; tel: 08 457 06 00; Teatermuseet, Duke Carl's Pavilion, open May–Sep daily).

Gustav's two great loves were theatre and French culture (he could write the French language better than he wrote Swedish), and it is said that he would have much preferred to be an actor or playwright than king. Gustav III was also a patriot, determined to turn Sweden's French theatre tradition into Swedish. He ejected the French actors from Drottningholm and replaced them with Swedes, and continued his aim of encouraging a Golden Age of the native arts.

Despite his enthusiasm for culture, Gustav's benevolent despotism was not popular with his unruly nobility. His assassination in 1792 at a masked ball inspired Verdi's *Un Ballo in Maschera*, a memorial Gustav himself might have approved of. On his death, the Court Theatre fell into disuse.

It was not until the 1920s that the building was used again, after Professor Agne Beijer discovered it, complete and undamaged, just waiting for restoration. That unlikely chance makes it the oldest theatre in the world which still uses its original backdrops and stage machinery for productions today. Attending a performance here on a warm summer evening is like experiencing magic from an earlier age.

The royal residence of Drottningholm Palace is surrounded by magnificent formal gardens.

BELOW: the Palace of Drottningholms on Lake Mälaren.

Island road

Drottningholmsvägen leads straight out to the main Mälaren islands. The first of these is **Kärsön**, which in the 13th century was part of a rich religious order, Klara Cloister, through Lovön and Drottningholm, and then on to **Svartsjölandet**, with its castle and the Hillehög runestone carving.

From there, the next island is **Ekerön** , an important trading centre in the fifth and sixth centuries, which archaeologists are now excavating. At the northern end of the island is **Munsö Church**, a "fortified church" used by the villagers in times of strife because it was usually the strongest building and the safest place to be.

Trade and church

Further west is **Björkö** , the site of Sweden's oldest city, **Birka** (see *Insight On The Vikings*, pages 24–5). Between AD 800 and 975, Birka was the trading centre for the 40,000 inhabitants of the rich Mälaren area, and the meeting point for traders from Russia and Arabia as well as from Central and Western Europe, at a time when the lake was still navigable from the Baltic.

This was also where Christianity first came to Sweden, when Ansgar, the Saxon missionary, landed in the early part of the ninth century. The Ansgar chapel, built in the 1930s, commemorates the missionary. Almost nothing is left of Birka above ground, but many archaeological digs have revealed the past at sites which include the old town, and the "sacrificial stones". Sadly for Ansgar, the sheer numbers of pagan graves show that he was largely unsuccessful in converting the island, and Sweden had to wait a further 200 years for Christianity to take a firm hold. A guide meets the boat at Björkö, which can only be reached

Map on page 188

TIP

The site of the Viking town of Birka is open May to September. Opening times correspond with the arrival of the boats, which depart from outside Stadshuset (City Hall) on Kungsholmen (details from Strömma Kanalbolaget, tel: 8 587 14 000).

BELOW: snaps at Drottningholms Palace.

by water. The new **Birka Museum** features the most recent archaeological findings (open May–Sep; entrance fee; tel: 08-560 514 45). The boat continues to **Strängnäs**, a pretty little town with a cathedral. There are also tours to other towns and castles on the lakeside.

Baltic gateway

Scots have their Scotch, Germans their beer and France its wine. Swedes have aquavit, or "snaps-pure", a hard liquor made from rye, flavoured with fruits, berries, herbs and spices.

To the east, the islands of the archipelago seem endless, almost as though every Stockholm family could have an isle of its own. A sense of freedom and distance begins the moment you start to skim through the skerries in a small boat or look down from the deck of a steamer.

Although now it is as easy to get there by underground (T–Ropsten) and bus, in summer you should grab the chance to take the boat to the island suburb of **Lidingö ㉞**, where you can visit **Millesgården**, the summer home of the sculptor, Carl Milles and his wife, the Austrian painter Olga Granner (Carl Milles väg 2; open May–Sep: 10am–5pm; Oct–Apr: Tues–Sun noon–4pm; entrance fee; tel: 08-446 75 90). Here, summer after summer, Milles patiently reproduced the statues that had made him more famous in his adopted country of America than in Sweden, though you can see a fine specimen in front of the Concert Hall at Hötorget. Milles' creations seem to evade gravity. They soar and fly, and step lightly over water, emphasised by their position on terraces carved from the steep cliffs of the island.

From Lidingö, the boat continues through the winding skerries as far as **Vaxholm ㉟**, to the northeast. The urban area of Vaxholm is the trading centre for the 60 or so islands in this group, with rail and train links to the mainland as well as the more leisurely boat and car ferries to nearby islands. It is all part of

BELOW: Vaxholm Fort, venue for herring picnics.

an elaborate transport network that manages to keep a remarkable number of islands in contact with the city of Stockholm itself.

Map
on page
188

Elegance from centuries past

Vaxholm still has many traces of the mid-18th century, when the wealthier Stockholmers began to turn it into an ideal summer resort and build elegantly decorated wooden summer homes. The island already had a 16th-century fortress built under the supervision of King Gustav Vasa, now a museum. A walk round the town reveals the old Saven Inn, now offices, the customs house, the battery on the ramparts, and the **Hembygdgårds Museet** (Homestead Museum) in a century-old fishing cottage with a pleasant café (open May–Sep: 11am–8pm; free; tel: 08-541 319 80).

You can also sail, canoe and wind-surf, or swim at several good bathing beaches. Fishing for your own Baltic herring from the town's quayside is popular but you could just sample them for lunch in the hotel near the harbour, or on one of the special Herring Picnics at **Vaxholm Fort**.

The cottages of the archipelago are designed with an appealing simplicity.

The journey out to Vaxholm takes about an hour and is a pleasant introduction to the archipelago. Though the Waxholmsbolaget boats are primarily designed to serve the islands, many have special day trips which allow you to stop, spend a day on an island and wait for the steamer's return.

The islands divide roughly into three areas which run parallel to the mainland: first, the big inner islands, then a belt of smaller skerries and, far out to sea, the isolated outer isles surrounded by pale, clear shallows. Each one is different, some wooded, some with heather, some scorched bare by the sea winds, and others steeped in silence and solitude. The bigger islands are ideal for cycling

BELOW: island hopping, and the parrot came, too.

Map
on page
188

and you can arrange a special excursion to **Ljusterö** ❸, an hour or so northeast from Vaxholm. Waiting for you there are a bicycle, a picnic box, a list of suggested routes and a map. In the evening the steamer *SS Storskär* returns for the journey to Stockholm, a beautiful trip in the long Scandinavian evening, winding in and out of the islands.

A similar cycling trip to **Utö** ❸, in the southern part of the archipelago reveals a hotel, restaurant, bakery, camping and bathing facilities and, though central Sweden was the traditional home of the iron and copper industry in Sweden, Utö claims the oldest iron mine in Sweden, with a museum.

Many islands are rich in wildlife – elk and deer, otters, mink, fox, badger and the occasional lynx. Others are a haven for birds and birdwatchers, with the rare white-tailed eagle, gulls, eiders, mergansers and velvet scoters, many wading birds such as turnstones and oystercatchers, with seabirds perching on the yellow lichen-covered rocks, and swans by the battalion.

Changing weather

The further east you go in the seaward skerries, the more peaceful and unchanged the islands become. In spring and summer many are beautiful with cowslips and wild pansies and orchids, and the scarlet of poppies. These outer islands are not always easy to reach and the weather can be fickle, but they repay any difficulty in getting there. Three of the most beautiful are accessible from Stockholm.

Gällnö lies in the middle of the archipelago. It has a year-round population of farmers and you will find youth hostels and camping sites, which stipulate a maximum stay of two days, though it may be possible to stay longer. Waxholmsbolaget boats serve Gällnö.

Svartlöga is also on the scheduled route, via Blidö towards the northern end of the archipelago, and you can combine it with a visit to nearby **Rödlöga**. Svartlöga has a small general store, open in summer, and there is excellent bathing near the quay.

Bullerön, just south of Sandhamn, is one of the remotest islands in the archipelago, part of a nature reserve that takes in some 900 islands, islets and skerries. An exhibition in an old studio on the island gives information about island culture and nature. You reach it by taxiboat from Stavsnäs, on the inner island of **Fågeltrolandet**, or direct from Stockholm.

In all this remoteness, the bigger island of **Sandön** is a surprise, ideal for a short stay or a day excursion. For, though Sandön is on the outer edge of the archipelago, the village of Sandhamn is a lively place with a restaurant and museum and a large harbour stuffed with the masts of visiting boats. It is the headquarters of the **Royal Stockholm Yacht Club**.

Despite the influx, which swells the island's winter population of around 100 by several thousand, on this island you feel you have really left the land behind. Sandhamn is part of the Baltic Sea, and a visit to the island will help you to understand what it was that from early times made the Swedes a maritime race, and what fires their present-day ambitions for a boat… and a star to steer her by. ❑

BELOW: music in the city.
RIGHT: winter in the archipelago.

STEAMING OUT AMONG THE SKERRIES

When summer comes, the Swedes set off by boat to the thousands of idyllic islands that dot the waterways between Stockholm and the Baltic

Every summer thousands of Swedes in boats navigate carefully through waters loaded with 24,000 islands, rocks and islets in the Stockholm archipelago. The brackish waters start in the centre of Stockholm and extend 80 km (50 miles) out into the open Baltic Sea. Close to the mainland, the islands are larger and more lush, the bays and channels wider. Hidden here are idyllic island communities, farmlands and small forests. But as you travel further out, the scenery becomes more rugged, finally ending in sparse windblown islets formed by the last Ice Age.

ISLAND RETREATS

In the middle of the 19th century affluent Stockholm families began to build their second homes along the shores of the various islands in the archipelago. Over the years, "commoners" had more money and leisure time and soon they, too, sought their way to the archipelago. The combination of wilderness, sea, fresh air and closeness to the city satisfied many leisure needs. Today, Swedes either own their cottages or rent them, and enjoy swimming, fishing, boating, nature walks and socialising with friends.

▷ **YOUNG VOYAGER**
Dressed for the ferry ride and a deck-side view of the steam boats and yachts that ply the waters.

△ **ON THE WATERFRONT**
More than 50,000 chalets offering varying degrees of comfort are spread throughout Stockholm's inner archipelago.

▽ **LAZY DAYS**
The archipelago is such an important factor in the Stockholmers' leisure time, that every tenth resident now owns a boa

▽ HOME FROM HOME

More than 10,000 people live year round on the 150 inhabited islands, working in farming, fishing, boat transport and retailing.

▽ WALK IN THE WILD

Escaping to the islands for summer weekends and holidays, mainly in July, is a perfect antidote to the bustle of city life.

A QUICK GUIDE TO ISLAND HOPPING

The archipelago can be explored on guided tours which can be picked up from Stockholm's city centre. But if you want to travel like the locals, then buy a *Båtluffarkort* (Inter-skerries card), which allows you to see as many islands as you can in 16 days, including:

● Sandön, with its attractive sailing centre village of Sandhamn, sandy beaches and some good restaurants (a 6-hour round trip).

● Fjäderholmarna, featuring a boat museum, aquarium, fish-smoking plant, restaurants and crafts shops (20 minutes by boat from Stockholm).

● Vaxholm, with its famous fortress (1 hour by boat).

● Utö, where a 12th-century iron mine is the principal attraction

ISLAND HARVEST

▸rry and mushroom ᴐking are popular ᴊstimes enjoyed by all ᴊes. Swedes also love ᴊture walks, bird ᴊtching and picnicking.

▷ PADDLE POWER

Swedes take time to enjoy the scenery by water. Although sailing is a very popular water sport, canoeing and kayaking come in a close second.

This is a also a great place for for bike-riding (3 hours by boat from the city).

AROUND STOCKHOLM

*Sweden's early history is firmly rooted around
the sparkling waterways of Stockholm's hinterland, in close
proximity to the ancient capital of Uppsala*

Maps:
City 202
Area 204

Three provinces surround Stockholm (Uppland, Södermanland and Västman-land) connecting with Gästrikland to the north and Östergötland to the south. Together they stretch from the ragged Baltic coastline of bays, inlets and islets to the thousands of lakes and streams glinting in the forests of the interior. In the centre are Lake Mälaren's waterways linking the districts and the capital with ribbons of water and chugging lake steamers. Along the banks castles, manors and palaces are reminders of hundreds of years of Swedish history.

This is the heart of Sweden today, a synopsis of the country's past, its natural wonders and its cultural riches. Its wealth stems from the area's mineral deposits that provided the iron for the Eiffel Tower and the copper for the roofs of Versailles. Sweden's excellent road system and fine-mesh network of ferries and cruise ships, make the riches of the region easily accessible.

Uppland culture

About 20 km (12 miles) north of Stockholm is **Vallentuna ❶**, the birthplace of King Gustav Vasa, with the greatest number of Viking rune stones in Sweden. Also worth seeing is the town's 12th-century church and **Angarnsjöangen**, a wetland area with the richest bird life in the Stockholm region.

Head 30 km (18 miles) west into the plain of Upp-land and where the sea meets the forest, you'll find **Sigtuna ❷**, Sweden's oldest town. In the 11th century this was the commercial centre for the Svea and Van-dal tribes. Merchant ships from as far away as Asia dropped anchor here; monasteries and abbeys com-peted with one another in building glorious churches. Today, Sigtuna is a sleepy town on the edge of the sea, with crooked lanes, quaint wooden houses and a miniature town hall. The ruins of the medieval monas-teries provide a cultural focus, as do the summer evening concerts at the gazebo on the green.

Less than an hour's drive north of Stockholm on the E4 lies **Uppsala ❸**, Sweden's ancient capital, last bastion of heathenism and seat of one of Europe's greatest universities. This is the birthplace of Ingmar Bergman and the setting for his film *Fanny and Alexander*. Visit the town on the last day of April for a rousing *Sista April*, with the students decked in evening dress and white "student caps" – the size, shape and tassel of which tells all about the wearer.

An early-morning speech by the university's head from the balcony of the library starts the day's fun with a stampede by the students downhill to the beer barrels set up in the halls of the 16th and 17th-century palaces, called *nationer* (student unions).

The town is also an Episcopal See and has the largest Gothic cathedral to be found in Scandinavia,

PRECEDING PAGES:
steam train at
Mariefred.
LEFT: a day out on
the Baltic coast.
BELOW: Uppsala's
Gothic cathedral.

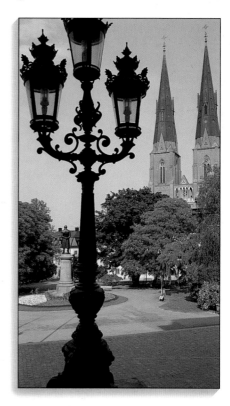

Domkyrkan (open 8am–6pm; tel: 018-18 71 77). Its vaults, from 1435, house the shrine of Saint Erik, a king and the patron of Sweden, as well as the graves of other early monarchs (including Gustav Vasa and his three wives), bishops, generals and a philosopher or two. The scientist and theologian, Emanuel Swedenborg, lies here in an enormous red granite sarcophagus.

Just across the road at Akademigatan 3 is the **Gustavianum** Ⓑ, an ancient, onion-domed edifice housing a 17th-century anatomical theatre built for the Renaissance genius Olof Rudbeck (open Mid-May–mid Sep: 11am–4pm, Thurs 11am–9pm; mid-Sep–mid-May: Wed–Sun 11am–4pm, Thurs 11am–9pm; entrance fee; tel: 018-471 75 71).

Cannon outside the imposing brick-built Uppsala Castle.

Across the town's lush parks rises **Uppsala Slott (Uppsala Castle)** Ⓒ, a typically squat, dominating brick fortress from the days of the Vasa dynasty (open mid-Jun–late-Aug for guided tours only; entrance fee; tel: 018-27 48 00). Its magnificent halls were the venue of the abdication of imperious Queen Kristina who preferred exile in Rome to "ruling a country of barbarians".

Linnaeus: father of botany

Another university genius from Uppsala was professor Carl von Linné or Linnaeus (1707–78), the father of our system of botanical classification (*see page 40*). His residence in the heart of town at Svartbäcksgatan 27 is now the Linnémuseum (open June–mid-Sep: Tues–Sun noon–4pm; May: Sat–Sun noon–4pm; entrance fee; tel: 018-13 65 40). Adjacent to the house are Linné's own botanical gardens, **Linnéträdgården** Ⓓ, with 1,600 different exotic plants set out to the botanist's own plan (open May–Aug: 9am–9pm, Sep: 9am–7pm; tel: 018-10 94 90).

BELOW: statue of the botanist Carl von Linné in Uppsala.

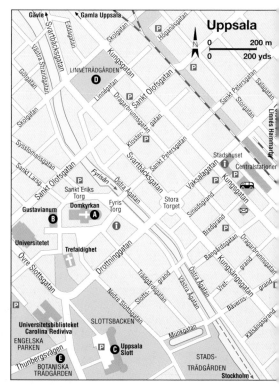

You can explore other botanical gardens, the **Botaniska Trädgården ⓔ**, at the castle at Villavägen 8 (open Mon–Thurs 9.30am–3.30pm, Fri 9.30am–2.30pm; entrance fee).

A few minutes north of the town lies **Gamla Uppsala (Old Uppsala)** the 5th-century bastion of the Yngling dynasty. The three huge grave mounds of kings Aun, Egil and Adils (described in the opening passages of *Beowulf*) dominate the evocative grave fields surrounding Gamla Uppsalakyrkan (Uppsala's parish church). This medieval brick construction replaced Scandinavia's last heathen temple (open 9am–4pm; free; tel: 018 327 081).

Around Uppsala

At **Härkeberga ⓸**, 30 km (18 miles) southwest of Uppsala, medieval mythology is illustrated on the ceilings of **Härkeberga Kyrka** (Church), where Albertus Pictor, an ambulating vault painter in the 1400s, recorded the lives and hopes of the parishioners. About 10 km (6 miles) east of Uppsala is Sweden's longest vintage railway, the Lennakatten, linking **Lenna ⓹** with Uppsala (open Jun–Aug weekends; entrance fee; tel: 018-13 08 00).

About 35 km (22 miles) north of Uppsala lies **Örbyhus Slott (Örbyhus Castle) ⓺**, a splendid baroque building. King Erik (XIV) was purportedly poisoned with pea soup while held here in house-arrest by his power-hungry brother. In the grounds are a "Turkish" orangery, stables and a spreading English-style park (open mid-May–mid-Sep by guided tour Sat, Sun 1pm; July–mid-Aug: Tues–Sun 1pm, 3pm; entrance fee; tel: 0295-214 06).

At **Älvkarleby ⓻**, another 50 km (31 miles) north, the Dalälven river tumbles into the Baltic over stunningly beautiful cliffs. This area is famous for

**Maps:
City 202
Area 204**

Linnaeus's last home, Linnés Hammarby, just southeast of Uppsala, is a pretty, 18th-century cross between a manor and a cottage (park open May–Sep: 8am–8pm; museum and café Tues–Sun noon–4pm; entrance fee; tel: 018-32 60 94).

BELOW: living near the water at Gräsö in Uppland.

Siggebohyttans
Bergsmansgård
(Manor) near
Lindesberg, 40 km
(25 miles) north of
Örebro, gives a taste
of the opulent life of
the iron-masters in
Victorian days (open
Jun–mid-Aug: 11am–
5pm; entrance fee;
tel: 0587-33 00).

salmon fishing and, despite the presence of a latter-day power station, the salmon still run thick here. There's an angling museum and a state game-fish research centre and a hatchery at Älvkarleby.

Along the Baltic coast

About 60 km (37 miles) northeast of Stockholm is **Norrtälje ❽**, a quaint fishing town where you can buy herring and salmon in the marketplace. Roslagsmuseet (Roslags Museum) shows life gone by in this island world (Faktorigatan 1; open mid–May–mid-Sep: Mon–Fri 11am–4pm, Sat 11am–2pm; mid-Sep–mid-May: Tues–Thurs noon–4pm; entrance fee). Try the nearby **Wallinska Gårdarna** (Wallinska Farm) for more heritage.

On a spit of land 30 km (18 miles) north of Norrtälje, sticking even farther into the Baltic Sea, is **Grisslehamn ❾**, the nearest point to Finland's Åland Islands. Boats can be hired here, and you can try the freshly smoked whitefish that is the speciality in the fishermen's huts.

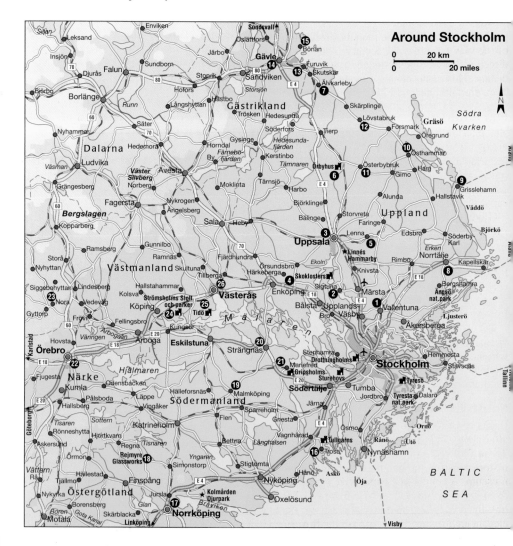

Neighbouring **Östhammar** , and Öregrund to the north, are summer retreats. Much of their 18th-century architecture is preserved. You'll get a good taste at the **Gammelhus Hembygdsgård** open-air museum in Östhammar (entrance fee; tel: 0173-170 05) and along narrow Tullports Street.

Map
on page
204

Iron prosperity

Sweden grew rich in the 17th and 18th centuries on its iron ore. Scots and Belgian Walloons emigrated here to found thriving forges, smelting ovens and dynasties. Their estates, actually small foundry villages (*bruk*), are found where forest, swift streams and the Baltic supplied the right conditions for smelting metal. About 30 km (18 miles) west of Östhammar is **Österbybruk** , the oldest iron foundry in Uppland, dating from 1443. The original Vallonsmedjan (Walloon forge), the last of its kind, is preserved and open to the public. See the manor house gardens and stables and the paintings of Bruno Liljefors in the main house (open May: Sat–Sun noon–4pm; Jun–Aug: daily 11am–5pm; early-Sep: Sat–Sun noon–4pm; entrance fee; tel: 0295-214 06/200 72).

Wealthy **Lövstabruk** , 20 km (12 miles) north, was Sweden's largest iron producer in the 1600s. The foundry street is immaculately kept and gives an idea of the hierarchy of *bruk* society. The villagers resided in bungalows, while directly across the street stretched the iron master's French *parterres* and, in the distance, his manor house, **Lövsta Herrgård** (open Jun–Aug for tours, noon, 3pm; entrance fee; tel: 0294-310 70).

The church of Gamla Uppsalakyrkan, Old Uppsala, houses the tomb of Celsius. An 11th-century rune stone can be seen on an outside wall.

Fun and games

About 20 km (12 miles) north into the forested landscape of Gästrikland is **Furuvik** , with a large amusement park, **Furuviksparken**, featuring a circus, ghosts' castle and other attractions (open mid-May–June: Mon–Fri 10am–4pm, Sat–Sun 10am–5pm; July–mid-Aug: 10am–6pm; mid-Aug–early-Sep: Sat–Sun 10am–5pm; entrance fee).

Gävle  is the main centre for entertainment and shopping. The old town is a knot of twisting lanes with wooden gingerbread houses from the past two centuries. **Sveriges Järnvägsmuseum** (Swedish Railway Museum), Rälsgatan 1, has some remarkable vintage steam locomotives and narrow-gauge rolling stock (open Sep–May: Tues–Sun 10am–4pm; Jun–Aug: daily 10am–4pm; entrance fee).

Out on the edge of the Baltic is **Bönan** , a fishing village famous for its *böckling* (smoked herring). You will smell it smoking before you see the town. Try the village's excellent restaurant, noted for its Baltic panorama and kaleidoscopic *smörgåsbord*.

BELOW: Gripsholms Slott, Mariefred.

South to Södermanland

If you head south from Stockholm, you will arrive after about 50 km (31 miles) at the seaside idyll of **Trosa** , where the attractions include the quaint, historic district, a handicrafts centre, and town museum. A couple of hours' drive south on the E4 from Trosa brings you to **Norrköping** , with its tree-lined avenues, outdoor café society, trams and elegant architecture. Near Norrköping flows the Göta

TIP

For camping in Västmanland, try the 13th-century Engsö Castle, where visitors can enjoy fishing, swimming, and canoeing (tel: 0171-44 40 12).

BELOW: Skoklosters Slott, near Sigtuna, venue for medieval pageantry.

Kanal with its attractive cruise boats (*see page 268*), but the town is most famous for the **Kolmården Djurpark**. This is Scandinavia's wildlife safari, natural habitat and amusement park supreme (open Apr–mid-May: 10am–4pm; mid-May–mid-Jun: 9am–5pm; mid-Jun–mid-Aug: 9am–6pm; mid-Aug–end-Aug: 10am–5pm; Sep: 10am–4pm; entrance fee; tel: 011-24 90 00).

About 25 km (15 miles) north you can visit **Rejmyre Glassworks** , the second oldest glass furnace in the country. You are welcome to watch the glassblowing (Mon–Fri 9am–2.45pm; mid-May–Sep: also Sat 10am–3pm; tel: 011-871 80), and the "seconds" shop is sensational (open mid-May–Sep: Mon–Fri 9am–6pm, Sat–Sun 10am–4pm; Oct–Apr: Mon–Fri 9am–5pm, Sat 10am–2pm, Sun 11am–3pm). Thirty km (18 miles) northeast you reach **Malmköping** ⑲ and the Museispårvägen i Malmköping (Tramway Museum), at Järnvägsgatan, with its colourful turn-of-the-century trains (open mid-May–early Sep: Sat–Sun; July–early Aug: Mon–Fri. Trams depart 11am–5pm; entrance fee; tel: 0157-204 30).

Continue north past Lake Mälaren's bays and inlets to **Strängnäs** ⑳, a delightful small town dominated by a magnificent Gothic cathedral. The church's altar screens are worth a detour. Next to the church at Boglösa, 20 km (12 miles) north, are hundreds of Bronze Age rock carvings.

About 15 km (9 miles) to the east lies idyllic **Mariefred** ㉑ and **Gripsholms Slott** (Castle). The impressive pile of the castle protects the royal portrait collections and a marvellous theatre from the late 1700s (open Oct–Apr: Sat–Sun noon–3pm; May–Aug: 10am–4pm; Sep: Tues–Sun 10am–3pm; entrance fee; tel: 0159-101 94). Best of all is the architecture of this fortress, begun in the 1370s and continually updated. Around the edge of the moat is a

SKOKLOSTERS SLOTT

Skoklosters Slott (Skokloster Castle) is what a castle is supposed to be: imposing, imperious, towered and abundantly endowed. Situated less than 70 km (43 miles) from Stockholm and 45 km (28 miles) from Uppsala, this is the family seat of the Wrangels, baroque lords who ruled over most of northern Europe. Their descendants live comfortably in the "old castle" and this majestic pile is open to the public. The collection of weapons, paintings, anthropologia, textiles and books from the early 1600s are among the best to be found (open Apr: 1–3pm; May–Aug 11am–4pm; Sep–Oct: 12.30–3pm; guided tour only; entrance fee; tel: 018-38 60 77). Every July the castle hosts the *Skokloster Spelen* (Skokloster Pageant). The medieval ages come alive with jousting tournaments, dancers, musicians, jesters and knights. In the four-day extravaganza, some 350 performances are given by different artists attracting thousands of visitors. Don't miss Skokloster Kyrka (Skokloster Church) and Skokloster Motor Museum, with its collection of vintage vehicles (open May–Sep: 11am–5pm; entrance fee; tel: 018-38 61 06). At Skokloster Wärdhus and Hotel, the castle's stables have been transformed into a restaurant and the dairy has become a health spa (tel: 018-38 61 00).

collection of rune stones – flat rocks carved in the deepest Dark Ages with serpents, ships and magic inscriptions in the runic alphabet. Mariefred is a lazy, summer lake town, with cafés and restaurants to suit all tastes.

Map on page 204

Mountain scenery

At the western end of Lake Hjälmaren lies bustling **Örebro ㉒**, capital of Västmanland and mountainous Bergslagen. This was where Swedish steel was born. The forests gave fuel, the rivers powered the trip hammers and the lakes provided transport for the swords, cannons and building materials produced by family-run forges. About 35 km (22 miles) north is **Nora ㉓**, a village of wooden houses which preserve the feel of the old days in its shops and tea houses.

To explore the eastern section of Bergslagen, start with the splendid, baroque **Strömsholms Slott och Parker ㉔**, a former royal residence and riding centre featuring a carriage museum, shop and restaurant (open May: Sat–Sun noon–4pm; Jun, Aug noon–4pm; July: noon–5pm; entrance fee; tel: 0220-430 35). Nearby are the Kolbäck River and Strömsholm Canal water sports areas.

On the next peninsula to the east rises **Tidö Slott ㉕**, the 1625 castle home of Axel Oxenstierna, a regent of Sweden and feared warrior. The present owners have converted part of their home into a toy museum with 35,000 exhibits. The wooded grounds offer a deer park and an inn (open May and Sep: Sat–Sun noon–5pm; Jun–Aug: daily noon–5pm; entrance fee; tel: 021-530 42).

On an inlet of the lake, 20 km (12 miles) east, **Västerås ㉖** is a 1,000-year old settlement with a 13th-century cathedral, a fortress of the same vintage. At **Anundshög**, 15 km (9 miles) east, are Sweden's largest Iron Age and Viking burial mounds and ship tumuli. Ferries run from here to Stockholm. ❑

Grafikens Hus, at Gripsholms Kungsladugård in Mariefred, is a modern art gallery which holds regular exhibitions of contemporary art (open May–Aug: daily 11am–5pm; Sep–Apr: Sat–Sun 11am–5pm; entrance fee; tel: 0159-231 60).

BELOW: the steamer *SS Mariefred* on Lake Mälaren.

SOUTHERN SWEDEN

*Home to the vibrant city of Malmö, the garden landscape of
Southern Sweden is not without charm. Castles and Stone-Age sites
abound, while bathers and birdwatchers head for Öland*

Map
on page
212

Skåne is Sweden's most southerly province, so close to Denmark across
the narrow sound that even the accent is faintly Danish. This isn't surprising because for centuries Swedes and Danes fought over this area,
along with the provinces of Halland and Blekinge, until Sweden established
its sovereignty in 1658.

As of May 2000, however, the two countries are one, joined by the Öresund
Fixed Link, a combined 16-km (10-mile) bridge and tunnel that links Malmö
and Copenhagen, the largest such connection in Europe. The project has
prompted a renaissance for southern Sweden as a centre of the Danish-Swedish
Öresund region, with a total of 3 million people and one-fifth of the total combined GNP of Sweden and Denmark. It also links four universities – Copenhagen, Roskilde, Lund and Malmö.

Skåne is often called Sweden's food store because of its rich farmland, mild
climate and good fishing. Although many think of the landscape as flat, there is
in fact a lot of variety. Along the coast it is undulating and lush and especially
spectacular in the southeast corner, Österlen. Inland, there are three large ridges,
Söderåsen, Romeleåsen and Linderödsåsen, with lovely walks and lakes.

History goes back a long way in Skåne: Stone-Age burial chambers can be
found at **Glumslöv**, north of Trelleborg, at **Tågarp**
and north of Kivik. The King's grave at **Bredarör**,
southeast of Kivik, dates from the Bronze Age and is
famous for its rock carvings, which differ from any
found in Sweden and the other Nordic countries from
the same period.

PRECEDING PAGES:
houses on Öland.
LEFT: overlooking
Kalmarsund.
BELOW: statue of
King Karl X Gustav,
Stortorget, Malmö.

Castles galore

The affluence of Skåne is obvious when you consider
the number of castles and manor houses. There are
said to be 240 in the province. Most are still in private
ownership and not open to the public, but it is usually
possible to walk round the gardens.

Among the most interesting are **Vrams Gun-
narstorp**, 8 km (5 miles) northeast of Bjuv (tel: 042-
830 55); **Vittskövle**, between Degeberga and Åhus
(tel: 044-35 30 43); **Kristinehov** in north Österlen
(not open for guided tours; tel: 0417-262 44/401 00);
Marsvinsholm near Ystad (castle closed to public;
gardens open; café and open-air theatre, open mid-
Jun–mid-Aug: Wed–Sun pm; entrance fee; tel: 0411-
776 81); **Bosjökloster** by Lake Ringsjön (open
Apr–Sep; tel: 0413-250 48; www.bosjokloster.com);
and **Övedskloster** by Lake Vombsjön, north of Sjöbo
(park open Apr–Sep: 9am–4pm; no entrance fee; café
in summer; book in advance to see castle; entrance
fee, tel: 046-63 001). **Sofiero**, 4 km (2½ miles) north
of Helsingborg, was built in 1857 and King Gustav VI

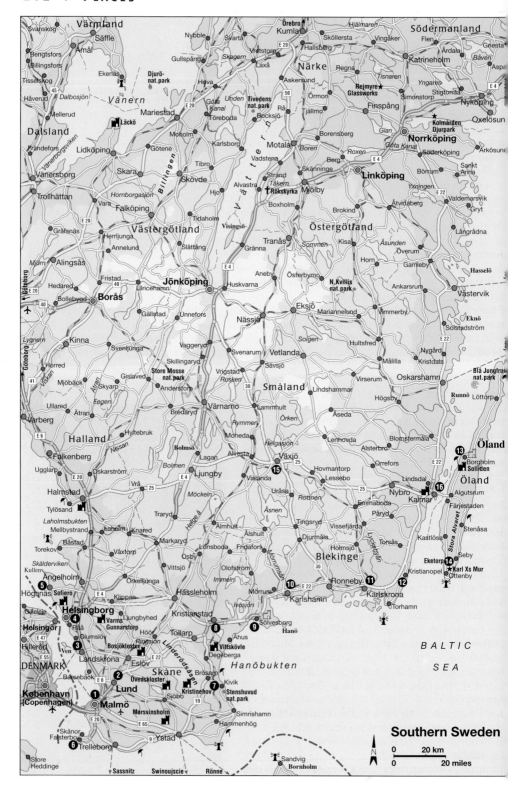

Southern Sweden

Adolf used it as his summer palace until his death in 1973. He was a keen botanist and made the gardens a real attraction (open Apr–Sep; tel: 042-13 74 00; www.helsingborg.se/sofiero).

Malmö: city of the south

Malmö ❶ is Sweden's third city, a lively place with a population of about 255,000. In the 16th century, Malmö competed with Copenhagen to be Scandinavia's leading capital, but in those days it was an important port on a major sailing route, not far from rich fishing grounds.

Today, the harbour is still busy with crossings to Denmark and other traffic, and many of the old buildings remain. **Malmöhus ❹**, the dominating castle built by King Christian III when Skåne was still part of Denmark, is Scandinavia's oldest remaining Renaissance castle. It houses the **Malmömuseer** (Malmö Museums), which includes the Art Museum, Museum of Natural History, City Museum, Science & Technology/Maritime Museum, and the **Kommendants Hus (Commander's House) ❸**, in Malmöhusvägen (open Jun–Aug: 10am–4pm; Sep–May: noon–4pm; entrance fee; tel: 040-34 10 00).

From the same period is **Rådhuset (City Hall) ❻**, which you will find in Stortorget, one of the largest squares in Scandinavia. Stadshuset, in August Palms Plats, was built in 1546 in genuine Dutch Renaissance style. In 1860 it was given a facelift by the architect Helgo Zettervall, with niches, bays, allegorical paintings, and colonnades (open Mon–Fri 8am–4:30pm; tel: 040-34 10 00; www.tourism.malmo.com).

Northeast from Stortorget is **St Petri Kyrka ❼**, Göran Olsgatan 1, built in the Baltic Gothic style and dating from the 13th century, although its towers were built in the 15th century and its copper spires in 1890. The cathedral is elegant, and probably its most beautiful feature is the altar area, Scandinavia's largest, created in 1611 by several sculptors. In the 1800s it was painted over with grey oil paint, which has fortunately been removed in recent years (Mon–Sun 10am–6pm; tel: 040-35 90 40).

Malmö also has a network of pedestrian streets, with many places to shop and coffee houses to sit awhile. A particularly idyllic place to sit and relax is **Lilla Torg (Little Square) ❺**, with its cobblestones, beautifully restored houses and 16th-century charm. Through an arch on the south side of the square is Hemanska Gården. Once a merchant's home and trading yard, it now houses the **Form Design Centre**, Lilla Torg 9, where Swedish industrial design and handicrafts are displayed (open daily).

When you get hungry, head for **Saluhallen**, on the northwest corner of Lilla Torg, where you can choose from fish restaurants, cafés, delicatessens, and an abundance of fresh food if you want to prepare your own picnic (open 10am–6pm; Sat 10am–2pm; last Sat of the month; 10am–5pm). After lunch, you can head southwest and stroll through **Pildammsparken ❻**, the largest landscaped park in Sweden, which houses Pildammsteater, a huge amphitheatre.

Walking east from Lilla Torg, a rewarding visit can be made to **Rooseum ❼** (Stora Nygatan), founded in

TIP

A *Malmökortet* (Malmö Card), available from the tourist office in Central Station, gives free museum entry, city bus journeys, discounted cinema tickets and reduced admission charges.

BELOW: Equestrian Week, Malmö.

Råå, on the outskirts of Helsingborg, is a picturesque fishing village with an excellent inn.

1988 by the Swedish art collector and financier Fredrik Roos. Here you'll see the art currently at the centre of international debate, like that of Jean Michel Basquiat, Julian Schnabel, Susan Rothenberg and Allan McCollum. Large-scale retrospectives of Sweden's foremost contemporary artists are held here (open Tues–Wed 11am–5pm; Thurs 11am–8pm; Fri–Sun 11am–5pm; entrance fee; tel: 040-12 17 16; www.rooseum.se).

Lund: university town

Heading north from Malmö, before joining the coast road you should visit Lund ❷, a university town with a beautiful cathedral, Domkyrkan, built in the 12th century. While in Lund, don't miss the fascinating Kulturhistoriska Museet (Cultural History Museum), Tegnérs platsen, an-open air museum with dozens of buildings, silver, textiles, ceramics and art (open May–Sep: 11am–5pm; Oct–Apr: Tues–Sun noon–4pm; entrance fee; tel: 046-35 04 00). Along with the University of Uppsala, north of Stockholm, Lund is one of the two ancient Swedish universities, both with their own traditions and customs.

About 30 km (19 miles) north along the coast, **Glumslöv** ❸ offers some very memorable views. From the hill above the church, on a clear day you can see 30 churches and seven towns: Helsingborg, Landskrona, Lund and Malmö in Sweden and Dragør, Copenhagen and Helsingør in Denmark.

Potters and artists

Helsingborg ❹ is an interesting town of cobbled streets, dominated in the centre by the remnants of an old castle, Kärnan, and with the 14th-century **St Maria Kyrka** and a bustling harbour. **Höganäs** ❺, 20 km (12 miles) north, is a town

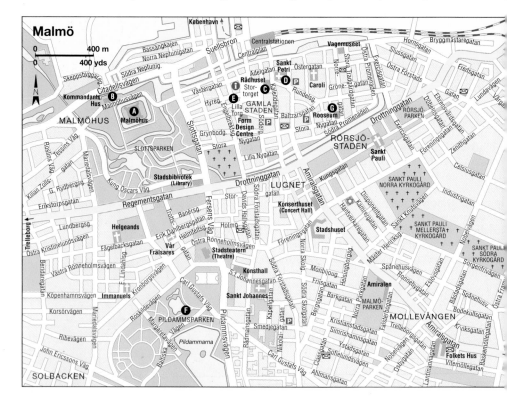

full of potters and artists. There are always a number of exhibitions and the large pottery is worth a visit.

Forty km (25 miles) southeast from Malmö are **Skanör** and **Falsterbo ⑥**, once important towns but now summer idylls. **Skanörs Ljung** is a must for bird-lovers, particularly in September and October, when a large number of migrating birds gather for their flight southwest. It is considered northern Europe's prime location for watching birds of prey.

Phoenician heritage

Follow the coast road east through Trelleborg and Ystad for about 85 km (53 miles) to **Kivik ⑦**, famous for its July market days, although they have lost their former glory. Southeast of Kivik is **Bredarör** (Kiviksgraven), one of Skåne's strangest prehistoric relics. Even 200 years after the discovery scientists wonder about the mysterious signs on the grave slabs. One theory is that Kivik may have been a Phoenician colony in AD 1200.

Kristianstad ⑧ is the birthplace of the Swedish film industry, which started around 1910. The original studio is intact and is now a museum where you can watch some of the old films on video (Filmmuseet, Östra Storg 53, open 1–4pm; tel: 044-13 57 29). The **Kristianstad Vattenriket** (Water Kingdom) is the name given to the catchment area of the Helge River with its rich wetland area, featuring a diversity of birds, wildlife and plants (www.kristianstad.se).

Blekinge is a tiny province with lovely sandy beaches along the coast and Sweden's most southerly archipelago. It is excellent for sea fishing of all kinds, from boat or shore. You can enjoy peaceful angling in some of the lakes, too, or good sport for salmon in the Mörrum River. Canoeing is also popular along

Map on page 212

A "stone ship".
Southern Sweden has
many burial grounds
of interest, including
those at Hjortsberga
and Hjortshammar,
near Ronneby.

BELOW: windmills
stand in line on the
island of Öland.

Kingdom of Glass

It's reassuring in a way that vandalism isn't just a 20th-century phenomenon. They even had the problem in 16th-century Sweden, when King Gustav Vasa's courtiers used to round off an evening of feasting and carousing by smashing as many expensive Venetian glasses as they could lay their hands on. The king, adopting a fatalistic attitude towards this medieval delinquency, invited Venetian glassblowers to his court, commenting that it would be cheaper in the long run to break home-blown glassware rather than the expensive imported variety. The first glass was melted in Sweden in 1556, but it was to be almost another 200 years before glassmaking really became established as an industry in Sweden.

The oldest works, Kosta, was founded in 1742 by Anders Koskull and Georg Bogislaus Stael von Holstein, provincial governors in Småland. Eager to make a little money on the side, they set up a glassworks, taking the first two syllables of their respective surnames to create "Kosta". The location was ideal because the dense forests between Växjö and Kalmar provided vast supplies of timber to keep the furnaces going.

Kosta has been a pioneer in the production of lead crystal glass with what is claimed to have the highest lead content – up to 30 percent – of any produced in Sweden (to qualify for the "crystal" description, there must be at least 24 percent lead oxide in the glass).

The second oldest glassworks is Rejmyre, founded in 1810 by Johan Jakob Graver. Today it specialises in the production of heat-resistant glass.

One of the best-known glass manufacturers is Orrefors. Orrefors started in the glass business by producing window-panes and bottles, but in 1913 the works was taken over by Johan Ekman, an industrialist from Göteborg. Ekman was one of the first to involve artistic talent in the design of glass, and during World War I he recruited two artists who were to transform Orrefors into one of the world's most renowned glassworks: Simon Gate, a portrait and landscape painter, and Edvard Hald, a pupil of Matisse. They were followed by new generations of designers. It is their creative flair, coupled with the centuries-old skills of the glassblower, that has put Sweden in the forefront of worldwide glass design and production.

Most of the 17 major glassworks are open every weekday to visitors (Mon–Fri 9am–6pm, Sat 10am–4pm, Sun noon–4pm: Orrefors Glasbruk, tel: 0481-341 95; Kosta glasbruk, tel: 0478-345 32; Boda glasbruk, tel: 0481-240 30; many have shops).

An old glass-country tradition – the *hyttsill* ("glassworks herring") evening – has been revived in recent years for the benefit of tourists. In bygone times the glassworks was also a social centre where the locals would gather for a chat and bake herrings and potatoes in the furnace, with music provided by an accordionist or fiddler.

During the summer some of the glassworks – including Kosta, Orrefors, Bergdala and Pukeberg – run updated *hyttsill* evenings. Reservations can be made on the spot. ❑

LEFT: the traditional skills of glassblowing are highly valued in southern Sweden.

the coast and on the rivers, and you can move from lake to lake by connecting canals. Driving to Blekinge from Skåne, you first reach **Sölvesborg** ❾, where the narrow streets and old buildings show their medieval origins and the ruins of 13th-century **Sölvesborg Slott** (Castle).

Map on page 212

Mörrum, 30 km (19 miles) north of Sölvesborg, is famous above all for its salmon fishing: at Laxens Hus, a salmon aquarium, you can see salmon and trout at different stages of their development (open Apr–Sep: 9am–5pm; Oct: 9am–4pm; entrance fee; tel: 0454-501 23). **Karlshamn** ❿, about 10 km (6 miles) to the east, is an old seafaring and market town with thriving industries. The Emigrants' Monument, entitled *Karl-Oskar and Kristina*, is a reminder of different times, when thousands of Swedes set off in search of a new life in the New World.

The biggest town in Blekinge is **Karlskrona** ⓫, a naval centre built in the 17th century, with wide streets and impressive buildings. In the **Björkholmen** district you'll find quaint 18th-century cottages built by ships' carpenters.

At **Hästhallen** in Möckleryd are fascinating rock carvings from the Bronze Age, while **Torhamn Point** is well known to ornithologists as the path taken by migratory birds and it is an excellent observation point. On the east coast of Blekinge is the village of **Kristianopel** ⓬, once a Danish stronghold on the border with Sweden. You can see the restored defensive wall and step-gabled church. These days it is more famous for its smoked herring.

Around Öland: an ornithologist's delight

The island of Öland, off the east coast, is one of the most heavily visited areas of Sweden, and, with its diverse landscape, is a paradise for birdwatchers, nature

BELOW: Kalmar Castle, Småland.

Map on page 212

The island of Öland is of great interest to botanists. Its flora is reminiscent of that of the tundra, and there are 30 types of orchid.

BELOW: glasswork by the artist Anna Ehrner for Kosta. **RIGHT:** Sweden has ample timber with which to supply the match-making industry.

lovers, and sun worshippers. The best beaches in Sweden are in northern Öland and attract some 2 million tourists a year.

Once you've crossed the Öland bridge from the coast of Blekinge, you soon see on the northwest coast the ruins of **Borgholm Slott** (Castle) rising above the main town of **Borgholm** ⓭, a once splendid residence from the 12th century. During the summer it is a venue for open-air concerts (open Apr and Sep: 10am–4pm; May, June, Aug: 10am–6pm; July: 10am–9pm; entrance fee).

Solliden Slott (Palace), just outside Borgholm, is the king's summer residence (park only open mid-May–mid-Sep: 1–5pm; entrance fee).

Öland is fascinating to not only to ornithologists and botanists but also gelogists. The island has many ancient burial places and there are remains of 16 fortified dwellings from earlier times. The most interesting is **Eketorp** ⓮, in the south, which has been partly restored.

Sweden's prime birdwatching can be enjoyed at the **Ottenby bird station**, on the island's southerly tip, where 10,000 to 20,000 birds are ringed every year and more than 350 species have been recorded. Ottenby is managed by the Swedish Ornithological Society (www.sofnet.org), which has established a science centre and museum and offers tours of the bird station. In southern Öland you can also see **Karl Xs Mur** (Karl X's Wall), impressive for its sheer size; it was built in 1650 to distinguish Ottenby's domain and keep out the peasants' animals. The entire island was a royal hunting park at that time.

Stora Alvaret, a great expanse of bare limestone soil covering 300 km (186 miles) of central southern Öland, is an unusual and starkly beautiful landscape. It offers the beauty of rare flowers, flocks of cranes in the autumn, and a sense of the earth as it must have looked at the time of creation.

The emigrants

During the late 19th and early 20th centuries, Sweden's population exploded, and many families could no longer eke out a living on the land. So began the years of migration to North America. Of the million who left, the majority came from Småland. Today, one of the most popular places to visit is Utvandrarnas Hus (House of the Emigrants) in **Växjö** ⓯, about 70 km (43 miles) west of Kalmar, which tells the story of the exodus (Wilhelm Mobergs Gata 4, open Jun–Aug: Mon–Fri 9am–6pm, Sat–Sun 11am–4pm; Sep–May: Mon–Fri 9am–4pm; entrance fee; tel: 0470-201 20).

Kalmar ⓰, one of Sweden's oldest cities, was of great importance in the Swedish-Danish wars. Sweden's best preserved Renaissance castle, **Kalmar Slott**, Kungsgatan 1, was in fact begun in the 12th century but was completely renovated during the 16th century by the Vasa kings Gustav I, Erik XIV and Johan III. The castle's beautifully preserved coffered ceilings, panelled halls, fresco paintings and magnificient stonework have inspired the Renaissance Festival, held every July. This features with tournament games, soldiers, craftsmen, a market, theatre and music, food and drink, and noble women and peasants walking the streets in native constume (open Jun–Aug: 10am–6pm; Sep–May: 10am–4pm; entrance fee). ❏

GOTLAND

Map
on page
224

*Ingmar Bergman favoured the Baltic island of Gotland's northern
outpost, Fårö, while holidaymakers are drawn to the sands
and cyclists meander lazily past fields of wild flowers*

Gotland is quite unlike the rest of Sweden. It is an island of gaunt rocks,
forests, wild flowers, cliffs and soft sandy beaches. Blessed with more
hours of sunshine than anywhere else in the country, Gotland is a favourite
summer holiday spot for Swedes. It is the largest island in the Baltic, about
120 km (75 miles) long by 56 km (35 miles) at its widest part. The island's
position 90 km (56 miles) off the east coast of Sweden makes the Republic of
Latvia its nearest neighbour to the east.

Gotland was created over thousands of years as the animals and plants of the
ancient Silurian Sea slowly sank into the sediment that was to become the limestone platform of modern Gotland. Million-year-old fossils and the island's
famous monumental sea-stacks (*raukar*), carved out of the soft limestone by
wind and water, can still be found around the coast.

In the Viking Age the island was a busy trading post. Later, Visby, the principal centre of population, became a prosperous Hanseatic town. It had strong
links with the German Hanseatic League in order to protect the Baltic trade
routes from widespread piracy. Despite its concentration on trade, Gotland
could not escape involvement in the wars between Denmark and Sweden
which ranged over the whole of the south of Sweden. In 1361, the Danish
King Valdemar Atterdag conquered Gotland but,
after some further changes in ownership, it finally
became permanently Swedish in 1679.

PRECEDING PAGES:
Almedalen in
Visby, the former
Hanseatic harbour.
LEFT: medieval
remains, Gotland.
BELOW: Medieval
Week, Visby.

Medieval Visby

During the 12th century, the former Viking trading
station developed into a leading commercial centre
for trade with the Baltic. Great stone houses were
erected in **Visby ❶**, churches were founded, and a
wall was built to protect its citizens. Today, 3 km (2
miles) of the medieval limestone **city wall** remain virtually intact, interspersed with 44 towers and numerous gates. The wall is one of the best preserved in
Europe and, because of its cultural value, Visby has
been included on UNESCO's World Heritage list.

Within the walls, the town has many step-gabled
houses and a network of little streets and squares, all
of which contribute to its atmosphere. The original
Hanseatic harbour, **Almedalen**, is now a park, while
the **Domkyrkan** (Cathedral of St Maria) is the only
medieval church in Visby that is still intact and in use.
By contrast, only ruins remain of the old Gothic
Church of St Catherine, next to the market square.

One of the most interesting buildings to survive is
Burmeisterska huset, the house of the Burmeister,
who was a German merchant. Today, it is the tourist
office. The town also has a particularly fine historical
museum, **Gotlands Fornsal**, at Strandgatan 14. The

TIP

Don't miss Gotland's Medieval Week in August. You'll be transported back to the year 1361 and experience Visby as a mighty Hanseatic city. The entertainment includes historical plays, tournaments, parades and typical handicrafts of the time.

BELOW: *raukar*, like these on the island of Fårö, can be seen around the coast of Gotland.

museum houses rich collections of artefacts spanning most of the 8,000 years of Gotland's history (open mid-May–Sep: 10–5pm; mid-Sep–Apr: Tues–Fri, noon–4pm; entrance fee; tel: 0498-29 27 15).

Tourism is vital to Gotland, and during the relatively brief but hectic summer season, the normal population of 58,000 is swollen by more than 650,000 visitors. The 450 km (280 miles) of coastline are a mix of sand and shingle beaches with cliffs and meadows stretching down to the water. There's a good beach 20 km (12 miles) south of Visby, at **Tofta ❷**.

Limestone features

Once the summer season is over, Gotland is quiet. The brevity of the season has little to do with the climate, which is milder even than that of Southern Sweden. This kindly climate and perhaps the limestone, is why many species of orchid, poppies and other rare plants can be found in Gotland.

Limestone has also created one of the island's major attractions – the impressive subterranean tunnels and stalactite caves of **Lummelundagrottorna ❸**, 13 km (8 miles) to the north of Visby – which should not be missed. Dress warmly, it's 8°C inside (open mid-May–Sep: 9am–4pm; July–mid-Aug: 9am–6pm for guided tours only; entrance fee; tel: 0498-27 30 50).

Bergman's hideout

About 50 km (30 miles) north of Visby lies **Fårö ❹**, the "island of sheep". Take a ferry (they run continuously) to the island from Fårösund, and enjoy sites such as **Gamlehamn**, a medieval harbour, and the ruins of a chapel to St Olof. You can also see one of Gotland's most bizarrely shaped *raukar*, called the

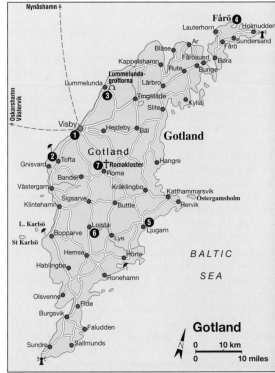

Camel. Or, if you are in the mood for another of Gotland's best beaches, visit **Sundersand**. After you have been here a while, you should begin to understand why Fårö is the favourite place of Sweden's world-famous film and theatre director Ingmar Bergman.

Gotland ponies

If you travel approximately 80 km (50 miles) southeast from Fårö, you come to **Ljugarn ❺**, an area which is often overlooked by visitors. This is Gotland's oldest seaside resort with its seaside villas and offshore *raukar*. The entire coastline also provides good opportunities for birdwatchers.

Sweden's most primitive horse, the Russ (Gotland pony), has lived in the forests of the island from time immemorial. Russ comes from Old Norse *hross,* and it is commonly thought that the horse is a descendant of the wild Tarpan. The oldest reference to the Russ is found in a legal code from the 13th century, where the "wild horses of Gotland" are mentioned. You can see these very small horses, 123–126 cm (46–52 inches tall), around the island. They are bred in **Lojsta ❻** at Lojsthajd, 20 km (12 miles) southeast of Klintehamn.

Ancient sites

Wherever you travel in Gotland you'll come across at least one of the island's 92 medieval churches. In the centre of the island is **Romakloster ❼**, 17 km (11 miles) southeast of Visby, a ruined 12th-century monastery. There are many other relics of the past including runic stones and burial mounds.

If you reach Gotland's southernmost tip, you'll see some of the most impressive *raukar* on the island. ❑

Medieval influence in the main town, Visby.

BELOW: thatching party on Fårö.

GÖTEBORG

Southwest Sweden is home to the country's second city with its café-lined boulevards, bustling harbour and a lively cultural and sporting scene

Map on page 230

Göteborg (Gothenburg) is Sweden's second city with some 450,000 inhabitants, but many visitors are surprised by its apparent low profile. The city, situated at the mouth of the Göta River on the Swedish west coast, is built on a bed of clay 120 metres (400 ft) thick in places – said to have the consistency of microscopic cornflakes, this is not the most suitable of foundations for building. High-rise buildings are few and far between in Göteborg.

As the city centre and its attractions are well concentrated, Göteborg is ideal for sightseeing on foot. If that doesn't appeal, there is a comprehensive network of buses, ferries and trams – you can use the same tickets for each – but the nature of the subsoil doesn't allow for an underground system.

Whether you arrive by sea or by train, one of the first buildings you'll notice is the mighty landmark of **Göteborgsutkiken Ⓐ**, Göteborg's lookout tower, situated just beside the Götaälv Bridge. Reaching 86 metres (280 ft) above sea level, this red and white layered tower looks almost like a giant Lego construction. For a great view over the city and especially the harbour, take the lift to the top of the building (open May–Aug: 11am–6pm; Sep–Apr: Sat–Sun 11am–4pm; entrance fee; tel: 031-60 96 60).

A favourable geographical position almost equally distant from the major population centres of Stockholm, Copenhagen and Oslo has helped Göteborg to become Scandinavia's largest seaport, now handling more than 11,000 ships a year. It is in the harbour area that you will find the soul of the city. A good place to start your sightseeing is by following the quay westbound for a while.

A look at the harbour

Just 200 metres (220 yds) west of the Göteborgsutkiken stands the bold new **Göteborgsoperan Ⓑ** (opera house), inaugurated in 1994. Built in a bold, ship-like style, it is well worth a visit for its architecture alone (Lilla Bommens Hamn; tel: 031-10 80 00).

A close neighbour of the Opera is Göteborg's **Maritima Centrum (Maritime Centre) Ⓒ**, on Packhuskajen. It is said to be the world's largest floating ship museum, featuring 15 ships, including a submarine, destroyer and a lightship (open Mar–Apr, Sep–Nov: 10am–4pm; May–Jun, Aug: 10am–6pm; July: noon–9pm; Dec–Feb: advance booking for groups; entrance fee; tel: 031-10 59 50).

To see an interesting example of how a redundant shipyard area can be rejuvenated, follow the quay westbound for another 700 metres (765 yds) to Rosenlund and take the Älvsnabben ferry west along the Göta river to **Eriksberg** on the opposite bank. This ex-shipyard area is now the site of the **Eriksbergshallen** complex containing concert and exhibi-

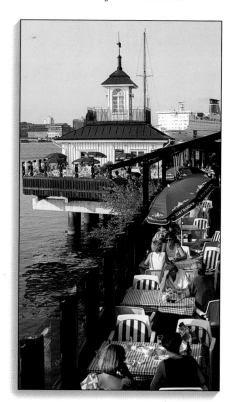

PRECEDING PAGES: the Tall Ships approach Göteborg. **LEFT:** Sjöfartstornet, near the harbour. **BELOW:** on the waterfront.

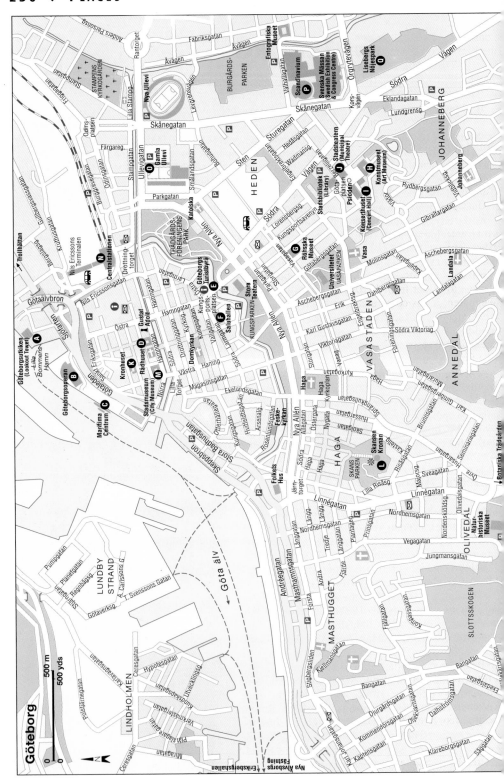

Göteborg

tions halls, a theatre, hotels and restaurants. There is still a shipyard of sorts here, the **Terra Nova** (open Mon–Fri 10am–4pm, Sat–Sun 11am–3pm; entrance fee; tel: 031-779 34 50). This is where a replica of the East Indiaman, *Götheborg III*, which sank outside the city in 1745, is under construction. When completed, she is expected to sail to China.

To explore the heart of Göteborg, take the Älvsnabben ferry back to the city and Lilla Bommens Hamn (harbour).

Map on page 230

Old and new

Starting at the northern end of **Östra Hamngatan**, heading south you will pass **Östra Nordstan**, one of northern Europe's largest covered shopping centres containing a huge variety of shops, supermarkets and restaurants.

Gustaf Adolfs Torg (Gustaf Adolf's Square) is named after the city's founder, Gustav II Adolf. In the square around the statue of the old king, facing the canal, are several historic buildings, all with official uses. The **Rådhuset (Town Hall)** ❿ was built in 1672 and extended in the early 19th century. It is now partly used as a courthouse.

Next is the **Wenngrenska Huset**, with the first two floors dating from 1759 and the top floor from 1820. Originally the home of a city councillor called Wenngren, it has come almost full circle and is now used as offices for the councillors. The **Stadshuset** (City Hall), built in 1758 as an armoury, was later used as a guardhouse and barracks for the city militia. It now houses the city council and administration department, which has spilled over into **Börshuset** (the former Stock Exchange, built in 1849) next door.

Cross Stora Hamnkanalen (Great Harbour Canal) and continue south to **Kungsportsplatsen**, where you can pop into the **Göteborgs Turistbyrå** ❺, the city tourist office (open Jan–Apr, Sep–Dec: Mon–Fri 9am–5pm, Sat 10am– 2pm; May: Mon–Fri 9am–6pm, Sat, Sun and holidays 10am–2pm; Jun and late-Aug: 9am–6pm, early-Aug: 9am–8pm).

Across the street is **Saluhallen** ❻, a large indoor marketplace built in 1886–89 and stocked with Swedish specialities such as seafood, cheese, veal, mutton and game. Immigrant-owned stalls sell exotic spices and vegetables. This is a good place to sit and enjoy a cup of coffee, a light snack or a full lunch.

Kungsportsplatsen is also the place to embark on a **Paddan**, one of the flat-bottomed sightseeing boats that cruise through the old moat, under some 20 bridges, along canals built in the 17th century, out into the harbour and back again (May–Sept: first departure 10am and then up to four times per hour; charge; tel: 031-60 96 70).

Where it all happens

From Kungsportsplatsen, cross the moat into Kungsportsavenyn – more commonly known as "**Avenyn**" (The Avenue). This, people claim, is Göteborg's answer to the Champs Elysées – or how the Via Veneto used to be. The Avenyn, 40 metres (130 ft) wide and just under a kilometre long, is a boulevard lined with trees, restaurants, pubs and cafés as well

A Göteborgskortet (Göteborg Card) gives unlimited travel on city buses and trams, a boat trip and free admission to many museums and to Liseberg.

BELOW: Feskekörka, the fish market.

Stora Teatern, at the northern end of the Avenyn, specialises in light opera and musicals.

BELOW: Göteborg's harbourfront lookout tower, Göteborgsutkiken.

as street musicians and pedlars of fruits and trinkets. It is one of the few opportunities to experience the more open side of the Swedish character. Young people monopolise many of the watering holes and restaurants, but a certain tradition does prevail as many of the establishments along the Avenyn have been the gathering place for successive generations of Göteborgers.

Halfway along the Avenyn, you are just a block away from the **Röhsska Museet** ⒢, the Swedish museum for design and handicrafts (Vasagatan 37–39; open Tues noon–9pm, Wed–Fri noon–4pm, Sat–Sun noon–5pm; entrance fee; tel: 031-61 38 50). The collection includes a rich mixture of furniture, glass, silver, china and textiles and is well worth a visit. There is a good shop and an excellent café.

At the southern end of the Avenyn is Göteborg's cultural centre, **Götaplatsen**, with the imposing Poseidon fountain by the famous Swedish sculptor Carl Milles. Götaplatsen is flanked by the **Konstmuseet (Art Museum)** ⒣, with an extensive collection of Scandinavian art, including Anders Zorn's *Bathers*, as well as work by Munch, Rembrandt and Pissarro among others (*see page 111*). It is open Tues–Fri 11am–4pm, Wed 11am–9pm, Sat–Sun 11am–5pm; entrance fee; tel: 031-18 91 75). On the west side of the square is the **Konserthuset (Concert Hall)** ⒤, home of the acclaimed Gothenburg Symphony Orchestra; and on the east the **Stadsteatern** ⒥ (Municipal Theatre) and the Stadsbiblioteket (Municipal Library), which has more than 400,000 volumes.

A city with a history

The Dutch engineers who built Göteborg for Gustav II Adolf in 1621 were aware of the unstable subsoil and advised against having any structure more than

two or three storeys high. Gustav II Adolf was, nevertheless, reported to be pleased with his choice of site since the same clay would prevent his arch-rival, Denmark's King Christian, from assaulting the city with his heavy cannon.

The Dutch builders naturally gave Göteborg a typical 16th-century Dutch look, with canals and a moated fortress. The centre of Göteborg retains its distinctive Dutch character, even though two of the canals were filled in long ago and are now called Östra Hamngatan and Västra Hamngatan.

Göteborg has nothing to compare to Stockholm's Old Town; five major fires over the years saw to that. The city's historic centre within the confines of the moat, grand canal and the Göta River is an architectural hotchpotch of styles and periods. The first town called Göteborg was actually on the other side of the Göta River in an area now called Hisingen. It was founded by King Karl IX. In one of the fierce internecine wars that broke out regularly among the Scandinavians, the Danes and Norwegians destroyed it in 1611 and cut Sweden off from the sea. A ransom of one million Riksdaler, equal to an entire year's grain harvest at that time, was eventually paid for the return of the Old Älvsborg fortress and an outlet to the sea.

To make sure it didn't happen again, King Gustav II Adolf enlisted the aid of Sweden's first guest workers, the Dutch, who were more experienced than the Swedes at building defences. The statue of Gustav II Adolf in the square of the same name points to the place where he wanted his new city to be built.

The day the king signed the Göteborg city charter, 2 June 1621, is not celebrated by the local citizens. Instead, they honour the day of his death, 6 November. Gustav II Adolf died at the battle of Lützen in 1632, during the Thirty Years' War, after eating small cakes with the king's image made of marzipan. It is a fit-

Map on page 230

Feskekörka (The Fish Church) in Rosenlundsgatan is a famous fish and seafood market. The building, which also houses a restaurant, resembles a church, hence the name (open Tues–Sat; Mon–Sat in summer).

BELOW: the city's new opera house beside the quay.

ting Göteborg answer to the Napoleon pastry since both were warrior kings or emperors, as the case may be.

Historical landmarks

Architectural remnants of Göteborg's earliest days are few and include only the Kronhuset, in the centre of town, the Bastion Carolus Rex at Kungsgatan and two small forts, Skansen Kronan and Skansen Lejonet.

Kronhuset ⓚ is Göteborg's oldest secular building, dating from 1643, and was originally the town's armoury. In 1660 it was briefly converted into the House of Parliament, so that the five-year-old Crown Prince could be sworn in as King Karl XI and succeed his father King Karl X Gustav, who died suddenly while visiting Göteborg. In an adjacent newer building, a little over 200 years old, is the **Kronhusbodarna**. It once housed various craftsmen's workshops and has now been restored into a living museum of turn-of-the-century shops, with a goldsmith, country store, handicrafts centre and a café.

Göteborg is a major port for both commercial and passenger traffic.

The other 17th-century structure open to the public is the fortress of **Skansen Kronan ⓛ**, now the Military Museum (open Tues–Wed noon–2pm, Sat–Sun noon–3pm; tel: 031-14 50 00). Situated on a hill in the city's Haga district, it also offers a fine view of Göteborg from its ramparts. Haga was Göteborg's first suburb in 1640, and as the city expanded it eventually became the workers' district during the 19th century. During the 1980s and '90s, Haga was heavily rebuilt. Many of the old houses were demolished and as the rents for the new flats were considerably higher, the impression of a workers' district faded. Still, some of the old atmosphere has been preserved, as the new buildings have been designed with the old architectural ideals in mind. Here, in the mainly pedes-

BELOW: café at Kronhuset.

THE GARDEN CITY

While Göteborg's canals and architecture reflect the early Dutch influence, its many parks give it an atmosphere reminiscent of 19th-century England. Göteborg has 20 parks, more than any other city in Sweden. At its heart, along the south and east side of the moat, is Trädgårdsföreningen (open daily 7am–7.30pm). The locals call it "Trägår'n" and it is Göteborg's answer to New York's Central Park or London's Hyde Park. It may not be as large, but it does have the Palmhuset, a greenhouse for tropical plants, and the Fjärilshuset (Butterfly House) where you can enjoy walking in a tropical climate among the fluttering butterflies.

Göteborg's other parks of note are all relatively close to the city centre. The largest is Slottsskogen, which covers 137 hectares (338 acres) and is a complete recreation centre with sports facilities, zoo and restaurants, as well as small lakes and lovely areas for walking and picnicking. Across the Dag Hammarskjöld highway from Slottsskogen is the Botanical Garden (open daily 10am–4pm; May–Aug 10am–5pm). It is one of the largest of its kind in the world, containing 12,000 species of plants (including 1,500 flower species). It's hard to believe that this green city is also a highly industrialised centre.

trianised streets you will find lots of small shops selling handicrafts and second-hand books, and a handful of small, cosy cafés and restaurants.

Göteborg became an economic force largely through the early efforts of the great merchant fleets and traders. Most notable was the Swedish East India Company, which brought great wealth into the city as early as the mid-1700s. Evidence of this wealth exists today in the buildings along **Stora Hamnkanalen** (Grand Canal).

The East India House itself, built in 1750, houses the new **Stadsmuseum** (City Museum) Ⓜ on Norra Hamngatan (open Tues–Sun 11am–4pm, Wed 11am–8pm; entrance fee; tel: 031-61 27 70). It's worth visiting to see the lavish interiors, oriental exhibits from the glory days of the East India Company, and a modern exhibition of 20th-century industrial history.

Most of the city's more historic structures are now used by the local government, either as offices or for official functions as well as museums. Along the Norra Hamngatan side of the canal is the **Sahlgrenska Huset**, built in 1753 and, among other things, the office of the Municipal Secretariat for Trade and Industry and the Göteborg Region Promotion Office. Across the canal on Södra Hamngatan is the **Residenset**, built in 1650 for Field Marshal Lennart Torstensson, although its present appearance dates from an extension in the 1850s. It is now the official residence of the governor for Göteborg and Bohuslän.

Maritime traditions

If you arrive in Göteborg by ship, you can't help noticing the **Nya Älvsborgs Fästning** (Fortress) on an island at the mouth of the Göta River. It was built in the 17th century to protect Sweden's western gateway against the Danes. Nya

The world's only stuffed blue whale can be seen at the Naturhistoriska Museet (Natural History Museum), Slottsskogen (open Tues–Fri 9am–4pm, Sat–Sun 11am–5pm; entrance fee; tel: 031-775 24 00)

BELOW: grocer's shop in the living museum of Kronhusbodarna.

TIP

CDs in Göteborg are available at what is claimed to be the lowest prices in northern Europe, thanks to two mega stores, Skivhugget (on Masthuggstorget) and Bengans (on Stigbergstorget).

Älvsborg witnessed its last taste of fire against the Danish fleet led by Norwegian Peder Tordenskiold in 1717 and again in 1719. It was last used officially as a prison during the 19th century and now serves as a venue for meetings and banquets, as well as weddings in the chapel. It is one of the few Göteborg tourist attractions that is not within walking distance or a tram ride from the city centre (open May–Aug: daily; Sep: Sat–Sun only). For a closer look it can be reached only by boat (departure from Lilla Bommen five to six times daily; tel: 031-609 660).

Göteborg's relationship to the sea was the reason for its coming into being. Its importance during the past century was even proclaimed by Sweden's most famous dramatist, August Strindberg. A character in the 1886–87 drama *The Maid's Son*, was to realise, after seeing Göteborg's busy harbour for the first time, that Stockholm was no longer the Scandinavian focal point and that Göteborg had taken the lead.

When Strindberg wrote those lines for the book, the city's harbour was alive with ships bound for, or returning from the four corners of the earth. The outbound traffic was also human, for at that time the flow of Swedish immigrants to America was still in full swing. For most of the nearly one million Swedes who made their way to the promised land across the Atlantic, the last they ever saw of their homeland was Göteborg.

Several decades later, Göteborg was the port for the Swedish American Line luxury liners *Gripsholm*, *Kungsholm* and *Drottningholm* that used to bring dollar-laden American tourists and some returning immigrants to Sweden. These liners eventually gave way to faster air travel. The port of Göteborg has nevertheless survived as a gateway to Sweden for people and cargo. More than 4

BELOW: graceful statue adorns a city park.
RIGHT: everyone loves an ice cream.

million passengers a year are carried by Stena Line and DFDS Scandinavian Seaways ferries to and from Denmark, Germany, England and Holland.

Bigness on the commercial side is closely related to Göteborg's being a seaport. Consequently, it is the home base for some of Sweden's largest and most internationally well-known manufacturing enterprises: Volvo cars and trucks, SKF ball bearings and Hasselblad cameras.

The largest industrial estate in Sweden is situated at the Högsbo/Sisjön area in the south of Göteborg. It houses some 1,000 companies, with around 14,000 employees, quite a large figure by Swedish standards. The main centre of the Scandinavian petrochemical industry can be found in the Göteborg region, as well as parts of the Swedish space industry.

Swimming in the city

Even though Göteborg is an industrial city, it takes pride in protecting its environment. The water in the Göta River is now as pure as it was 100 years ago, and fish such as salmon are thriving once again. As for swimming in Göteborg, there are bathing lakes just a few kilometres from the city centre, and the beach is less than half an hour away.

Take tram 5 to Bögatan, 6 km (4 miles) east of the centre. From here, a 15-minute walk brings you to the **Delsjön**, where you can sunbathe on the rocks before jumping in the water. You can also hire a canoe for an hour or two. Or you can go by tram 7 to terminus **Bergsjön**, the name of both the district and the lake, 10 km (6 miles) northeast of the centre, to enjoy the rocks and the water.

If you prefer the sea, jump on the Express Blå (blue) bus at Nils Ericssons terminal, just beside **Centralstationen** ⓝ (Central Station), and go to the Askims-

Map on page 230

Liseberg amusement park (see page 238) – *fun for all.*

BELOW: Göteborg is a working port.

Map on page 230

TIP

Useful websites:
tourist information:
www.gbg-co.se
Liseberg amusement
park: www.liseberg. se
official Göteborg:
w3.goteborg.se
culture links:
w3.goteborg.se/kultur

BELOW: fish
hanging out to dry.
RIGHT: Carl Milles'
statue of Poseidon.

badet (Askim Beach), 10 km (6 miles) south of the city centre. Here you will find a lovely sandy beach with a jetty, café and kiosks.

Bus 19 from Brunnsparken will take you to **Näset**, 11 km (7 miles) southwest of the city, where there is a rocky beach with some grassy areas.

Sporting Göteborg

Göteborg is the sports capital of Sweden. Football is the biggest sport and the leading team is IFK Göteborg, well known all over Europe. Throughout the 1990s, Göteborg had at least three teams in *Allsvenskan*, Sweden's first division. IFK Göteborg play all its national games at **Ullevi** ⊙, situated just a few hundred metres southeast of the Centralstationen. Just a free kick away, you will find Nya ("New") Ullevi, Sweden's largest outdoor stadium. Built for the football World Cup in 1958, today with a capacity of 50,000, this is not only the venue for many international sport events (speedway world championship 1991, European championship in football 1992 and world championshps in athletics 1995), it is also on arena for performing superstars, which have in the past included the Rolling Stones, Elton John, Pink Floyd and David Bowie.

Some 600 metres south of Nya Ullevi is **Scandinavium** ⊙, a large indoor arena which seats 12,500 spectators and where Göteborg's ice hockey pride, Frölunda Indians, play their games. This arena's flexibility is worth mentioning. Not only can it be used as a tennis arena, concert hall or for equestrian events; in 1997 a swimming pool was built for the world championship in short-track swimming. Two days after the final, it was back once more to its normal use, with not a trace of the pool to be seen. Between Nya Ullevi and Scandinavium you will find the Heden grounds, where the annual Gothia Cup, the world's largest youth football tournament, is played. In 1998, around 28,000 boys and girls from more than 50 countries participated.

Just for fun

One of the main attractions for these young players – and indeed for any visitor to Göteborg – is the **Lisebergs Nöjespark** ⊙, an amusement park which ranks as one of the largest tourist attractions in Europe with more than 2½ million visitors a year. Liseberg not only offers candy floss, popcorn and thrilling rides for both adults and children, here you can also see and listen to many of the best Swedish artists on the main stage. Furthermore, the park has 29 restaurants, a theatre and also spectacular gardens. You will also find out about the green rabbit that you might have seen all over town: it is the symbol of the amusement park – not the city. The park is open mid-May–late Aug: Mon–Fri 3–11pm, Sat 11am–11pm, Sun 11am–8pm; Jul–mid-Aug: Mon–Fri open from 11am Sep–May: Fri 5–11pm, Sat 11am–11pm, Sun 11am–8pm; entrance fee; tel: 031-40 01 00).

Opposite Liseberg is the **Svenska Mässan**, the Swedish Exhibition and Congress Centre, where about 40 trade fairs and public exhibitions are arranged annually. Among the major events are the Book and Library Fair and the International Travel and Tourism Fair.

THE WEST COAST

From the sandy beaches of Halland to the pink-tinged rocks and islands of Bohuslän, the West Coast has long been a summer playground for the Swedes

Map on page 244

he West Coast of Sweden, generously dotted with beaches and fishing villages, is 400 km (250 miles) of glorious coastline divided in two by the city of Göteborg. To the south is the province of Halland, where the best beaches lie. North of the city, in the province of Bohuslän, the coast is majestic: granite rocks, islands and skerries. The Swedes discovered the West Coast as a favourite holiday spot early in the century, and its popularity has never waned. The E6 runs along the coast, separating it from the hinterland. Although the highway connects all the larger cities, you will have to take to the small coastal roads to discover the gems. Starting along the coast in the northwestern corner of the county of Skåne, a number of small towns offer views into the past. Gamla Viken ❶, about 15 km (9 miles) north of Helsingborg along highway 22, is a picturesque old fishing village. Continuing up the coast, the furthest point out on the peninsula, Kullen ❷, offers a beautiful seascape. And Mölle, the town closest to Kullen, has a lovely summer bathing spot. Torekov sits at the tip of the next peninsula. Here, there is a seaside golf course (one of the oldest on the west coast), and Värdhus Hovs Hallar, a hotel surrounded by countryside, and Kattegatt Gastronomi & Logi, whose chefs, Rikard and Robert Nilsson, are two of Sweden's finest, both winners of prestigious cookery prizes.

PRECEDING PAGES: West Coast sailing. LEFT: evening light in Bohuslän. BELOW: inland to farm and forest.

A natural barrier

A ridge running inland from the coast forms a natural border between Skåne and Halland. This part of the coast has an abundance of sandy beaches, such as those at **Skummeslövstrand** and **Mellbystrand**, while inland if you cross the busy E6, it is quietly pastoral with woodlands, farms and winding rivers.

Halmstad ❸, the largest town in Halland, lies on the River Nissan and is the home town of the rock duo The Roxettes. The river here is now a spawning ground for salmon. **Halmstads Slott** (Halmstad Castle), the provincial governor's residence, was built in the 17th century by the Danish king, Christian IV. In front of the castle is moored the old sail-training vessel *Najaden*, built in 1897 (open Jun–Aug: Tues, Thurs, 5–7pm, Sat 11am–3pm). Other sights include the remains of a city wall and St Nikolai, a 13th-century church.

The local museum, Museet i Halmstad, Tollsgatan, has an important marine section and a large-scale model of the town (open Mon–Fri 10am–4pm, Wed also 7–9pm, Sat–Sun noon–4pm; Jun–Aug: weekdays until 7pm, Wed until 9pm). See also Sweden in miniature at **Miniland**, Gamla Tylösandsvägen 1, which has models of more than 100 famous Swedish buildings on a scale of 1:25 (tel: 035-10 84 60).

Tylösand, 6 km (10 miles) west of Halmstad, is a

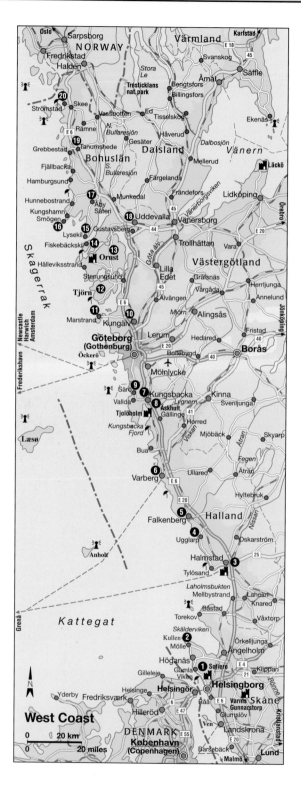

popular holiday resort with a predom
nantly sandy beach. There are also goo
beaches at **Östra Strand**, **Ringenäs** an
Haverdalsstrand. Tylösand is dom
nated by the massive complex of th
Nya Hotel Tylösand, which has all th
trappings of a major modern holida
centre. There are lots of spors facilitie
too, including two 18-hole golf course.

The next town north along the coas
25 km (15 miles) north of Halmsta
towards Falkenberg, is **Ugglarp** ❹
where you will find **Svendinos Biloc
Flygmuseum** (Car and Air Museum
open June and late Aug: 11am–4pm
July and early Aug: 10am–6pm
entrance fee; tel: 0346-431 87). It's
bit untidy, but is bursting at the seam
with 140 old cars and 31 old and nev
aircraft which delight the enthusias
and the engineer. The bigger, moder
aircraft sit outside; inside the rest ar
crammed bumper-to-bumper and wing
tip-to-wingtip. Treasures include suc
exotic names as a Bullerbilen ca
which was built in 1897.

Salmon galore

Falkenberg ❺ is on the Ätran, a rive
famous for its salmon. The British wer
the first to enjoy the sport of anglin
here in the 1830s, when English an
Scottish immigrants who had settled i
Göteborg invited friends to join then
for hunting and fishing. For many year
in the 19th century the fishing rights o
the river were leased to a Baron Osca
Dickson, who belonged to one of th
best-known families in Göteborg.

A London solicitor, W.M. Wilkinson
was so moved by the quality of th
fishing that in 1884 he wrote and hac
published privately a little book for th
benefit of his Swedish and Englis
friends. Called *Days in Falkenberg*, i
reveals that the going rate for salmo
was 3s. 6d. a pound (18p/25 US cent
for 500g). One salmon smokehous
remains; it is now the local museum.

The old part of the town with it
18th-century wooden houses and cob
bled streets is centred on the 14th-cen
tury St Laurenti Church. There is an ol

ll bridge (*tullbron*) from 1756 and the oldest pottery in Sweden, Törngrens rukmakeri, which has been run by the Törngren family since 1789 (Kruakaregatan 4; open Mon–Fri tel: 0346-103 54). Good beaches are found at lofsby (north of the town) and **Skrea Strand** (south of the town).

Map on page 244

arberg: popular resort

ontinuing 30 km (19 miles) up the coast on the E6, the next large town is arberg ❻, which, in contrast to the rather restrained atmosphere of Falkenerg, is a bustling sort of place combining spa, resort, port and commercial entre with a ferry service to Grenå in Denmark.

It looms impressively beside the water, with a fortress, **Varbergs Fästning**, hich houses a youth hostel, restaurant, apartments and a museum with 35,000 xhibits. Pride of place goes to the Bocksten Man, who demonstrates what the vell-dressed 14th-century male should be wearing. He is the only preserved igure in the world to be wearing a complete costume from the Middle Ages. nother prize possession is the bullet (a button) which, according to legend, illed King Karl XII in 1718. There is also the Museum of Communications in ing Karl XI's stables, which has a collection of carriages, boats and – from a omewhat different era – bicycles. The museums open Mon–Fri 10am–4pm, at–Sun noon–4pm; July–early Aug: daily 10am–6pm (entrance fee).

Varberg also has two reminders of its late 19th-century development as a wedish holiday resort – and both are in use today. One is the 1883 **Societethuset** in the park, an elaborate wooden pavilion, which is now a restaurant nd a site for outdoor concerts. The second is the 1903 bathing section, where ou can indulge in gentle sea- and sun-bathing. A little bridge leads from the

Falkenberg is a town full of quirky sights and is well worth exploring.

BELOW: a sandy beach in Halland.

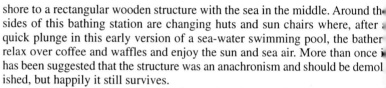

Lighthouses keep watch over the coast of Halland.

BELOW: woodlands at Hallands Väderö, an island nature reserve north of Helsingborg.

shore to a rectangular wooden structure with the sea in the middle. Around the sides of this bathing station are changing huts and sun chairs where, after a quick plunge in this early version of a sea-water swimming pool, the bather relax over coffee and waffles and enjoy the sun and sea air. More than once it has been suggested that the structure was an anachronism and should be demolished, but happily it still survives.

Around Varberg there are several more beaches. At **Apelviken** the beach shelves gently and is safe for children, but **Träslövlägen's** beach is disappointing. The island of **Getterön**, 5 km (3 miles) to the north, has beaches, a nature reserve and bird sanctuary. It is reached by a bridge from the mainland

North towards Göteborg

Heading north towards Kungsbacka you will pass what is probably the most out-of-character building along the entire coast. **Tjolöholm Castle** was built as recently as the beginning of the 20th century, but in an English Tudor style. I looks for all the world as if it has been transported lock, stock and leaded light from some corner of England, stands at the centre of a large park, and has a splendid art nouveau interior (open mid-Jun–mid-Aug: daily 11am–4pm; late Aug–Sep and Nov–mid-Jun: Sat–Sun only 11am–4pm; Oct: Sun only 11am–4pm; entrance fee; tel: 0300-54 42 00).

The original way of cleaning the interior of this architectural aberration was as unusual as the castle itself. Teams of horses dragged a huge and primitive vacuum cleaner up to the building, where cleaner, horses and all came in through the windows. Today, the City of Göteborg owns Tjolöholm, and the cleaning methods are more conventional, but less interesting.

Kungsbacka ❼ is the most northerly town in Halland. Lying only 30 km (18 miles) south of Göteborg, the town was inevitably reduced to becoming a dormitory for Big G. However, when it was established as a wooden city in the 13th century, Kungsbacka was a separate town with its own identity. In 1676, it briefly knew royal patronage when King Karl XI made Kungsbacka his headquarters during a war with Denmark.

Less than 10 km (6 miles) inland from Kungsbacka a high ridge runs parallel with the coast. It is called **Fjärås Bräcka**, and was the result of action by glaciers many thousands of years ago. From the top of the ridge there are good views over the Kungsbacka Fjord. On the other side of the ridge is an equally attractive view of **Lake Lygnern** which, before the Ice Age, was part of the same fjord. Towards the southern end of the ridge there are some Bronze Age graves and about 125 *menhirs* (grave stones) from the Iron Age. The most impressive is the Frode stone which gets its name from a Danish fairy king who legend says, is buried there.

From Tjolöholm, along the E6/E20 towards Gällinge, signs indicate the route left to Fölanda i Gällinge and the hamlet of **Äskhult** ❽ – a group of buildings from the 18th and early 19th centuries, gathered around a common courtyard. It is one of the few surviving examples of an undivided hamlet and is now

Map
on page
244

museum (open May–Aug: 10am–6pm; Sep: 10am–5pm). Take a minor road on our return to Kungsbacka and you pass **Gåsevadholm**, a privately owned castle built in 1757 by Niclas Sahlgren, then manager of the East India Company. The moment you reach the little seaside resort of **Särö ⑨** (immediately north of Kungsbacka), you realise the coastline has changed. Apart from some small sandy coves, the beaches have gone and instead, as you near Göteborg, a more dramatic landscape of rocks, inlets and islands takes over.

As early as the first years of the 19th century, Särö was a fashionable resort and, when it became popular with the Swedish royal family, its name was made. Both King Oskar II, and the tennis-playing king, Gustav V, liked to spend time here each summer and Gustav was a frequent player on the same tennis courts which you can use today. This was the resort where the wealthier inhabitants of Göteborg had their summer villas, charming wooden houses with verandas, balconies and an abundance of carved woodwork which still remain.

Fortunately Särö has resisted development and remains in something of a time warp with its turn-of-the-century atmosphere. You can walk along the Strandpromenaden and through **Särö Västerskog**, one of the oldest oak woods along the west coast. There is one small sandy beach on the south side of the town, otherwise it is smooth granite rocks. The pace is leisurely and summer excitement is restricted to going out in a boat to fish or watch the basking seals.

The 12th-century church at Gällinge, on the E6, 25 km (15 miles) south of Kungsbacka, is worth visiting for its beautiful ceiling paintings dating from the 18th century.

The rugged coast

The province of **Bohuslän** begins on the north side of Göteborg and already the coastal scenery has set a pattern that continues all the way to the Norwegian frontier: rocks, islands and skerries. There are few major towns in Bohuslän, but

BELOW: Tjolöholm Castle, built in an English style.

10 km (6 miles) north from Göteborg, is **Kungälv** , an old Viking centre which occupies a key strategic position on the Göta Älv (river). It is now within easy commuting distance of Göteborg and so, like Kungsbacka, it ha become a dormitory town.

To start seeing the coast, head 15 km (9 miles) west from Kungälv on road 168 past Tjuvkil, where you can catch a short ferry over to **Marstrand** ⓫. A town without cars, Marstrand is a popular holiday resort and sailing centre. Ir summer it is also a good place to buy crafts. **Carlstens Fästning** (Carlster Fortress), which is unfortunately spoiled by obtrusive radar equipment on its tower, dominates the town and offers the best views of the island. King Oska II used to come here every summer to holiday and his statue stands in front o the Societetshuset. As a link with the past, a quartet often plays in Paradis parken (Paradise Park) in the season.

Beyond Marstrand lie two major islands, Tjörn and Orust, and a number o smaller ones. You reach Tjörn over a bridge near **Stenungsund**, 22 km (1: miles) north of Kungälv. A second bridge links Tjörn with Orust and a thir bridge gets you back to the mainland.

This area is known as the Bästkusten ("Best Coast"), the heart of Bohuslän **Tjörn** ⓬ is beautiful with some barren areas inland, but a fascinating coastline Off the southern corner of Tjörn is **Klädesholmen**, a tiny island, linked by ye another bridge (this area is full of examples of Swedish bridge-builders' skills) Klädesholmen is a colourful jumble of tightly packed wooden houses whicl seem to cling to the rocky surface. Like the majority of these villages, they ar not just pretty places for the holidaymaker but are working fishing villages too. Views may be spoiled by industrial-style buildings connected with fish

BELOW: the fishing island of Smögen is a favourite place for summer sailing.

NEWS SET IN STONE

Concentrated around Tanumshede, in Bohuslän, is Europe's richest collection of Bronze Age rock-carvings. They are included on UNESCO's World Heritage list. These were the original tabloid newspapers: all the news in pictures and no text – a strip cartoon that's 3,000 years old. The carvings show battles, ships, hunting and fishing scenes, warriors, sun-wheels, mating couples and footprints. These images hold many mysteries, but they also provide an enormous amount of information about everyday life, beliefs and practices from 1500–500 BC. The abundance of ships, as well as the close proximity to the sea of all the carvings, indicates a reliance on the sea and the ships are also believed to have been important as religious vehicles. There are numerous wedding and mating scenes, possible evidence that couples mated in public as part of the ceremonies. Many of the pictures are related to themes of fertility, spring and the afterlife. At nearby Vitlycke the carvings cover 204 sq metres (2,200 sq ft). Opened in 1998, the Vitlycke museum provides information, exhibitions and tours (Apr–Sep: daily; Oct–Dec: Thurs–Sun; Jan–Mar: Sat–Sun; tel: 0525-209 50). There is also a reconstructed Bronze Age village. Other carvings are at Fossum, Tegneby and Litsleby.

processing or the repair of trawlers and their gear, but this is part of local life. A magnificent curved bridge, which provides good views in either direction, links Tjörn and **Orust** ⑬. This island, the third largest in Sweden, has its quota of fishing villages including Mollösund, Halleviksstrand, Gullholmen, Ellös and Käringön. Inland from the deeply indented coastline with its succession of rocks and coves, there is fertile farmland.

Map
on page
244

Crossing the fjord to Lysekil

As you cross yet another bridge, you have the impression that you are on yet another island, but it is in fact a long jagged promontory and part of the mainland. From the fishing village of **Fiskebäckskil** ⑭ a ferry crosses the Gullmarn, Sweden's only genuine fjord, to **Lysekil** ⑮.

Lysekil has been Swedish for 300 years; before that it was Norwegian. In the 19th century it became a summer resort and its popularity has continued to the present day. During the summer it comes to life and is full of bustle and activity with boat excursions to the islands and sea fishing trips. **Havets Hus** (Sea Aquarium), at Strandvägen 9, is one of the star attractions and includes sea life from Gullmarn and the Skagerrak. The most impressive exhibit, the tunnel aquarium, holds 140,000 litres of water and creatures such as rays, sharks, halibut and cod (open 10am–4pm; entrance fee; tel: 0523-165 30).

North of Lysekil on the **Sotenäs peninsula** are yet more fishing villages. **Smögen** ⑯, another small bridge-connected island, is particularly attractive with its brightly painted houses near the water's edge. During the summer months, this town's lovely small harbour is packed with leisure boats making their way up and down the coast. One of the main attractions of the town is the

Skärhamn, a pretty fishing village on the island of Tjörn, is the site of a new water-colour museum, due to open in 2000 and featuring children's studio, exhibitions and a centre for research.

BELOW: Bronze Age rock carvings at Tanumshede.

Map on page 244

Bohuslän is noted for its fine Bronze Age rock carvings. The "Bridal Pair" at Vitlycke, near Tanumshede, is among the best-known of the rock carvings in the area.

BELOW: sunbathing on the smooth rocks of Bohuslän.
RIGHT: sailing into the sunset.

boardwalk, where you can shop, stroll and lounge. Here, numerous shops open just for the summer in the old, wooden fishing huts, selling mostly clothing and souvenirs. The other attraction of Smögen is fresh shrimp. Smögen is a working fishing village and it's worth watching a fish auction and then going round the corner to buy some of the fresh catch from the fishmongers (fish auctions Tues–Thurs 7am, 5pm, shrimps 8pm; Fri auction at 7am only).

At **Åby Säteri** ⓱, about 17 km (12 miles) northeast of Smögen on route 171, is **Nordens Ark**, a nature park featuring endangered species (open 10am–4pm; Jun–Aug: 10am–6pm; entrance fee; two-hour guided tours available; café open May–Sep; tel: 0523-522 15). All the animals are kept in large sections of the natural wooded habitat, so the walk is pleasant but finding the animals can be a challenge .

As you travel north along this coast of smooth, pinkish granite rocks the combination of fishing village and holiday centre is repeated. Inland from Lysekil, east of the E6, lies **Uddevalla** ⓲, the biggest town in the province. It was once a major shipbuilding centre, but like so many others in Europe, the shipyard closed and has been partially replaced by other industry. If the town has little to interest the visitor, then there is a place on the outskirts which has greater merit. **Gustavsberg** claims to be Sweden's oldest seaside resort and it was mentioned by the botanist Linnaeus in his book *Westgötha Resa*, published in 1746. Like many of the other resorts, it has its **Societetsalongen** – another of these grand, richly ornamented wooden buildings – which continues as a restaurant. The original spa building is now a youth hostel and this and other buildings are all set in a delightful park that leads down to the water's edge.

Towards Norway

Tanumshede ⓳, a small town on the E6 60 km (37 miles) north of Uddevalla, lies inland from the fishing village of Grebbestad and has two claims to fame. One is **Tanums Gestgifveri**, an inn established by Royal decree and which has been welcoming visitors since 1663. The modest-looking wooden building, painted in the traditional buff colour, belies an interior of cosy rooms and outstanding cuisine. Fish dishes naturally rank high on its list of specialities. Tanum's second claim to fame is of much greater historical importance since nearby is Europe's largest collection of Bronze Age rock carvings (*see page 248*).

The last town before the Norwegian frontier is **Strömstad** ⓴. This old health resort was one of the first places in Sweden to provide saltwater and seaweed baths. It is also said to have more hours of sunshine than anywhere else in northern Europe and is known as the town of the shrimp: Strömstad shrimps are considered by the local inhabitants to be in a class of their own, with a distinctive mild flavour.

The Strömstad district has more than a touch of Norwegian about it which is not surprising. In the past, the histories of Denmark, Norway and Sweden were inextricably linked, and for many years Strömstad was part of Norway. At last, in 1717 at the Battle of Strömstad, the Swedes finally succeeded in defeating Tordenskiold and his Danish fleet. ❏

THE GREAT LAKES

At the heart of southern Sweden lie the two great lakes, Vänern and Vättern. In this region of forests, farmland and rivers, pretty villages, castles and painted churches abound

Map on pages 256–7

Two enormous lakes, Vänern and Vättern, dominate the map of Sweden. The larger of the two is Vänern, a vast stretch of water with an area of 5,585 sq km (2,156 sq miles). It is not only the biggest lake in Sweden but also the largest in Western Europe, and its western shore embraces two provinces, Dalsland and Värmland.

Dalsland is a province of neat farms and prosperous small towns and villages, with empty roads running through its forests. From a bus or car, you may be lucky enough to catch a glimpse of an elk sliding out of the trees. This gentle countryside with its sprinkling of lakes and rivers stretches from the fertile Dalboslätten in the southeast to the northwest slopes of the Skogsdal. The nearer you go to the Norwegian border, the more barren it gets. No province in Sweden can be described as "small" but, by the standards of this large country, everything in Dalsland is on a modest scale – hence the title "Sweden in Miniature".

The greatest attraction in Dalsland is its nature and, thus, the most interesting activities are outdoors: namely, camping, hiking and canoeing. West of Mellerud is **Kroppefjällen ❶**, an upland area which is a nature reserve and popular with botanists. One of the best ways to explore the region is to hike along the 15-km (9-mile) Karl XIIs väg (trail) through Kroppefjällen; maps obtainable from the tourist office in Mellerud (tel: 0530-183 08).

On the waterways

The major feature in the county is the **Dalslands Kanal**, a network of interconnected lakes and rivers. Very little of its 240 km (158 miles) had to be excavated. The canal was designed by Nils Ericsson and built between 1864 and 1868 to provide better transport for the ironworks and sawmills of the area. Today, it is used only for pleasure and is popular for sailing and canoeing.

The most dramatic piece of engineering is the aqueduct at **Håverud ❷**, 14 km (9 miles) north of Mellerud. Made of iron and 33 metres (108 ft) long, it carries the canal over the rapids of the river Upperud. Held together by 33,000 rivets, it is still watertight after 130 years. Apart from the aqueduct there are road and rail bridges and locks at Håverud, and the best view of this unusual combination is from the hill above the roadway. Håverud has a small Canal Museum, **Håverud Kanalmuseet**, which describes the various sets of locks (open Jun–Aug: daily 10am–7pm; Sep–May: group bookings only; entrance fee; tel: 0530-306 24).

King Karl's genius

Along highway 164, which runs between the two lakes, Stora Le and Lelång (Big Le and Long Le),

PRECEDING PAGES: an artist at work. **LEFT:** fishing on tranquil waters. **BELOW:** 13th-century wooden church in Hedared, near Borås.

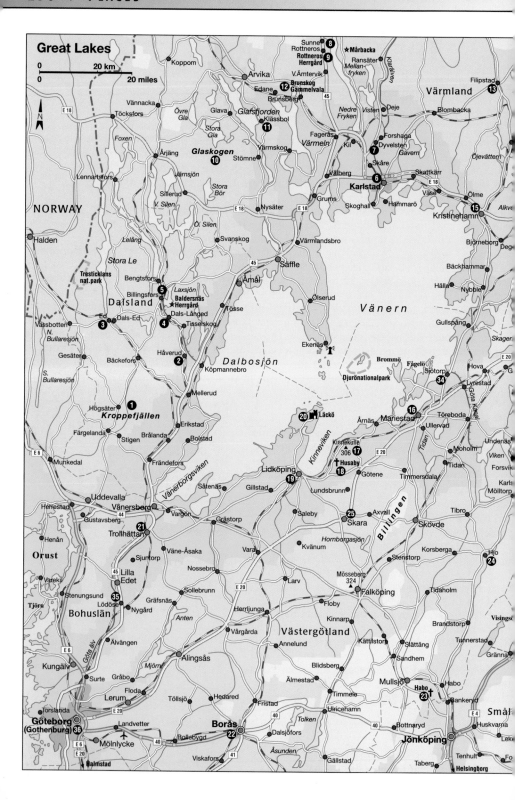

Great Lakes

0 ___ 20 km

0 ___ 20 miles

N

Värmland

NORWAY

Dalsland

Vänern

Dalbosjön

Kroppefjällen

Bohuslän

Orust

Västergötland

Småland

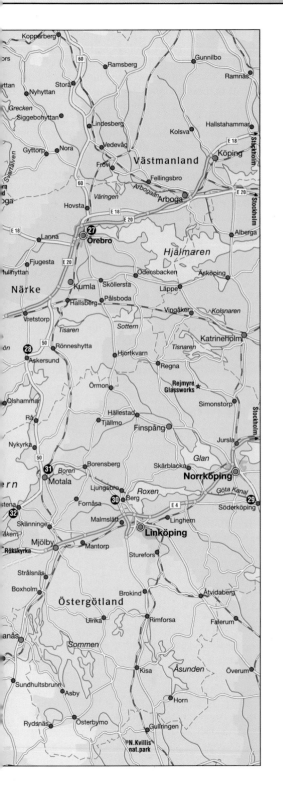

stand the twin villages of **Ed** and **Dals-Ed ❸**, nowadays so close that it is hard to tell where one ends and the other begins. The views of water and forest are lovely, and this has long been a popular holiday centre.

The area's earlier history was more dramatic because of its links with Sweden's 17th-century military genius, King Karl XII and his final campaign against Norway *(see box, page 258)*. The **Dals-Ed museum** (tel: 0534-190 22) touches on the community's involvement in these great events. It is housed in the town's oldest building, dating back to 1790, a charming wooden structure with verandahs, first-floor balconies and windows facing both lakes. There is also a craft shop (open Jun–Aug: 10am–6pm, closed Sun; Sep–May: 10am–6pm, closed Sun–Tues).

Dals-Ed should not be confused with **Dals-Långed ❹**, which lies 23 km (14 miles) to the east and is an art and handicrafts centre. About 4 km (2½ miles) south towards Håverud is **Tisselskog**, whose many Bronze Age rock carvings are the province's principal historical attraction.

North of Dals-Långed on Lake Laxsjön is **Baldersnäs Herrgård**, a manor set in a lovely Edwardian park. The original house was built in 1796 and then pulled down in 1910 when the present building, now a restaurant and hotel, was erected. There is a handicrafts and nature centre in the park (open May–Aug: daily 10am–6pm; entrance fee for special events; tel: 0531-412 13).

To the northwest are **Billingsfors ❺**, an area of pulp and paper mills (with a distinctive smell) and **Bengtsfors**, which has an open-air museum, Gammelgården, devoted to local history and culture (open mid-Jun–mid-Aug: 11am–7pm; mid-Aug–mid-Jun: advance booking only; entrance fee; tel: 0531-126 20).

Along the Klaralven River

An old parish register in Western Värmland states: "Between Sweden and Norway lies Värmland", which shows a certain rugged independence that still

TIP

Trips on the Klarälven
River can be arranged,
May–Sep, from
Likenäs or Branäs in
northern Värmland.
Nights can be spent
on a raft or ashore.
Contact the Torsby
Tourist Office, tel:
0560-105 50;
www.torsby.se

BELOW: Valle Harad,
between the lakes.

asserts itself today, plus a slight Norwegian accent. It is a region with strong traditions and which has produced a rich crop of writers of both prose and poetry.

Spruce and pine forests cover seven-tenths of the county and are often referred to as "Värmland's gold". Forests, fast-running water and the discovery of iron ore all played an important part in the economic development of the province, although the old ironworks are now just a part of history.

Värmland is criss-crossed with narrow lakes and rivers, and the Klarälven River can claim to be among its most beautiful. It begins turbulently enough in Norway, where it is called Trysilelva, but gradually becomes broader, winding and sluggish before emptying into Lake Vänern near the province's largest town, **Karlstad** ❻. The town is 400 years old and stands on the site of a trading post called Tingvalla. Karlstad has a cathedral (consecrated in 1730), a school museum and a popular park, Mariebergskogen.

From **Hammarö**, on the outskirts of Karlstad, you can follow the route of the pilgrims of old, up the valley of the Klarälven. They crossed Lake Vänern by boat to Hammarö, where they prepared themselves for the next stage of their journey. Then, they set off on the road north, to follow the Klarälven throughout its 240 km (168 miles) on their long pilgrimage to the grave of St Olav the Holy, at Trondheim, on the west coast of Norway.

The Klarälven was the last Swedish river used for floating logs. The practice ended in 1991, but in **Dyvelsten** ❼ (17 km/10 miles north of Karlstad), the Flottningsmuseet shows how it was done (open early Jun–mid-Aug: daily 10am–5pm; Sep–May: Mon–Fri guided tours bookable in advance; entrance fee; tel: 054-87 12 26).

At Ransäter, 83 km (51 miles) north of Karlstad on the Klarälven, is a well-

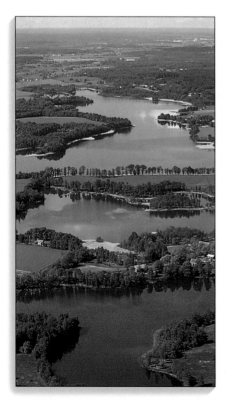

THE MYSTERY BULLET

Karl XII was one of Sweden's greatest military leaders. Considered invulnerable to normal bullets, some speculated he could only be killed with a bullet from his own coat. In 1718, during a battle in Sweden's last campaign against Norway, Karl XII was shot through the head by a mystery bullet while inspecting the trenches at the border fortress of Fredriksten. Given that Karl XII was such a seasoned war veteran, there has always been debate whether the bullet came from the enemy or from an assassin. A legend grew around a soldier who claimed to have seen Karl XII killed, and had picked up the bullet. He later threw it away, near Varberg on the west coast. In 1924, a farmer found a button near Varberg and remembered the legend. The king's body has been exhumed four times (1746, 1799, 1859 and 1917) to examine the wound. Although it is unlikely that the button is the bullet in question, the possibility can not be ruled out. The button is of the right calibre. And did it come from the king's coat? Well, that is also possible. Researchers say it is the sort of button used by the Russian and Polish armies; and Karl XII was known to cut off the buttons of dead soldiers and put them on his own clothes. The Dals-Ed museum on Stora Le recounts the events.

arranged heritage village, **Hembygdsgården**, which includes four museums devoted to mining, forestry, agriculture and rural life. Together they provide a fascinating picture of the Värmland of yesterday (open May–Aug: 9am–5pm, closed Sat–Sun; Sep–Apr: group bookings; entrance fee; tel: 0552-303 43). Ransäter holds an annual festival with a local folk play in the open-air theatre.

The Klarälven is no longer used for floating logs, but many Swedes holiday on the river – drifting along on the gentle current on a raft they assemble themselves. It is regarded as an opportunity for overworked executives to become adventure-loving children once again (*see page 130*). Contact Värmlands Turisttråd in Karlstad (tel: 054-22 25 50; www.varmland.org) for more details.

Nobel prize-winner

To the south, almost parallel to the river, are three lakes, Övre Fryken, Mellanfryken and Nedre Fryken, which together are 80 km (50 miles) long. Between the first two is the little town of **Sunne ❽**, which makes a convenient base from which to explore this area.

High on the list of places to visit is **Mårbacka**, the manor house home of the Swedish writer Selma Lagerlöf, the first woman to receive a Nobel prize (for literature), in 1909 (*see page 120*). Through her books, including her best-known works *The Wonderful Adventures of Nils* and *The Story of Gösta Berling*, she made the Fryk valley and lakes famous. The house is exactly as it was when she died (open mid-May–mid-Sep: daily 10am–5pm; Oct–Apr: guided tours on Sat; entrance fee; tel: 0565-310 27).

On Mellanfryken is **Rottneros Manor ❾**, which appears as Ekeby in Selma Lagerlöf's *The Story of Gösta Berling*. One of Sweden's most beautiful parks,

Map on page 256–7

The Klarälven River offers wonderful opportunities for fishing, especially for salmon, trout and grayling.

BELOW: first build your raft, then sail it down the Klarälven.

the 40-hectare (98-acre) grounds contain an arboretum and 100 works by famous Scandinavian sculptors, including such luminaries as Milles, Eriksson and Vigeland. The manor and park are open mid-May–early Jun: and last three weeks Aug: Mon–Fri 10am–4pm, Sat–Sun 10am–5pm; mid two weeks Jun: Mon–Fri 10am–5pm, Sat–Sun 10am–6pm; late Jun–early Aug: daily 10am–6pm; entrance fee; tel: 0565-602 95.

At **Fryksdalshöjden**, on road 238 to Arvika, there is a bird's eye view of the valley and lakes below. Midway along Övre Fryken, to the west, the mountain of **Tossebergsklätten** also gives wonderful and wide-ranging views. Further to the southwest is another region with a patchwork of lakes. This is where you will find **Glaskogen** ⑩, a vast area rich in wildlife and with 241 km (150 miles) of trails, where you can hike, fish, bathe, camp or go canoeing. Most of it is unpopulated and its forests are dominated by the Stora Gla and Övre Gla lakes.

Two other places of interest within this area are Klässbols Linneväveri and Brunskog Gammelvala. The linen mill at **Klässbol** ⑪ is a small traditional linen and damask weaving mill, the last of its kind in Europe. Among other things, it provides all the table linen for the Swedish diplomatic corps. Visitors are welcome and there is also a shop (open Mon–Fri 8am–6pm, Sat 10am–3pm, Sun May–Aug: 10am–3pm; tel: 0570-46 01 85).

Brunskog Gammelvala ⑫ (Old World) is a collection of 15 old buildings on a picturesque site by Lake Värmeln. Each summer it comes to life for a brief period, when all the traditional crafts and skills are practised (about the last week of July: daily noon–9pm; entrance fee; tel: 0570-522 08).

The western part of the province is comparatively empty, except for elk – Värmland has Sweden's biggest elk population.

BELOW: Rottneros Manor, Värmland.

Inventors remembered

North of Lake Vänern, the bedrock is rich in minerals and this area has long been associated with Sweden's early industrial development. It is dotted with the remains of old disused ironworks, of interest to industrial archaeologists.

Many Americans make the pilgrimage to **Filipstad** ⑬, which has the mausoleum of John Ericsson. Also, along the lake, there are two cannons from the *Monitor*, the warship designed by this gifted inventor and engineer. The *Monitor*'s greatest fame is that it is said to have won the American Civil War for the North. Ericsson also invented the ship's propeller, and his brother Nils was equally talented. They were born at Långbans Herrgård to the north of the town.

Björkborn Herrgård ⑭, near Karlskoga, was the home of another well-known Swedish inventor, the world-famous Alfred Nobel. The manor house is now a museum, Nobelmuseet (open Jun–Aug: daily 1–5pm; entrance fee; tel: 0586-818 94), while Karlskoga is dominated by Bofors, the armaments manufacturer. At **Kristinehamn** ⑮, 50 km (32 miles) to the west of Karlskoga, a 15-metre (49-ft) high sculpture by Picasso is the most striking navigational feature on Lake Vänern.

Between the lakes

The region separating Lake Vänern from Lake Vättern offers rich pickings for the visitor. This is the province of Västergötland which extends beyond the lakes, spreading southwestwards until it diminishes almost to a point at Göteborg. It includes mountain tablelands, which look out over the Västgöta plain, one of Sweden's finest castles, Läckö, and the weavers' country centred on Borås. In 1746 the indefatigable Linnaeus said: "Truly no one could ever imag-

"My factories may make an end of war sooner than your congresses. The day when two army corps can annihilate each other in one second, all civilised nations, it is to be hoped, will recoil from war and discharge their troops."

— ALFRED NOBEL

BELOW: history in the open-air at Brunskog Gammelvala.

ine such splendour as in Västergötland who had not seen it for himself." Such praise may be a little over the top, but nevertheless it is a pleasant area.

Heading south along the eastern shore of Vänern, you come to **Mariestad** , on the River Tidan. The silhouette of the town is dominated by the spire of the 17th-century Renaissance-style cathedral, one of the few churches of this period remaining in Sweden. There are interesting little streets around the cathedral, which conform to the 17th-century town plan.

About 30 km (19 miles) south of Mariestad is **Kinnekulle** ⓱, which rises 306 metres (1,000 ft) above the surrounding countryside and is locally known as the flowering mountain. As such, it attracted paeans of praise from Linnaeus. For good views, you can drive virtually to the summit.

Most Swedes learn at school that the king who first united the Svea and Göta tribes, Olof Skötkonung (994–1022), was baptised in 1008 at **Husaby Källa** (Husaby Spring) at the southern tip of Kinnekulle. Some experts dispute the place and date, but other researchers would like to establish Husaby as the cradle of the Swedish state. **Husaby Church** ⓲ has an imposing stone tower with three spires (open May–Aug: daily 8am–8pm; Apr, Sep: daily 10am–6pm; tel: 0511-34 30 10). At **Flyhov**, to the north, there are 350 rock carvings from the Bronze Age.

Mariestad Slott, on the eastern shore of Lake Vänern.

BELOW: ancient rune stone, Motala.

Porcelain and pottery in Lidkoping

Nestled into Kinneviken (Kinne Bay) is **Lidköping** ⓳, a town renowned for its porcelain and pottery. The leading maker is Rörstrand, which has its own pottery museum featuring royal pieces, plus a large shop (open Mon–Fri 10am–6pm, Sat 10am–2pm, Sun noon–4pm; tel: 0510-823 46/45). The original town dates from 1446 when it was on the east bank of the River Lidan, but the present town on the west bank owes its existence to Magnus Gabriel de la Gardie. In 1670 he laid down a grid plan for the streets, an innovation at that time. The dominant feature is the large square with the old town hall in the centre, housed in a former hunting lodge.

For such a modest sized town, Lidköping has several fine cafés. The best is **Garströms Konditori**, established in 1859, in the main square. The interior gives a real feel of café life in the early 20th century, and the selection and quality of goods are unbeatable (open daily). On the opposite corner of the block you can visit one of the finest millinery shops in Sweden.

Vänermuseet (Lake Vänern Museum) is located away from the centre of town at Framnäsvägen 2, on the edge of the lake. The museum, opened in 1996, includes information and exhibitions about the environment and activities in and around the lake (open Tue–Fri 10am–5pm, Thur 10am–8pm, Sat–Sun noon–5pm; entrance fee; tel: 0510-77 00 65). The shore around Lidköping is very shallow and perfect for wading and bathing with small children.

Lovely Lacko, super Saab

Make the pleasant 20-km (12-mile) drive from Lidköping north to the tip of the beautiful Kållandsö peninsula, which juts into Lake Vänern and ends in a

fringe of islets and skerries. There sits **Läckö Slott (Castle)** ❷, one of the most impressive castles in Sweden (open mid-Jun–mid Aug: daily 10am–6pm; May–mid-Jun and mid-Aug–Sep: guided tours only; entrance fee; tel: 0510-103 20). Built in the 17th century in baroque style, Läckö has 248 rooms. In recent times it has been completely restored and is now an important attraction in this part of the country. Every summer it holds major exhibitions relating to Sweden's cultural heritage as well as outdoor concerts and dramatic productions.

On the western side of the peninsula is **Hindens Rev** (reef), which is 5 km (3 miles) long and has a nice sandy beach. This thin finger stretching out into the lake is a remnant of the glacial era 11,000 years ago.

Trollhättan ❷ is 65 km (40 miles) southwest from Lidköping along highway 44, and Vänersborg lies nearby, just within the borders of Västergötland at the southern tip of Lake Vänern. Trollhättan is the home town of Saab Automobile, which has a museum dedicated to it at the newly revitalised Nohab industrial area (where train engines were made), just south of the town centre. It is open mid-Jun–mid-Aug: daily 10am–6pm; mid-Aug–mid-Jun: Mon–Fri 10am–5pm (entrance fee in summer; tel: 0520-843 44). Next door there is a new science and industry centre, **Innovatum Kunskapens Hus**, with lots of hands-on experimental activities for children (closed Mondays; entrance fee; tel: 0520-48 84 80).

Trollywood

Although the dominating presence of Saab and Volvo Aero have given Trollhättan a reputation as an industrial town, it has a new claim to fame of an entirely different character. Also located at Nohab is **Film i Väst** (West Films), which,through financing and practical support, works to develop film produc-

Map on page 256-7

Lidköping's square is said to be the largest in northern Europe. A big market is held in the square on Wednesday and Saturday mornings.

BELOW: peaceful spot for a lakeside summer picnic.

TIP

On the east of Lake Vättern, historic sites of note include the stone of Rök at Rökeskyrka with its 800 runes (E4 north of Ödeshög) and Alvastra Kloster, Sweden's first Cistercian monastery (Road 50, 15 km/20 miles north of Ödeshög).

tion in western Sweden. As of 1999, films made in Trollhättan accounted for 40 per cent of all the films made in Sweden.

But Trollhättan was famous long before the invention of the motor car or celluloid because of the magnificent falls of the Göta River. The water level drops by about 32 metres (105 ft) and when the Göta Kanal was built, an impressive flight of locks was required to give ships access to Lake Vänern. Today, the river is diverted to generate electricity and the falls are silent. But during the annual Falls Festival in July, it is released to follow the old course, providing an impressive spectacle. The best view is from Oscarsbron (Oscar's Bridge).

Boras: textile territory

The southern part of Västergötland was the heartland of Sweden's textile industry, with the focal point at **Borås** **㉒**. This is not an elegant town by any yardstick but it does have factory shops, bargain stores and trendy boutiques. There is a **Textilmuseet** (Textile Museum) in Borås (open Tues, Thurs noon–8pm, Wed, Fri–Sun noon–4pm, closed Mon; entrance fee; tel: 033-35 76 72), while **Rydal** has a well-preserved mill, together with textile workers' houses. **Borås zoo** features about 400 animals in a natural habitat (open May–mid-Jun: Mon–Fri 10am–4pm, weekends and public holidays 10am–5.30pm; mid-Jun–mid-Aug: daily 10am–6pm; mid-Aug–mid-Sep: daily 10am–4pm; enquire for other times of the year; entrance fee; tel: 033-35 32 77).

Habo's painted church

BELOW: lakeside autumn colours.

Lake Vättern, the second largest lake in Sweden, covers an area of 1,912 sq km (738 sq miles). Near the southern tip of the lake, on the west side, is **Habo**

Kyrka (church) **㉓**, just southwest of Habo village. This is perhaps the most remarkable timber church in Sweden. Probably built in the 14th century, it was enlarged in the 1600s, and then rebuilt in 1723. What makes this church so distinctive is the painted interior, the work of Johan Christian Peterson and Johan Kinnerus, both of Jönköping. It is open May–Aug: Mon–Sat 8am–8pm, Sunday 9am–8pm; Mar, Apr, Sep: Mon–Sat 9am–6pm, Sun 10am–6pm, Oct–Feb: Mon–Sat 9am–4pm, Sun 10am–4pm (tel: 036-404 90.)

Between 1741 and 1743, Peterson painted the northern half and Kinnerus the southern half. Their paintings illustrate Luther's catechism, with the Ten Commandments on the walls (even numbers north side, odd numbers south side), the Lord's Prayer above the gallery and the Baptism and the Lord's Supper on the ceiling of the nave. There you will also find the Confession and Absolution. The overall effect is outstanding. The church also has a 1731 organ built by Johan Niclas Cahman, a renowned Swedish organ builder, and there is a separate and elegantly proportioned bell tower.

Hjo to Karlsborg

Further north along the coast, the small lakeside resort of **Hjo ㉔** has been popular since the turn of the 20th century. It has some attractive preserved wooden houses in the centre of town, a pretty lakeside park, and a pool and beach area right by the marina. You can partake of the famous freshly smoked whitefish, and you can tour the town sedately in a horse-drawn carriage, or cruise on the lake in the 1892 steamer, *Trafik*.

Situated 50 km (31 miles) to the west of Hjo, following roads 49 and 194, is the town of **Skara ㉕**. It has Sweden's second oldest cathedral (after Lund)

Women's history buffs may be interested to visit Strand, 10 km (6 miles) north of Ödeshög. This is the home of Ellen Key, a feminist writer well-known for her suffragette activities (tel: 0140-195 04).

BELOW:
Örebro Slott, a lake island castle.

Map
on pages
256–7

TIP

Fun for all the family: Gustavsviksbadet, near Örebro, is one of Scandinavia's biggest indoor adventure pools (open daily; entrance fee; tel: 019-19 69 01).

BELOW: shopping in the town of Hjo.
RIGHT: rural scene in Västergötland.

dating from the 11th century. **Västergötlands Museet** (Provincial Museum), at Stadsträdgården, includes *Skaramissalet* (Skara missal), a book written between 1100 and 1150 by monks in Sweden describing Catholic church rituals, probably the oldest book in Sweden (open Tues–Fri 10am–5pm, Wed 10am–9pm Sat–Sun noon–5pm; entrance fee; tel: 0511-260 00).

Skara Sommarland, 8 km (5 miles) from Skara on road 49, is an activity park with more than 70 attractions for children, from lunar vehicles to a giant water park (open May–Aug: daily 10am–5pm; Jul–Aug: closes 6–7pm; entrance fee; tel: 0511-640 00). For more relaxed pursuits, head 10 km (6 miles) south-east of Skara on road 184 to **Hornborgasjön** (Hornborg Lake), a wildlife area with more than 100 species of birds. The biggest attraction is the annual mating dance of the crane, a graceful long-legged bird, best seen in April.

Karlsborg ㉖, on the western shore of Lake Vättern, 30 km (19 miles) north of Hjo, is dominated by its huge fortress, **Fästning**. In 1809, when the Swedes lost Finland to the Russians, they realised that a new defence strategy was required and decided to build two massive fortresses. These were to house the Government and the Treasury. The first, at Karlsborg, was started in 1819 and required 250,000 tons of limestone. It was quarried by prison labour on the eastern side of the lake and ferried across by boat. The castle has walls 2 metres (6½ ft) thick with 5 km (3 miles) of ramparts, but by the time it was finally finished in 1909 fortresses were out of fashion (open Jun–Aug: daily guided tours; entrance fee; tel: 0505-188 30). The second castle was never built.

Island castle

North of Västergötland and east of Värmland is Närke, one of Sweden's smallest provinces, and **Örebro** ㉗, its principal town, is worth a visit. It lies on the plain between Kilsbergen and Lake Hjälmaren (Sweden's fourth largest) and is bisected by the meandering River Svartån. In the centre, on an isle in the river, is the castle. Despite its massive appearance, the castle dates only from the late 1800s, but there has been a castle here since the 13th century (open Jun–Aug: daily, guided tours; Sep–May: Sat tour 1pm only; entrance fee; tel: 019-21 21 21).

Beside the River Svartån is **Wadköping**, a preservation area with a collection of buildings, which includes the house of the cookery writer Cajsa Warg the Swedish "Mrs Beeton" (open Tues–Sun daily 11am–5pm; tel: 019-21 62 20). For good views take the lift up the **Svampen** (the mushroom), a water tower 58 metres (190 ft) high.

Karlslunds Gård on the outskirts of the town is a splendidly proportioned country house with 90 preserved 18th- and 19th-century buildings ranging from a cowshed to a tavern within its spacious grounds. The grounds are open to the public.

The other town of note in Närke is **Askersund** ㉘ a quiet little place at the northern end of Lake Vättern which was established by Queen Kristina in the 17th century. The **Landskyrkan church** is worth visiting. Founded in 1670, it was designed by Jean de la Vallée – one of Sweden's most important baroque architects – and Erik Dahlberg.

Map
on pages
256–7

GÖTA KANAL

*A leisurely cruise along Sweden's "Blue Band"
between Stockholm and Göteborg offers one of the most relaxed
ways of sampling the country's history*

The challenge of linking the lakes and rivers through the interior of Sweden from Stockholm on the east coast to Göteborg on the west coast had exercised the minds of many industrialists, statesmen and kings before Baltzar von Platen actually succeeded at the beginning of the 19th century.

For 22 years, 58,000 men laboured to build the Göta Kanal, many of them soldiers who worked with little to help them but steel-reinforced wooden spades. It was a massive undertaking and nothing like it has been built in Sweden since. At the time, the country needed this new artery from east to west to transport timber, iron, food and a range of other goods, and also to build up industry along its banks. One of the advisers to the plan was the famous Scottish engineer, Thomas Telford.

In 1998, the Göta Kanal was designated an "International Historic Civil Engineering Landmark," giving it the same status as the Statue of Liberty, the Golden Gate Bridge and the Panama Canal.

A choice of ways

Today, there is no commercial traffic, but many Swedes travel the canal each summer in their own motor and sailing boats. For the visitor there are many ways of seeing the Göta Kanal. The classic way is to take a four- or six-day cruise between Stockholm and Göteborg on one of the vintage vessels operated by Göta Kanal Rederiaktiebolaget (the Göta Kanal Steamship Company). The oldest of the three vessels is *MS Juno*, built in 1874 and now the world's oldest registered passenger vessel with overnight accommodation. She is complemented by *MS Wilhelm Tham*, built in 1912 and *MS Diana*, a mere stripling dating from 1931.

There are also a number of passenger boats which take you along part of the way, and small boats to provide sightseeing trips at various points along the canal (tel: 0141-535 10; www.gotakanal.se). Along both sides of the canal there are towpaths, which make excellent cycle tracks. Bikes can be transported across the lakes on the passenger boats and ferries.

Setting sail

Travelling along the canal gives you a whiff of Swedish history. The four-day westbound Göta Kanal Steamship Company cruises start from Stockholm at 9am and head down the Baltic coast for most of the first day before entering the first lock on the canal at **Mem** – where the canal was officially inaugurated in 1832 – in the early hours of the next morning. The first major town on the canal is **Söderköping** ❷⁹, a medieval trading town with

BELOW: the vessel
MS Wilhelm Tham
negotiates a lock
on the Göta Kanal.

number of beautiful churches and a restored town hall. At lunchtime on the second day you reach **Berg ㉚**, with its impressive flight of seven locks, where there is time to visit the historic monastery church at nearby **Vreta**, once the richest religious establishment in Sweden.

Birds and more besides

The route crosses two picturesque lakes, Asplången and **Roxen**, where there are good chances of spotting ospreys and herons during the breeding season. After Lake Roxen the canal takes you through 15 locks in 3 km (2 miles), lifting you 37 metres (120 ft). You spend most of the next night moored at **Motala ㉛**, a town founded by Baltzar von Platen, who drew up the town plans and started the now thriving engineering industry. The **Kanal och Sjöfartsmuseet** (Motala Canal and Maritime Museum) tells the story of the canal and its construction (open mid-May–mid-Jun and early Aug: 9am– noon, 1–5pm; late Jun–Jul: daily 9am–6pm; entrance fee; tel: 0141-535 10).

A magical moment on the first night of the eastbound cruises, weather permitting, is when the boat inches through a tortuous channel towards the floodlit 17th-century Läckö Castle.

The schedules for the Göta Kanal cruises are constructed so that some sightseeing stops included on the westbound itineraries are not included on the eastbound route and vice versa. The eastbound cruises make a stop of several hours at **Vadstena ㉜**, 15 km (9 miles) south of Motala, a delightful small town with wooden houses lining its narrow streets. The town is famous for its associations with St Birgitta and grew up around a 14th-century convent. The Abbey was built to the design of St Birgitta and consecrated in 1430.

Early next morning on the westbound cruise, you cross Lake Vättern from Motala to Karlsborg, site of a huge fortress built at the same time as the canal, and **Forsvik ㉝**, an old metal-working village and the site of the canal's oldest lock, built in 1813. Vättern, the fifth largest lake in Europe and the second largest in Sweden, is deep and cold and rich in fish.

The Göta Kanal boats are often greeted at Forsvik by a local family singing hymns and offering passengers freshly picked wild flowers. This 100-year-old custom originated as a blessing for passengers as they embarked on what was then regarded as the hazardous crossing of Vättern.

For the rest of the day the route follows the western section of the canal, passing Tåtorp, which has the only manually operated lock, and Lyrestad, another town founded by von Platen. In the evening you reach **Sjötorp ㉞**, marking the end of 58 locks and the beginning of Lake Vänern, Sweden's largest lake.

BELOW: canalside room with a view at the Göta Hotel.

At the south side of Lake Vänern, you pass through **Vänersborg** before reaching the gorge at Trollhättan early the next morning. Once there were 11 locks here; today, there are only four. Now you start the last stage of your journey down the Göta älv (river), passing through the final lock at **Lilla Edet**. There is also time to visit the fascinating Medieval Museum at **Lödöse ㉟**, which depicts the area, its people and the crafts of early times (open Oct–Mar: Tues–Fri 1–4pm; Sat–Sun 11am–4pm; Apr–Sep: Tues–Sun 10am–6pm; entrance fee; tel: 0520-66 10 10).

Göteborg ㊱, with its four bridges, lies ahead. You have arrived on the west coast. ❑

DALARNA

Dalarna is the folklore province, as famous for its scarlet Dala horses as its Midsummer festivities. Artists have made their homes here and industrialists their fortunes

Map on page 274

Dalarna is often regarded as the heart of Sweden's folklore district, and indeed, it represents all that is quintessentially Swedish. With its colourful costumes, centuries-old traditions of music and dance, Midsummer festivals, and evocative rural landscape, its folklore and beauty attract an increasing number of visitors each year.

Dalarna is the third-largest tourist site in Sweden, after Stockholm and Göteborg. In the country's southernmost mountain landscape, both summer and winter activities beckon, with Dalarna fast becoming a popular European ski destination. The culture that gave us the red-painted *Dalahäst* (Dala horse) and inspired two of Sweden's most beloved artists, Carl Larsson and Anders Zorn, can best be experienced in the twilight of *fäbodar*, the old pasture cottages nestling in the hills of Dalarna, in the company of some elderly but amazingly energetic fiddlers; or at the magic of Midsummer, when a young woman places nine different flowers under her pillow to dream of the man she will marry.

Music-making

Music is one of the most defining characteristics of Dala culture. **Music on Lake Siljan** and the **Falu Folk Music Festival** are two annual festivals that attract visitors from all over Sweden and abroad. Distinctly Dala are the *spelmansstämmor*, folk musicians' rallies, particularly the one held each summer in **Bingsjö ❶**, 30 km (19 miles) east of Rättvik, where fiddlers in their eighties turn the classic polka into a musical performance that rivals any blues master.

An exotic setting for listening to music is **Dalhalla**, a cavernous outdoor concert arena set in the depths of an abandoned limestone quarry near the town of **Rättvik ❷**. The quarry, abandoned in 1990, was inaugurated as a music arena in 1994, with the first performance, of Wagner's *Der Ring des Nibelungen*, held two years later. The annual summer festivals feature artists of international standing. (Guided tours of the arena, accompanied by music to sample the marvellous acoustics, are available from mid-June–Aug: 10am–5pm; other times of year, by appointment, tel: 0248-79 79 50.)

Pastoral scenes

For a change of pace, explore the gentle quiet of the region's *fäbodar*, which offer a taste of back-to-the-land living. These pasture cottages and surrounding buildings, dating from the 15th and 16th centuries, are found all over Sweden but are most often associated with Dalarna.

They constitute a living museum, where cows are milked, butter is churned, *messmör* (a type of goats'

PRECEDING PAGES: sunset, Lake Siljan. **LEFT:** autumn colours. **BELOW:** all dressed up in Dalarna.

At the bear park of Orsa Grönklitt, 10 km (6 miles) north of Orsa, bears roam with lynx and wolves in their natural habitat (open May–early Sep: daily; entrance fee; tel: 020-462 00).

BELOW: folk-art telephone boxes are still in use.

cheese) is made, and the classic *tunnbröd* (thin bread) is baked, in the same way that it has been done for centuries. Many *fäbodar* are open for visits by tourists and sell products or serve food.

One worth visiting is **Ljusbodarnas Fäbodar**, about 20 km (12 miles) south of **Leksand** on Route 70 towards Mockfjärd, where children can pet the cows, calves, hens, sheep and pigs, and you can enjoy a meal of *sill* (herring) on some nights (open Jun–Aug; tel: 010-255 59 57/0247-330 80).

If trying your own hand at 15th-century farming appeals, **Prästbodarna Fäbodar**, 40 km (25 miles) east of Rättvik, near Bingsjö, has a variety of native Swedish farm animals, and offers one-day courses in butter churning, milking and cheese-making (book in advance; open Jun–mid-Sep, tel: 0248 141 59). The farming life seems a natural accompaniment to the breathtaking scenery of the province, two-thirds of which is forested.

At the northern extremity of Dalarna is the deceptively gentle start of the mountain range which marches north, gaining height all the time until it culminates in the snow-topped peaks of the Kebnekajse range in Lapland. Dalarna is a transition zone between the softer landscapes of southern Sweden and the more dramatic, but harsher landscapes of the north. It is even divided within itself between the more densely-populated area south and east of Lake Siljan (dense by Swedish standards) and the relatively uninhabited zones to the north and west of the lake.

Industrial traditions

However, Dalarna is by no means an exclusively rural area. The provincial capital, **Falun ❸**, has been a centre of industry for probably 1,000 years, and

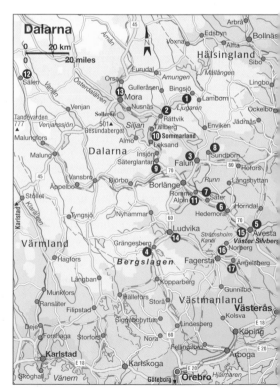

is an attractive town, well worth a stroll to the central square. The **Bergslagen** area to the south has been a noted centre for mining for several hundred years and covers not just Dalarna but also parts of Värmland and Västmanland. This district is well worth exploring if you are interested in industrial archaeology (*see page 278*).

About 60 km (37 miles) south, near Ludvika, is **Grängesberg ④**, where a large iron-ore mining complex and the railway serving it were financed by capital from the City of London in the 19th century. The mine is working to this day. Steam enthusiasts will not want to miss the **Lokmuseet (Railway Museum)** with its vintage locomotives which used to handle the iron-ore trains (open June–Aug 10am–6pm; entrance fee; tel: 0240-204 93).

Fifty km (31 miles) east is **Avesta ⑤**, another centre with a long industrial tradition, this time dating back to the 14th century. It was once the home of the Swedish Mint and the **Myntmuseet (Mint Museum)** contains what is claimed to be the world's largest copper coin, weighing 20 kg (43 lb) and dated 1644. The museum is open Apr–May and mid-Aug–Dec: Wed 10am–noon, some Sundays 2–4pm; June–mid-Aug: Wed–Sat 1–3pm (tel: 0226-507 83).

Hedemora ⑥, 20 km (12 miles) north, claims to be the oldest town in Dalarna, with a charter dated 1459; its privileges as a market town go back even earlier than that, while parts of the church are 13th-century. The locals have devised Husbyringen, a 56-km (35-mile) "museum trail" which you can take by car through the area northeast of the town to see a number of industrial archaeology sites.

About 10 km (6 miles) further north, **Säter ⑦** is claimed to be one of the seven best-preserved wooden towns in Sweden. But compared with Hedemora

Map on page 274

The work of one of Dalarna's acclaimed peasant painters, Mats Persson Stadig, is visible on ceilings, walls and furniture at Dössberget, a beautifully situated museum at Bjursås, 20 km (12 miles) east of Leksand.

BELOW: Midsummer celebrations are an annual highlight.

Around Lake Siljan

Legend has it that Siljan, the huge lake in the centre of Dalarna, was formed when a giant meteorite crashed to earth 360 million years ago. Siljan is something of a symbol for the local folklore traditions. Driving around the lake is an excellent way to see many of the most notable attractions.

Some of Sweden's typical Midsummer celebrations are held around the lake, notably at **Rättvik**, where the long "church-boats" bring hundreds of villagers to church for the annual service, dressed in their local costumes. **Rättvik Kyrka** (church) features folk-art paintings showing Biblical scenes in a Dalarna setting.

About 20 km (12 miles) along the north shore, as you approach Mora, is the small village of **Nusnäs**, headquarters for the production of the brightly painted Dalarna wood-carved horses which became almost a Swedish national symbol after they were shown at the New York World Exhibition in 1939. You can watch the horses being made and painted.

Mora is a pleasant lakeside town. It is best known as the home of the Swedish artist Anders Zorn, who was a close friend of another Dalarna artist, Carl Larsson. Zorn's paintings are more varied in subject and treatment than those of Larsson, whose works usually reflect family life. Mora has a museum devoted to Zorn's work and you can also visit his house and studio (**Zorngården**, Anders Zorns House, open Sep–mid-May: Mon–Sat noon–4pm, Sun 1–4pm; mid-May–mid-Sep: Mon–Sat 10am–4pm, Sun 11am–4pm; entrance fee; tel: 0250-100 04; **Zornmuseet** open mid-Sep–mid-May: Mon–Sat noon–5pm, Sun 1–5pm; mid-May–mid-Sep: Mon–Sat 9am–5pm, Sun 11am–5pm; entrance fee; tel: 0250-165 60).

Heading 10 km (6 miles) along the west side of the lake, make a detour to the island of **Sollerön**, which is claimed to have the sunniest climate in the region. The island is one of the places where the church-boats (direct descendants of the Viking longships) are constructed.

Back on the mainland is an excellent mountain-top viewpoint, **Gesundaberget**. On the slopes of Gesundaberget is **Tomteland** (Santaworld). Children can meet Santa and see his animals, including the rare musk-ox, and visit the toy workshops (open mid-Jun–mid-Aug: 10am–5pm; late-Nov–early Jan: 10am–5pm; Christmas Eve, New Year's Eve 10am–2pm; entrance fee; tel: 0250-212 00).

Leksand, at the southern tip of Siljan, is a bustling little community and the centre for many cultural attractions in summer, including a traditional mystery play, *Himlaspelet*, which is performed in an open-air theatre. **Leksands Kulturhus** (Culture House) provides a spotlight on local folk culture (open Tues–Sat 11am–4pm; entrance fee; tel: 0247-802 45).

One of the best-known resorts on Siljan is the village of **Tällberg**, 11 km (7 miles) from Leksand, a typical Dalarna village, complete with maypole and timber buildings. A quiet stroll down to the lakeside here at sunset is a good a way to round off the day. ❏

LEFT: decorated maypole on the shores of Lake Siljan, a centre for Midsummer festivities.

it is quite an upstart, with a town charter dated 1642. The ravines of the **Sater Valley** were created at the end of the Ice Age and are of interest for their flora.

Map on page 274

Cradle of Larsson and Swedish culture

Just 13 km (8 miles) east of Falun is **Sundborn ⑧**, a picturesque small village which was the home of a much-loved Swedish artist, Carl Larsson, in the early part of the 20th century. His work and that of his wife, Karin Larsson, a textile artist, still inspire the interior design of Swedish homes today and their influence has spread internationally as well. About 60,000 people from all over the world visit Carl Larssongård at Sundborn each year. The house, beside a small lake, has been authentically preserved and is open for tours. Larsson's paintings reflect his happy family life and were strongly influenced by the local Dalarna folk-art traditions (open May–Sep: 10am–5pm; other times by appointment; entrance fee; tel: 023-600 53; www.clg.se).

If you want to read more about the enormous influence that Carl Larsson had on design in Sweden, turn to the special feature on pages 112–113.

Local handicrafts

In the province that inspired the distinctive *Dalahäst* (Dala horse), a more readily recognised Swedish symbol than the flag, it is not surprising that the region is known for its abundance of carvers, potters, silversmiths, weavers, painters and bakers. This is a mecca for *hemslöjd* (crafts), all of which have their ancient roots in the farming culture.

At **Säterglantan ⑨**, 3 km (2 miles) south of Insjön lake, **Hemslöjdens Gård**, offers a wide array of handicrafts as well as week-long courses (tel: 0247-402 73; info@saterglantan.se; www.Siljan-Dalarna.com/fi/saterglantan). At **Nittsjö Keramik**, 6 km (4 miles) north of Rättvik, clay goods are made following a 100-

BELOW: Dala horses are carved from wood at Nusnäs.

year-old tradition. You can save a great deal on the seconds, with barely noticeable blemishes (open Mon–Fri 9am–6pm; Sat 9am–2pm; Jun–Jul: Sun noon–4pm; tel: 0248-171 30).

The province offers many attractions for families with children, including **Sommarland** , **Vattenland** (Waterland) and **Motorland**, three parks with just one entrance fee, grouped in an adventure park on Lake Siljan's shores and featuring more than 80 different activities (open Jun–mid-Aug: from 10am; entrance fee; tel: 0247-139 39/137 38).

Cross-country ski challenge

Dalarna's ski resorts are the principal winter tourist attraction, both for cross-country skiing and downhill. **Romme Alpin** ⓫, 10km (6 miles) south of Börlange, is Sweden's most visited ski resort outside the proper mountain areas, with some 110,000 visitors annually. **Sälen** ⓬, in northwest Dalarna, is the well-known popular resort in the higher mountains with longer and harder pistes. Together, Sälen and **Idre**, 100 km (62 miles) further north, have almost half of Sweden's skilift facilities. There are also many other smaller resorts in the province.

Sälen is also famous for being the starting point for a 53-mile (85-km) cross-country skiing race to **Mora** ⓭: the **Vasaloppet**, the most popular sporting event in Sweden, held in March each year to commemorate King Gustav Vasa's flight from his enemies in the 16th century. Each year the race includes more than 15,000 competitors, who in the past have included the present king, Carl XVI Gustaf. The first Vasaloppet was run on March 19, 1922.

A victory in Vasaloppet is regarded by most of the world's best skiers as highly as a podium place in the Olympic Games or the World Championships. Nils "Mora Nisse" Karlsson has won the race a record nine times. Women first began competing in 1981; in 1988, the **Tjejvasan** (Women's Vasa) was inaugurated, and has grown to include some 7,500 female skiers each year. For more about the fascinating history of this race, stop by Vasaloppet Museet (Vasaloppet Museum) in Mora and Vasaloppethus (Vasaloppet House) in Sälen.

The **Vasaleden** (hiking route) allows hikers to walk the famous Vasaloppet course during the summer months. The course is marked with orange circles on poles, which are also branded with a portrait of Gustav Vasa. There are five chalets along the course where hikers can spend the night free of charge. Information about sightseeing is also available. Maps and a commemorative pin can be purchased in Sälen and Mora (for more information, www.vasaloppet.com).

BELOW: a quiet moment near Lake Siljan.

The Old Mines of Dalarna

Few countries have preserved the places that laid the foundations of their prosperity like Sweden. In tracing the nation's industrial archaeology, you can follow a direct line which has led to what is today one of the most successful industrial countries in the world.

The heart of Sweden's mining region forms a broad swathe across the centre of the country, from east to west, containing the majority of the nation's industrial archaeological treasures. The catalyst for this development was the 17th-century discovery of minerals, including iron, copper and silver, which, combined with water power and timber (for charcoal), led to furious activity in the region. The manufacture of steel and other metals has continued, largely with the use of imported ores and powered by hydro-electricity.

Map on page 274

Copper Mountain

A good place to start exploring the industrial treasures is Falun, Dalarna's capital and the jewel in the crown of Swedish mining history. The 1,000-year- old town is renowned as a great copper centre. At its peak, it produced two-thirds of the world's copper.

The town is the headquarters of Stora, the corporate name for **Stora Kopparberg** (Great Copper Mountain), with a history going back at least to 1288. Falun's main claim to fame for the past 300 years has been a huge hole in the ground which was formed in 1687 when the whole copper mine caved in, creating The Great Pit, 99 metres (325 ft) deep and 396 metres (1,300 ft) wide. No one was killed, as it happened, because it was Midsummer and all the miners were carousing, but production never returned to previous levels.

In fact, Stora Kopparberg wanted to close down **Falu Gruva** (Falun Mine) in the 1880s, but then gold was discovered in the workings. It is still mined today, along with lead, zinc and the original copper ore. An interesting by-product is the red ochre which forms the basis for the distinctive paint which is used on buildings not just in Dalarna but over much of the rest of Sweden as well. Access to the mine is by a lift which takes visitors down to the 55-metre

Lugnet, northeast of Falun, is site of the Nordic Skiing World Championships. There is a 90-metre (295-ft) high ski jump, an observation tower and a sports museum.

BELOW: Falu Gruva, still being mined today.

Map on page 274

(180-ft) level. There, a tunnel leads to the oldest part of the workings, the Creutz shaft. This was opened in 1662 and is 207 metres (680 ft) deep. All the shafts, drifts, and chambers have names, such as the Christmas Gift, discovered at Christmas, and the General Peace, named after the short-lived peace treaty between Britain and France in 1801.

The mine offers guided tours – complete with helmets and raincoats. Wear warm clothes, it's 5°C inside (open May–Aug: 10am–4.30pm; Sep–mid-Nov, and Mar–Apr: weekends only 12.30–4.30pm; entrance fee; tel: 023-158 25).While there, visit **Stora Kopparberg Museet** next to the mine. The museum has an outstanding collection of exhibits of the industrial past (open 12.30–4pm; from 10am in summer; entrance fee; tel: 023-71 14 75).

Touring the mines

Sweden's biggest mining region was in Bergslagen to the south of Falun. Here, in the country's most important industrial region, the foundations for modern Sweden were laid. In recognition of this historical background, the Swedes have created the **Eko-Museum Bergslagen**, an award-winning eco-museum, covering 49 cultural and historical sites within a 150-km (93-mile) area. The area encompasses seven rural districts, two in Dalarna, five in Västmanland and two provincial museums. It is mainly concentrated along the River Kolbäcksån, where the **Strömsholm Kanal** links mines, blast furnaces and ironworks.

The eco-museum also includes workers' dwellings, homesteads, mansions, power stations, railways, canals, inns and restaurants – all in their historical settings. To see this area, your best bet is to hire a car, choose a few days in the summer when the sites are sure to be open, pick up an Eko-Museum Bergslagen guidebook from one of the tourist offices in Ludvika, Smedjebacken, Norberg, Skinnskatteberg, Fagersta, Surahammar or Hallstahammar, and follow the map (for information, tel: 240-66 30 82). Below are a few examples of what you can expect to see:

Ludvika ⓮ Ludvika Mining Museum, the first open-air museum of industrial history in the world.

Silvberg ⓯ Legendary Väster Silvberg silver mining district from the Middle Ages, 20 km (12 miles) northeast of Ludvika; a varied cultural landscape complete with hiking trails through valleys dotted with the ruins of abandoned mines, forges, cottages, mill ponds and furnaces.

Norberg ⓰ The most important producer of iron during the Middle Ages. Mossgruvan Mining Museum shows working life at a mine at the end of the 19th century. At the Svinryggen Mines is the famous Polhem's Wheel, an industrial invention that captured water to drive the mining pumps.

Ängelsberg ⓱ About 20 km (12 miles) south of Norberg, the Engelsberg Ironworks is one of the world's most important remains of the early industrial era and is included on UNESCO's World Heritage list. The blast furnace and forge are unique in that the water wheel, the crusher, the blower and the hammer are still in working order. Visitors will also find various industrial buildings, gardens, and the manor house from 1746. ❑

BELOW: old cart once used in the copper mines.
RIGHT: Lake Siljan from the west shore at Gesunda.

THE CENTRAL HEARTLANDS

In an area where towns and villages are few and far between the landscape is awe-inspiring and attracts numerous hikers, skiers and anglers

Map
on page
286

Five provinces stretch across central Sweden. In the east are Gästrikland, Hälsingland and Medelpad, which share the long coastline from Furuvik and Sörfjärden, known as Jungfrukusten (Virgin Coast). Further inland come Härjedalen and Jämtland, which stretch west to the Norwegian border, the land of lakes and coniferous or birch forests. Härjedalen marks the beginning of the great northern mountain ranges and the further north you go, the more dramatic the scenery.

The small province of **Gästrikland** has one major town, **Gävle ❶**, in the southeast corner of the region. Though the history of this coastal town goes back over 500 years, on the surface this busy commercial centre is unexceptional. But don't let this note of discouragement overshadow Gävle's attractions. It has a castle, built by Johan III (not open to the public), a town hall built by Gustav III, and a sizeable provincial museum, **Länsmuseet**, which requires four floors to display its 16,000 varied exhibits. Gävle was one of Sweden's great shipping towns, and the most treasured exhibit is the Björke boat, built in AD 100 and among the most notable finds in Northern Europe (open Tues–Sun noon–4pm, Wed 4–9pm; entrance fee; tel 026-65 56 00).

Railway magic

Sveriges Järnvägsmuseum (Railway Museum) occupies a spacious site on the outskirts of Gävle. The railway collection embraces a total of 400 exhibits, including 29 gleaming locomotives, 30 coaches and wagons, the 1874 coach of King Oscar II, plus a multitude of smaller exhibits from tickets to scale models. It is a paradise for railway enthusiasts (open Tues–Sun 10am–4pm; Jun–Aug: Mon–Sun 10am–4pm; entrance fee; tel 026-14 46 15).

The **Gamla Gefle** area has preserved wooden houses with an artists' quarter. Beside the Gävle river are the **Stadsträdgården** and **Boulogneskogen**, which together form one of the largest municipal parks in Sweden. A park of a different kind is **Furuviksparken**, on the coast 10 km (6 miles) south of the town, which combines extensive zoological gardens and a variety of attractions for children (open mid-May–late Jun: Mon–Fri 10am–4pm, Sat–Sun 10am–5pm; late Jun–mid-Aug: daily 10am–6pm; entrance fee; tel 026-19 90 00). People from a wide area flock to Gävle for sporting events, shopping and theatre. It is also a place for a good night out.

Gästrikland is at the eastern end of the swathe of land which gave Sweden its early mining and smelting industries, and moving only a few kilometres inland to **Sandviken** you are in an area which saw the development of the Swedish steel industry. Sand-

PRECEDING PAGES: Tännforsen, to the west of Åre. **LEFT:** ski-break at Åreskutan. **BELOW:** winding River Ljusnan.

TIP

Discover more about Sweden's greatest natural resource – its forests – at Silvanum, the forestry museum at Gävle (open Tues, Thur, Fri 10am–4pm, Wed 10am–7pm, Sat–Sun 1–5pm; free; tel 026-61 41 00).

viken grew up with the development of the Bessemer process in the 1860s and Sandviken steels are well known today.

Jädraås ❷, 80 km (50 miles) to the north, is the starting point for a vintage railway with steam trains running for some 4.5 km (2.8 miles) to **Tallås**. This is typical of therailways used to haul minerals or timber, and it has the coach used by King Oscar II when he went hunting bears in Dalarna.

Only 10 km (6 miles) northeast of Gävle and also on the coast, **Bönan** is famous for its golden-brown smoked herring, cured over spruce wood. **Engeltofta** is a good restaurant at which to sample it – in summer you can catch the boat over from Gävle (11am daily mid-Jun–mid-Aug). Grilled herring and potatoes with dill butter are favourites all along the Virgin Coast, which also has small fishing villages and working harbours such as **Skärså**, where catching the Baltic herring is still an important industry.

Choral tribute

The main highway north, E4, skirts two coastal towns in **Hälsingland**: Söderhamn and Hudiksvall. **Söderhamn ❸**, set between two hills, was founded in 1620 as an armoury for the Swedish army, and the museum is situated in part of what was the gun and rifle factory. Although a commercial centre, the town has an impressive town hall, plus a church to match, a pleasant riverside park and boat trips around the archipelago. On top of the hill on the eastern side of the town is **Oskarsberg**, a look-out tower built in 1895, which – for reasons not immediately apparent – was paid for by the members of the choral society.

Next to Gävle, **Hudiksvall ❹** is the second oldest town in northern Sweden; it celebrated its 400th anniversary in 1982. Some 100 years ago, when the tim-

BELOW: folk dancers prepare for the *Hälsingehambo* at Järvsö.

ber industry was at its peak, the town had a reputation for high living. Today it has no buildings erected by unusual benefactors but it does have a theatre of distinction, which was opened in 1882. It also has a group of the best preserved 19th-century wooden buildings in Sweden, the **Fiskarstan** (Fishermen's Town). Strömmingsundet's wooden wharves and warehouses also merit a glance.

About 10 km (6 miles) south of Hudiksvall, at Iggesund, is **Bruksmuseet**, an impressive ironworks museum. Its blast furnaces and the Bessemer steelworks can still be seen (open early Jun–early Aug: Mon–Sun 11am–5pm; Sep–May guided tours by appointment; free; tel: 0650-280 00).

The interior of the province has the best scenery, particularly the valley of the Ljusnandalen (River Ljusnan), which is laced with lakes along its entire length. West of **Ljusdal ❺**, where the Ljusnan meets the Hennan river, the forests begin. The life of the early charcoal burners who lived in these forests was not easy, but at **Albert Vikstens Kojby** (Albert Viksten's Cabin Village) at **Lassekrog**, 40 km (25 miles) northwest of Ljusdal, you can discover what it is like to spend a night in a charcoal burner's cabin and bake your own "charcoal bread" over the fire (tel 0651-212 75).

Map on page 286

Hikers still use the traditional Sami hut for shelter.

Folk dancing festival

About 12 km (7 miles) south of Ljusdal, and halfway between the river's source and the sea, is **Järvsö ❻**, a small town in farming and forestry country and a minor holiday and winter sports centre. Once a year, this peaceful routine is broken by an unforgettable festival: the **Hälsingehambo**, a competitive event which involves around 3,000 folk dancers. At dawn on a July morning, groups of competitors in traditional costumes begin to dance. To the tune *Hårgalåten,*

BELOW: the railway stretches north to Kiruna in Lapland.

Stenegård manor at Järvsö, site of the Hälsingehambo folk dancing festival's grand finale, is also a handicrafts centre featuring potters, silversmiths, glass-blowers, blacksmiths and woodworkers.

they dance all the way up the Ljusnan valley, north from Bollnäs and Arbrå, to a grand finale in Järvsö, in front of **Stenegård** manor house.

Today the "Hambo" is a joyous event but its origins are much more macabre, with something of the Pied Piper of Hamelin about them. Legend has it that a sinister fiddler seduced the dancing couples, who did not realise that he was the Devil. Lured by the music, they danced to their own perdition at the top of the **Hårgaberget** mountain. By the time the night ended, only their skulls remained, whirling around to form a visible ring in the solid rock.

On an island on the river between the manor and village is the parish church. When it was built in 1832, it was the largest country church in Sweden, seating 2,400, which may say something about the piety of the local people of that era. Later this was reduced to 1,400. The pulpit comes from an earlier church and the parsonage, built in 1731 and used until 1879, is now a museum.

Bollnäs ❼, 50 km (31 miles) south of Järvsö, has a tradition of sweet-making. In 1919, in a little cottage at Hållbo, southeast of the town, Olof Käller invented a special peppermint sweet. Today, the factory uses the most modern techniques to produce these popular sweets, but during the summer you can still watch them being boiled, rolled and stretched out in the old way at **Källers Karamell-museum** (open late Jun–end Jul: 2–5pm; tel: 0278-800 23), and the general store has the whole range piled high from floor to ceiling.

Of the mountains around Järvsö, **Gluggberget**, 515 metres (1,689 ft), has a viewing platform at the summit, while **Öjeberget**, 370 metres (1,314 ft), has the advantage that you can drive to the top.

BELOW: hundreds of musicians converge on Delsbo for the fiddlers' festival.

To absorb this region you need to drive first along the minor road 30 km (18 miles) east from Järvsö to **Delsbo ❽**, which attracts an enormous number of folk

fiddlers for the annual Delsbostämman, and then on the secondary road through Friggesund and Hassela and back to the coast. Surrounded by dark forests, this is Dellenbygden, rural Sweden at its best, and includes the Dellen lakes area, with boat trips and canoe trails, and walking trails.

Map on page 286

The most northerly coastal town of this central area is **Sundsvall ❾** in Medelpad, which has only a small area of coastline. Mainly industrial, Sundsvall still enjoys a fine location, partly on the mainland and partly on the island of **Alnö**, connected by bridge. It has a 13th-century church and Hembygdsgård, an open-air museum with some 20 old buildings.

South of the town at **Galtström** is another restored ironworks, complete with blast furnace, works office, chapel and forestry museum (open daily; free). Drive 60 km (37 miles) west on the E14, which starts at Sundsvall, and you will come to **Torpshammar ❿**, which is claimed to be the very centre of Sweden.

The "Stone City" of Sundsvall, Medelpad, earned its nickname after a devastating fire in June 1888 destroyed the wooden town. Architects from Stockholm were called in to rebuild Sundsvall in stone.

Anglers' paradise

Together the provinces of **Härjedalen** and **Jämtland** are as big as Denmark. Though they cover an area of 50,000 sq km (19,300 sq miles), their population is only 135,000. Since 55,000 live in Östersund, the principal town of Jämtland, this means that outside the main towns people are few and far between. To the east and southeast are extensive forests with low hills, rivers and lakes. The higher mountains begin in Härjedalen and spread north and west.

This heartland has four main rivers, the Ångermanälven, Indalsälven, Ljungan and Ljusnan, all well stocked with fish, especially trout and grayling, and 4,000 lakes and watercourses make these provinces a fishing Utopia. Perch, pike and whitefish are the most common in the forested regions, but many tarns

BELOW: when the wind blows, it's time to seek refuge in a snow hole.

have been stocked with trout in recent years. Most fishing waters are open to the general public though you may need a permit, bought cheaply nearby or at the tourist offices. The vast tracts of near uninhabited territory are also home to wildlife such as bears, wolverine, lynx and the ubiquitous elk.

When tourism was in its infancy, Härjedalen was one of the first Swedish provinces to attract skiers, who still return to pit their skills against its varied terrain, and come back in the summer for mountain-walking.

The scenery is impressive and, north of **Funäsdalen**, not far from the Norwegian border, the province has Sweden's highest road over the **Flatruet Plateau**, up to 1,000 metres (3,280 ft) high. Close to the Norwegian border is the Rogen area, a remnant of the Ice Age with scratched and furrowed boulders.

For a driver, mile after mile of forest road stretching ahead can be mesmeric, and the art is not to fall asleep. But roads are not plentiful, apart from a few minor ones. At the cross of the north-south route, Highway 45, and east-west, Highway 84, is **Sveg**, a small town, but the province's largest at around 4,000 people. **Vemdalen ⓫**, 60 km (37 miles) northwest, has an eight-sided wooden church with a separate onion-domed bell tower. Beyond the village the road climbs steeply between two mountains, the Vemdalsfjällen, before crossing the provincial boundary.

Lakes and islands

Jämtland is by far the biggest province in central Sweden, a huge territory of lakes, rivers and mountains. Its heart is **Lake Storsjön**, the fifth largest stretch of inland water in the country. North of Storsjön, on the north bank of Lake Alsensjön at **Glösa ⓬** are *hällristningar*, primitive rock carvings. At the cen-

BELOW: a hard-earned rest from elk-hunting.

THE INLAND RAILWAY

A trip on the Inlandsbanan (Inland Railway) is an enjoyable way of seeing some of Sweden's most dramatic scenery. The route stretches through the Central Heartlands from Mora in Dalarna to Gällivare in Lapland. The idea of building such a long railway through a harsh and inaccessible landscape was first promoted in 1894, but it was to take another 40 years of hard labour before it was completed. The 1,100-km (680-mile) line was finally inaugurated in Jokkmokk in Lapland on 6 August 1937, and a monument was erected to commemorate the event. Today, the train often makes stops along the way so passengers can visit local artists and craftspeople or simply admire the views. Sometimes it has to stop to avoid running into herds of reindeer resting on the track. With luck, passengers may also see elks or bears on the lineside. It is possible to make stopovers along the route and stay for a night or two in local towns and villages to do some walking in the mountains, or just to enjoy the magnificent landscape. Various packages are available combining rail travel with hotel accommodation, or trekking. For more information: Inlandsbanan AB, Box 561, SE-831 27 Östersund, Sweden. Tel: 063-10 86 72; fax: 063-10 86 70; www.inlandsbanan.se/england.html

tre of this network of water is the largest town, **Östersund ⓭**, connected by a bridge to the beautiful island of **Frösön**, which has been inhabited since prehistoric times. According to legend, it was dedicated to Frö, the god of fertility, a place of pagan sacrifice, and the most northerly spot where a rune stone has been found. Today, its oldest religious building is of another faith, Christianity. The church dates in part from the 12th century, with a nave and porch added in 1610, the altar in 1708 and the pulpit in 1781. The separate bell tower is 18th-century, though one of the bells is 400 years older.

Map on page 286

From the island there are magnificent views over countless lakes and waterways towards Norway. Five minutes' walk from the church you'll find **Stocketitt**, which combines a local museum and a good viewpoint.

The island was home to the noted Swedish composer and critic Wilhelm Peterson-Berger (1867–1942). This prolific composer produced a total of five operas, five symphonies and a violin concerto, as well as choral works, chamber music, piano pieces and songs. His most popular major work, the opera *Arnljot*, is performed every summer on the island.

Frösön also has a 21-hectare (52-acre) zoo, **Frösö Djurpark**, with 600 animals and a challenging golf course, kept in impeccable condition even though it spends several months a year covered in snow (open late May–late Jun: Mon–Sat 10am–4pm, Sun 11am–4pm, late-Jun–early Aug: Mon–Sat 10am–6pm, Sun 11am–6pm; closed in winter; entrance fee; tel: 063-51 47 43).

All over Sweden you come across open-air museums which may be merely a handful of local buildings re-erected on one site, perhaps with a café, some indoor exhibits or traditional craft demonstrations. In a different league is **Jamtli** in Östersund, one of the oldest and biggest open-air museums in the country. It

Deer, bears, lynx, wolverine and elk inhabit the Central Heartlands.

BELOW: fast-flowing river in Jämtland.

Map on page 286

contains 60 buildings and was established in 1912 (open end Jun–mid-Aug: 11am–5pm; late Aug–Jun: Tue–Sun 11am–7pm; entrance fee; tel: 063-15 01 10). In summer, local people perform bygone tasks using traditional implements and equipment and visitors can also have a go. The buildings are from the 18th and 19th century and include a *fäbod* (summer farm), a baker's cottage, a smithy, and an old inn. The food in the café is first class.

Sweden's Loch Ness monster

The E14 from Östersund to the Norwegian frontier is an age-old route once used by pilgrims on their trek to the grave of St Olaf at Trondheim.

Lake Storsjön is reputed to have its own monster, a Swedish version of the world-famous Scottish "Nessie", the serpent-like creature supposed to inhabit the depths of Loch Ness. Lake Storsjön's monster is said to vary in length from 3.6 metres (12 ft) to 27 metres (90 ft) and to have eyes like saucers, large ears, a tail and horns. Among its 40,000 exhibits, Östersund's provincial museum has traps with hooks and cables which were owned by a company set up in 1894 to find the monster. After failing to catch anything, the company went into liquidation and donated the implements to the museum. Present-day monster seekers can take a cruise on the lake in the 1875 steamer *Thomee*.

In western Jämtland, the peaks rise up to nearly 1,800 metres (6,000 ft). It is a splendid area for trekking in summer and skiing in winter. Centuries ago, melting ice left many strange and unusual formations such as the deep canyon between the Drommen and Falkfångarfjället mountains (the nearest road ends at Höglekardalen). An equally impressive Ice Age landscape is near **Vallbo**, at the end of a minor road from Undersåker.

BELOW: sorting the day's catch.
RIGHT: Lockne Kyrka, Jämtland.

The E14 is the main highway west from Östersund to the Norwegian frontier. It was the scene of frequent fighting between Norway and Sweden, marked today by the remains of some fortifications. In 1718 the Swedes suffered a major defeat along this route. When Sweden's great warrior king Karl XII made his last fatal attack against the southern Norwegian fort of Fredriksten, he ordered his general Carl Gustav Armfelt to attack Trondheim from the north. It was a tragic failure. The king was killed at Fredriksten and, in the northern retreat, 3,000 men froze to death in a desperate attempt to withdraw into the safety of Sweden. You will find memorial stones to this disaster at Handöl, Ånn, Duved and Bustvalen.

In the 18th century, the area was the scene of frantic activity after the finding of copper – a boom period that lasted around 100 years.

Between Östersund and the border is **Åre** ⑭, a popular winter sports resort. A funicular railway goes from the town centre part-way up the local mountain **Åreskutan**, and a cable car goes almost to the summit. Lakes and mountains on every side make a superb view.

Western Jämtland is also rich in waterfalls, such as **Ristafallet** near Hålland or **Storfallet**, northwest of Höglekardalen, and **Tännforsen**, west of Åre.

Monotonous? Yes, to a degree. You need to be at ground level to absorb the immensity of the region: the brilliant blue lakes, their waters gently rippled by the breeze, the mysterious outlines of the distant mountains, the open space and the glorious silence. ❑

LAPLAND

Map
on page
298

*Under dancing northern lights and a golden midnight sun,
Lapland beckons the traveller north to the land of
the Sami where the taxi service is by dog sled*

n the great search for natural landscapes and the open air Lapland, Sweden's
largest and most northerly province, becomes more and more popular each
year. To some, this could be a two-edged "benefit" because of the danger of
)o many people in a fragile environment, but the Swedes are among the most
ware of the need for conservation.

Baedeker's *Guide to Norway and Sweden*, published in 1892, said: "The vast
wedish Norrland is rarely visited by travellers, the points of interest being
ew, the distances great and the communications imperfect." Today this dis-
nissive statement couldn't be further from the truth. Distances may be great but
nodern communications are easy, with a rail link to the far north and good
uality roads. As for "the points of interest being few", what about the mag-
ificent scenery? Lapland's uplands, lakes and mountains are among the finest
n Europe and remarkable enough to put any human attraction in the shade.

The best way to absorb the immensity of Lapland is to take the inland road –
Highway 45 – from south to north. In that way, this scenic extravaganza will
uild up like a highly-polished piece of drama into a climactic grand finale.

PRECEDING PAGES:
stunning scenery
rewards hikers in
the north.
LEFT: outlook from
an ice cave.
BELOW: traditional
Sami dress.

outhern Lapland

Dorotea ❶ is named after Queen Fredrika Wil-
elmina Dorotea, consort of King Gustav IV Adolf,
nd its best claim to fame is the Dorotea Hotel which
s renowned for its cuisine.

Vilhelmina ❷ (which also gets its name from the
ame queen) lies on the Ångermanälven river, 100 km
50 miles) north, and is of greater interest. Off the
nain road on a hillside is its well-preserved church
illage with an imposing church. The wooden houses
ow provide accommodation for tourists.

A secondary road heads west at Vilhelmina, along-
ide the Malgomaj lake, and gives access to some
plendid fell country, notably the **Kittelfjäll** region
round **Klimpfjäll ❸**. This is a largely uninhabited
rea with untouched mountain scenery where the
eaks rise to 1,375 metres (4,500 ft).

Eventually this road crosses the Norwegian fron-
er at Skalmodalen and links up with the E6 near
1osjøen. The E6 runs up the Norwegian west coast
nd the east-west roads in Sweden all feed into it,
llowing the itinerant traveller to criss-cross from one
ountry to the other with few formalities.

Storuman, 120 km (75 miles) north of Vilhelmina,
s a more important road junction, where Highway 45
s bisected by the E12, known as the **Blå Vägen** (Blue
lighway) because it follows a succession of lakes
nd the Umeälven river. It starts on the Swedish east
oast at **Holmsund**, on the Gulf of Bothnia, and

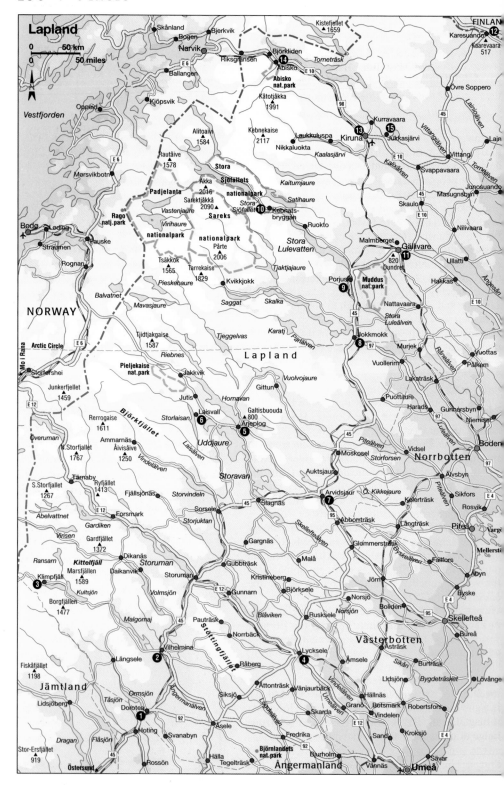

Lapland

0   50 km

0   50 miles

passes **Lycksele** ❹,where there is a zoo, **Lycksele Djurpark**, which concentrates on Nordic species including bear, elk, musk-ox, wolves and reindeer (open daily mid-May–Jun: 10am–4pm; Jul–mid-Aug: 10am–5pm; mid-Aug–mid-May: 10am–3pm; entrance fee; tel 0950-163 63). From Storuman the road continues through Tärnaby where it joins the E6 at Mo-i-Rana.

Map on page 298

Sami heritage

At **Slagnäs**, 75 km (47 miles) west of Arvidsjaur, there is a secondary road through glorious, peaceful lakeside scenery to **Arjeplog** ❺ and this is an enjoyable alternative to the main road (Highway 95). Arjeplog is one of Lapland's most interesting little towns and it is almost surrounded by the waters of lakes Uddjaure and Hornavan, which at 221 metres (725 ft) is Sweden's deepest lake.

The main attraction at Arjeplog is the **Silvermuseet** (Silver Museum), Torget. Housed in an old school, a typical beige-coloured wooden building, it provides a fascinating insight into the region's history and, above all, the Sami – the correct name for the Lapps (open mid-Jun–mid-Aug: daily 9am–6pm; mid-Aug–mid-Jun: Mon–Fri 10am–4pm, Sat 10am–2pm; entrance fee; tel 0961 612 90). It owes its existence to Einar Wallqvist, "the doctor of the Laplanders", a most remarkable man who came to the town in 1922.

Besides his medical work, Dr Wallqvist began to collect all kinds of cultural objects as a hobby. Later he decided to establish a museum in the old schoolhouse and today it has the finest collection of Sami silver in existence plus a host of artefacts relating to the life and times of the settlers and the Sami. He wrote books, lectured widely, was a gifted linguist and had a sparkling wit. He continued as the museum's curator until his death in 1986. Arjeplog's local church, which is 17th-century and quite impressive, was founded by Queen Kristina.

Red crosses mark the routes taken by snow scooters in winter.

BELOW: camping in Lapland in summer.

The Silver Road

Arjeplog is roughly halfway along Highway 95, which is the historic **Silver Vägen** (Silver Road) stretching from Skellefteå on the Gulf of Bothnia to Bodø on the Norwegian west coast. In the 17th century there were silver mines around **Nasafjäll** and the ore was transported, first by reindeer sleigh and then by boat, to the Swedish east coast. Not until 1972 did it become an asphalt-surfaced highway throughout its length, to open up an area of outstanding beauty.

About 60 km (37 miles) west of Arjeplog and to the south of road 95 is the isolated community of **Laisvall** ❻, where the inhabitants work in one of the biggest lead mines in Europe, **Laisvallsgruvan**. It extends below Lake Storlaisan (open Jul–early-Aug: Tue and Thur noon for guided tours; free; children under 15 years not admitted; tel 0920-202 62).

One of the finest viewpoints in this area is from the top of **Galtisbuouda**, 800 metres (2,624 ft) above sea level. It is 15 km (9 miles) north of Arjeplog and there is a good road to just below the summit. The outlook is magnificent with a network of lakes and range upon range of mountains stretching to infinity.

The wide main street of **Arvidsjaur** ❼ has something of the atmosphere of a frontier town which, to some degree, it is. Once a trading post, it is now a junction of both roads and rail-ways and has grown and expanded within the past 100 years. The major historic attraction is **Lappstaden**, the Sami village with nearly 80 buildings, including both the *kåtor*, the tent-shaped wooden huts, and the *härbren*, the distinctive wooden storehouses (open in July; guided tours available; tel 0960-175 00)

Although not permanently inhabited, the village is still used from time to time by the Sami people and is the oldest surviving example in Sweden, dating from the late 1700s.

In summer, Arvidsjaur is a tourist centre with all the essential adjuncts: hotels chalets, camping site, swimming pool, putting green, tennis courts and sports ground. In winter, when it is intensely cold, it is taken over by Europe's auto-motive industry which uses the area to test the ability of its products to perform satisfactorily in sub-zero temperatures. The Swedish Army has a year-round presence in Arvidsjaur, where there are barracks and a major base on the town's outskirts. The camp has modern chalets, which double as holiday homes for visitors in summer and rooms for Swedish conscripts in winter.

Across the Arctic Circle to Jokkmokk

The Arctic Circle is marked by a multilingual sign beside the road, 156 km (97 miles) north of Arvidsjaur. At a nearby café you can buy a suitably inscribed certificate to prove you have crossed the line. Only a short dis-tance further north is **Jokkmokk** ❽ which is the principal town in the *kom mun* (local-authority district) of the same name.

BELOW: Arjeplog's
Silver Museum is a
treasure trove of
Sami artefacts.

The Jokkmokk *kommun* is the biggest in Sweden covering an area of about 19,425 sq km (7,500 sq miles), equal to the whole of Wales, or Connecticu

and Delaware put together. The population, however, is a meagre 7,000, about half of whom live in Jokkmokk itself.

The word Jokkmokk was the name of a group of Sami and it means "a bend in the stream". It is the only place where you will see nomadic Sami in summer, but the big event is the market which takes place every February. This attracts thousands of people not so much to buy or sell but to experience the unique atmosphere (*see page 307*). If you need accommodation at the time of the fair you have to book at least a year in advance, and it is no time for camping out with the temperature often dropping to –35°C (–31°F). Other smaller fairs take place in various parts of this country.

Jokkmokk is a centre for the Sami culture, which can best be studied at the **Ajtte Svenskt Fjäll-och Samemuseum** (Swedish Mountain and Sami Museum), one of Sweden's most modern museums. As its name implies, the museum portrays not just the local culture but also the mountain world, placing mankind in a natural, cultural and ecological perspective. Geographically, it covers the whole of the mountain region and the areas where the Sami traditionally live (open mid-Jun–end Aug: Mon–Fri 9am–7pm, Sat–Sun 11am–6pm; late Aug–mid-Jun: Mon–Fri 9am–4pm, Sat–Sun noon–4pm; Oct–Apr closed Sat; entrance fee; tel 0970-170 70).

The next stretch of Highway 45 goes through a sparsely populated area to **Porjus ⑨**, 75 km (47 miles) north. It lies at the southern end of Lake Lulevat-ten and is a major centre for the generation of hydroelectric power. The original switchgear building is a monumental edifice and today Porjus is the headquarters for the state-owned power stations which are on the upper part of the Store Lule river. From Porjus a very minor road follows Lake Lulevatten for

Map on page 298

BELOW: preparing for an expedition.

DOG-SLEDGING IN LAPLAND

Sweden's northern wilderness is an amazing area, particularly in winter, and dog-sledging is a fascinating way of exploring it. A sled team usually consists of 5 to 12 dogs, most of them Siberian or Alaskan huskies. The dogs enjoy the work: indeed, showing a sled to a husky is like showing any other dog a lead and calling "Walkies". Once clipped in, they become extremely impatient to get going, leading to a crescendo of yelping until, at last, the driver releases the anchor and they're off like a flash. Most expeditions travel 25–50 km (15–30 miles) a day, but the dogs can cover far greater distances. In one of the highlights of the dog-sledging season, the Nordic Marathon, dozens of teams compete in a 250-km (150-mile) circular race from Abisko around Kebnekaise, Sweden's highest mountain. The fastest teams complete the course in about 16 hours, which includes a compulsory rest-stop.

Husky teams are based at a number of settlements, including Jukkasjärvi and Abisko. Passengers need to be well wrapped up against temperatures that could be –20°C (–4°F) or less. At Jokkmokk you can visit the local sledge-dog kennel, meet the huskies, inspect the sledges and watch a slide show (open Mon, Thur 6–9pm; entrance fee; tel 0971-122 20).

Gamla Kyrka (church) in Gällivare was built in 1747. Its bell tower, however, dates from 1768.

6 km (3.7 miles) to **Stora Sjöfallet** , which is the largest waterfall in Sweden. This should not be confused with Storforsen, north of Älvsbyn, which claims to be the largest unrestricted waterfall in Europe.

Bear country

To the east of Porjus and the E45 is a wild, untouched area which is the **Muddus National Park,** home of bear, lynx and wolverine. It is open to the public but visitors are not allowed in some of the more sensitive areas of the park during the breeding season, mid-March to the end of July (tel 0971-121 40).

A relatively short drive brings the bulk of the **Dundret Mountain** in sight, beyond which is Gällivare, one of the two major centres of population in northern Lapland. High on the side of Dundret is an extensive holiday centre, with a hotel, self-catering facilities, restaurants, nightclub, indoor pool and caravan park. Like all of northern Lapland, in summer it also has rapacious mosquitoes with an appetite for foreign blood. Don't forget the insect repellent.

Mosquitoes aside, the bustling **Dundret Centre** is something of a cultural shock after the peace and solitude of the area. But it gives you the chance to ride, walk, windsurf, fish, play golf, go white-water rafting, or even pan for gold. Although the track is rough in parts, you can also drive right to the top of the mountain. At an altitude of 820 metres (2,690 ft) the views are marvellous and, from early June to early July, this is the place to see the Midnight Sun.

End of the line: Gallivare

BELOW: hanging out in Gällivare, it's hot in Lapland, too.

Gällivare owes its growth to the discovery of iron ore and now has a population of 22,000. The main mining area is in its twin town of **Malmberget**

here most of the mineworkers live. Here, too, you find the contrast of a suburban small town at odds with the grandeur of the countryside all around it.

Gällivare is the end of the **Inlandsbanan**, a railway line which has faithfully followed the E45, give or take a few miles, all the way from Östersund. Construction began in 1907 and the line was completed in 1937. At one time its future was in doubt, but the line was saved by a decision to turn it into a tourist route. Today, with new diesel trains, it has regained its youth as a useful alternative way into the far north.

Gällivare has a mining museum, a mid-18th century Sami church (**Lapp-kyrkan**), a park with some preserved buildings and a Sami camp which appears to exist purely for the tourists. The town is also the jumping-off point for treks into the vast region to the west which includes the Padjelanta and Stora Sjöfallet national parks. Only a few minor roads penetrate into this enormous area and it is very much for those who want to trek.

Beyond Gällivare, road 45 joins up with highway E10 and together they go north to **Svappavaara**, a former mining centre. Here the E45 goes off to the northeast to Karesuando, just short of the Finnish frontier. Many of the place names in northern Lapland owe more to Finnish than to Swedish. In Kiruna, for example, a fifth of the population are Finnish immigrants.

Across the tundra

Karesuando ⑫ has two main distinctions. It is home to the most northerly church in Sweden, 250 km (155 miles) inside the Arctic Circle, and it also has the dubious honour of producing the coldest average winter temperatures in the country. All around the village is Sweden's only tundra scenery, and about

Map on page 298

TIP

A word of caution: reindeer are regarded as currency to the Sami. It is not "done" to ask a Sami how many reindeer he owns, because it is like asking him how much he earns a year.

BELOW: helicopter pick-up at the end of a day's walking.

4 km (2½ miles) to the south is **Kaarevaara Mountain**. The summit is no higher than 517 metres (1,696 ft) but from the top you can see Sweden, Finland and Norway. Better still, you can drive up there.

Distances in the far north between towns and settlements and places of interest are often great. Shared driving is a great advantage, particularly when the road runs mile after mile through an unchanging landscape. This happens beyond Svappavaara, where the E10 swings northwest through uninspiring scenery to **Kiruna** ⓭. With 22,000 inhabitants, this is the biggest centre of population in Lapland. Like Gällivare it grew and developed through the discovery and extraction of iron ore. Mining on a large scale began in 1900 and though it has declined since, it is still the main industry. The **Kirunavaara** (mine) is the world's largest deep mine, with more than 400 km (248 miles) of two-lane underground roadways. In summer, you can tour it by bus.

Tribute to Gällivare's miners. In summer, tours can be made of the iron-ore and copper mines at nearby Malmberget.

BELOW: Muddus National Park, south of Gällivare.

Kiruna is at the south of Lake Luossajärvi and dominated by the iron ore mountain which brought it into being. Although most mining is now underground, there is also a huge opencast site. The mine led to the opening in 1903 of the town's railway line, to take iron ore either to the port of Luleå on the Gulf of Bothnia to the east, or across the Norwegian border to the ice-free port of Narvik on the Norwegian west coast. In 1903, this was an outstanding feat of engineering and, until 1984 when Kiruna and Narvik were joined by road, the railway was the only cross-border link in this remote area.

With the decline in mining, Kiruna has switched its emphasis to tourism and scientific research. The **Kiruna Geophysical Institute**, among other things, investigates the phenomenon of the Northern Lights, while on the banks of the Vittangi river is **Esrange**, a rocket testing station. Esrange sends research rockets and balloons into different layers of inner space while beside Tarfalasjö lake, scientists research the Ice Age. **Abisko** ⓮, 150 km (93 miles) north of Kiruna, has a natural sciences research station.

Apart from a visit to the mine, try not to miss **Samegård**, Brytaregatan 14, which provides a glimpse of the life and history of the Sami (open mid Jun–Sep: daily 8am–6pm; Oct–Jun: Mon–Fri 8am–4pm; entrance fee).

A hotel made of ice

A secondary road just outside Kiruna takes you to the village of **Jukkasjärvi** ⓯, a centre for winter and summer excursions. In recent years Jukkasjärvi has acquired fame with its **Ice Hotel** which is rebuilt every winter. In winter the dog-sledging is truly Arctic, in a snow-covered wilderness. In summer Jukkasjärvi provides the stomach-churning thrill of white-water rafting through the rapids in an inflatable boat. You can choose from day and week-long trips using the Torne, Kalix and Kaitum rivers. The village also has a modest but quite interesting wooden church and a small open-air museum.

Tourism received its biggest boost in 1984 with the opening of road 98 from Kiruna via the Norwegian frontier to Narvik. This is the **Nordkalottvägen**, an outstanding piece of road building which penetrates for 170 km (105 miles) through one of Europe's last

wilderness areas. It starts undramatically, but by the time you have **Lake Torneträsk** on the right with distant mountains, and even more impressive mountains rising up to 2,000 metres (6,500 ft) on the left, the journey changes from interesting to spectacular. The clarity of the air sharply etches the outlines of the mountains, some snow-capped even in midsummer against the sky, while the lake is a brilliant blue.

The mountains to the southwest of the highway can only be reached on foot or by pony and it is in this hinterland that **Kebnekaise**, Sweden's highest peak at 2,117 metres (6,945 ft), reigns supreme.

The king's trail

Abisko is a popular base from which to set out along the **Kungsleden** (King's Trail), a long-distance footpath which, for almost a century, has enabled even inexperienced walkers to see something of the most mountainous region of Sweden. Abisko, Björkliden and Riksgränsen (the last place before the frontier with Norway) all have hotels.

This area presents wonderful opportunities for the angler and an inexpensive permit allows you to fish in 3,000 lakes. Apart from walking and fishing, there are trips on Lake Torneträsk and sightseeing flights by seaplane or helicopter. From Riksgränsen the highway crosses the frontier and descends to meet the E6 at the edge of the Rombak fjord, and on to the coast at Narvik.

Despite these engineering feats, the abiding impression of Lapland must be that however clever are human achievements they are all upstaged by nature. This awe-inspiring combination of rivers, lakes and mountains cannot fail to leave its mark on the visitor. ❑

Map on page 298

A large part of northern Sweden forms Laponia, an area which is now on UNESCO's World Heritage List. It covers four national parks, including Sarek, Sweden's oldest, founded in 1909.

BELOW: offbeat accommodation, the Ice Hotel at Jukkasjärvi.

ARTS AND CRAFTS IN THE FAR NORTH

Living in isolated communities across Lapland, the Sami have developed distinctive handicrafts using reindeer, wood and silver as raw materials

Sami handicrafts have a long tradition. The raw materials are often derived from everyday items found in the mountainous northern landscape, such as birch wood. Antlers and skins from the reindeer herds are used to make knives, tools, clothes and decorative objects.

The products have developed from simple household items to the sophisticated handicrafts of today. Many objects are round in shape. This is because the Sami are a nomadic people who roam over wide areas with their reindeer herds, and angular items cannot be packed so easily.

SAMI SILVER TRAIL

A silver mine was established in Lapland in the 17th century, since when the Sami have become particularly noted for their silverware – including richly decorated drinking vessels, bowls and adornments. Today, their silverware is almost always made by silversmiths in the cities to Sami specifications. Embroidery is also used to exquisite effect in Sami handicrafts.

Sami products are sold in craft shops and markets in Lapland. Prices and quality vary, so be sure to hunt around before you buy.

▷ **PLAY-TIME**
Sami have always used whatever materials came to hand. These are traditional dolls made from reindeer horn.

▷ **FANCY FOOTWORK**
A pair of children's boots made from reindeer skin. Reindeer bones are used for sewing. The woven band is typically Sami and is tied around the boot.

▽ **WATER CARRIER**
The inside of this water flask is made from leather. The outer basketry is woven from flattened and softened birch roots.

△ **PRIMARY COLOURS**
A tapestry featuring typical Sami colours, including red and blue. Pewter thread is used for the decorative embroidery.

▽ **DRINKING MUG**
The *kåsan* is the classic Sami drinking vessel. It is usually made from birch wood. This is a more exclusive silver version.

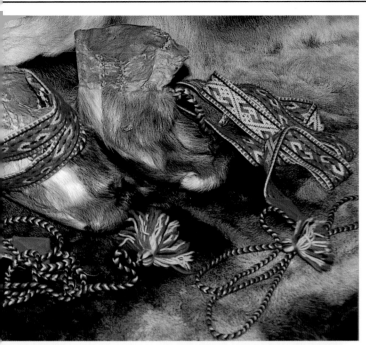

JOKKMOKK'S WINTER MARKET

The annual winter market in Jokkmokk (*see page 300–301*) takes place over the first weekend in February. This tradition started in 1605, and the market soon became a meeting place for the Sami and the merchants from the coastal communities. The merchants were generally looking for supplies of furs, in exchange for the everyday items which the Sami people needed for their harsh life looking after the reindeer herds.

Over time, the market became not just an occasion for buying and selling goods but also for special events such as weddings, baptisms and funerals. For many years it was staged over two weeks, but this was gradually shortened to just a weekend. During the 1930s, the market consisted of just 20 stalls; today, there are at least 500, and it is estimated that 30,000 people visit Jokkmokk during the market, some coming from abroad. It is still very much a Sami occasion, with the accent on traditional arts, handicrafts and music. For many visitors the most spectacular event is the reindeer drive.

△ **MARKET DAY**
In a land where national frontiers are not a barrier to free movement, Sami women from Russia visit an annual market in Jokkmokk, Lapland.

▷ **LOCAL DISH**
The richly decorated handicrafts are often best seen in the setting of a traditional Sami tepee. This is a bowl or serving tray made from birchwood.

THE NORTHEAST COAST

Map
on page
312

The Bothnian coast of the northeast is Sweden's best-kept secret.
Uninhabited islands, sheltered coves and historic towns
await the traveller on the journey north

Bottenviken (the Gulf of Bothnia), the stretch of water that separates Sweden from its eastern neighbour, Finland, forms the common bond between the three provinces of the northeast – Ångermanland, Väster-botten and Norrbotten – which share its seaboard. For the most part, the coast-line is low-lying and ranges from polished rock to sand and shingle beaches, and from wide bays to small coves and inlets.

All the major towns are on the coast, a harking back to the days when the sea was the easy way to travel, compared with the dense forests and rolling hills further inland. Most of these coastal towns grew up as trading settle-ments and today, particularly in the west, there are still few people and towns in the endless expanses of forest.

The coast is fringed with islands which at times form an almost continuous archipelago. Only a handful are inhabited and, even on those, few of the descen-dants of the early fishermen who established these small settlements now seek a livelihood from the sea. The boats are still there but today their owners are holidaymakers, who have turned the islands into a playground to indulge the Swedish passion for sailing and the sea. Only the occasional small, simple chapel, which you come across on the islands, speaks of the past.

Inland, lakes provide tranquil blue oases in the dense forests, while river valleys cut swathes through the trees. The greatest charm of the area is its rich wildlife, with bear, lynx, elk and beaver in abundance.

PRECEDING PAGES:
the forested north.
LEFT: Ullvöhamn
in Ångermanland.
BELOW: a taste of
the outdoors.

Seafaring town

Starting in the south of this great stretch of empty land, the main coastal town of Ångermanland is **Härnösand ❶**, 50 km (30 miles) north of Sundsvall in Medelpad. In 1585, King Johan III not so much granted, but forced, a charter on the old trading and seafaring centre.

The king was looking for duties and taxes, and threatened the inhabitants with deportation to Russia if they did not agree to create a permanent trading centre. That threat was enough to turn Härnösand into a successful commercial town.

The town is part island, part mainland, with the major section on **Härnö Island**, 7 km by 10 km (4 miles by 6 miles). In the 17th and 18th centuries, it blossomed into the cultural and administrative centre of northern Sweden.

Although it is now a commercial and industrial town, its splendid location makes it attractive. The fine town hall, with its classic lines and impressive pillared entrance, was completed in 1791, and the equally handsome cathedral, **Domkyrkan**, built between 1843 and 1846, is in the same style. It

Northeast Coast

0   50 km
0   50 miles

replaces an earlier building which in 1721 was burnt down by marauding Russians during a turbulent time in Sweden's history. There are some well-preserved 18th-century wooden houses in **Östanbäcken** but the rest of the town is modern.

Overlooking the town and harbour is the **Murberget**, which has one of the largest open-air historical museums in Sweden (open Jun–Aug: daily 11am–5pm; entrance fee). An exhibition at the nearby **Länsmuseet** shows how people settled in the area more than 2,000 years ago and contains a collection of hunting weapons (open daily 11am–5pm; free; tel: 0611-886 00).

The High Coast

One of the most important attractions along this road is the new **Höga Kusten (High Coast) Bridge**. It is 1.8 km (1.1 miles) long and has a vertical clearance of about 40 metres (130 ft). The bridge's supporting pillars stretch out 180 metres (590 ft) over the sea. At its northern end there is a restaurant and visitor centre. It is an impressive structure, modelled partly on the Golden Gate Bridge in San Francisco, and is well worth a visit. It has now replaced the old Sandö Bridge, which itself once attracted sightseers.

About 40 km (25 miles) northwest of Härnösand, on the Ångermanälven river, is **Kramfors ❷**, the home of the musician Frans Berwald, one of Sweden's best-known composers, and Kalle Grönstedt, a musician who made the town the country's leading centre for accordionists.

In the vicinity of Kramfors, near **Ytterlännäs** on Highway 90, look out for a 13th-century church, regarded as an antiquarian wonder. The 16th-century golden Madonna is by Haake Gulleson; the ornate vaults and walls were decorated by an unknown farmer-painter in the 1480s.

Between Härnösand and Docksta, 60 km (37 miles) to the north, the coast changes dramatically to form the Höga Kusten (High Coast), where the low-lying shoreline gives way to one with a much higher profile. This beautiful area with its impressive coastal landscape is Sweden's best-kept secret, which does not seem to be widely known or appreciated even by Swedes, and few foreigners ever reach it.

Map on page 312

The heart of the High Coast is the **Nordingrå Peninsula** ❸, where the bedrock is an intense red *rapakivi* granite– this word is Finnish and means "rotten stone", because of the way it weathers easily into gravel and shingle. To get to the High Coast, leave the E4 north of Härnösand and take the short ferry crossing over the estuary to **Nydal**. Coming from the north, you reach the peninsula by leaving the E4 at either Lockestrand or Sundborn. Offshore are several attractive islands, such as **Mjältön**, which achieves the record for the highest Swedish island with its peak at 236 metres (774 ft).

The peninsula has a variety of scenic treasures – the wide sweep of Omne bay, the villages of Måviken, Norrfällsviken and the view from the church over Vagsfjärden. Bönhamn is a tiny little place tucked away among the rocks, where Arne's Sjöbad (Arne's Boathouse) justifies its popularity as a rendezvous for meals of salmon or fresh grilled herrings and mashed potatoes. Equally popular is the Café Mannaminne, near Häggvik, run by Anders Åberg; it provides sustenance, including a variety of home-baked delicacies, in addition to handicrafts and musical evenings.

The **Höga Kusten walk**, a 25-km (16-mile) footpath through the peninsula, starts at Fjördbotten. There are bathing places at Storsand, Norrfällsviken, Hörsång and Noraström.

On the inland side of the E4 is another surprise, the looming outline of the **Skuleberget**, some 295 metres (968 ft) above sea level. If approaching from

On the menu, typical dishes in the north include smoked reindeer, which has a beef-like flavour, followed by a dessert of cloudberries and ice cream.

BELOW: the road north, Sansbron at Kramfors.

TIP

The best way to explore the island of Norra Ulvön is to rent a bike in the village of Ulvöhamn, where the ferries tie up. Simple cabins are available for overnight stays, bookable on the island. Sailors arrive in force in July for the Ulvön Regatta.

BELOW: stoking up the fire.

the north, it rises suddenly just before Docksta, and the easy way up is by chairlift to the top.

Behind Skuleberget is the **Skuleskogen National Park** ❹, noted for its birds and mammals, which include the rare white-backed woodpecker, grouse, Siberian jay and waxwing, as well as a whole range of mammals – elk, deer, lynx, fox, badger, marten, ermine, blue hare and squirrel (open all year).

Örnsköldsvik ❺, commonly called Övik, is the nearest town to the High Coast and is twice the size of Härnösand, with 60,000 inhabitants. The town itself is industrial but there are some good views from the **Vansberget** hilltop (accessible by car) and it has a beautiful archipelago. In bygone years, many of the local people were fisher-farmers, combining the two jobs to make ends meet – the counterparts of the west-coasters. Örnsköldsvik is one of Sweden's leading winter-sports areas, particularly for ice hockey and ski jumping. There is also an attractive adventure swimming pool in the town centre.

Island hopping

There are two attractive islands to the south of Örnsköldsvik, **Södra Ulvön**, which is uninhabited, and **Norra Ulvön**. Södra has one of the oldest fishermen's chapels in Sweden, built in 1622. It has well-preserved paintings on the walls and ceiling. Another attractive island just to the north is **Trysunda**, a favourite with the sailing fraternity because of its lagoon-like bay. Norra Ulvön can be reached by boat from Docksta and is linked by ferry to Trysunda.

Umeå ❻, on the Umeälven river at the junction of the E4 and E12 roads, 110 km (68 miles) north of Örnsköldsvik, may be larger than Övik but, thanks to its layout and location, is undoubtedly more attractive. Like so many towns in

Sweden, it was founded by King Gustav II Adolf, in 1622. After a devastating fire in 1888 – a commonplace event in a country where virtually all the buildings were made of wood – the town planted avenues of birches as protective firebreaks, and these have created a gracious appearance which goes well with its riverside location. Umeå is the principal town of Västerbotten and has a population of more than 100,000.

Map on page 312

It was not always peaceful. Between 1808 and 1809, at the time when Sweden lost its 800-year-old rule over Finland, the Russians crossed the winter ice from Finland and attacked the town, which resulted in bitter fighting. The town's main attraction is **Gammlia Friluftsmuseum**, yet another open-air museum, but distinguished by the fact that it was established as early as the 1920s (open late Jun–late Aug: daily 10am–5pm; free). Apart from a variety of old buildings, it includes the provincial museum of Sami culture (open late Jun–late Aug: Mon–Fri 10am–7pm, Sat–Sun noon–7pm; Sep–Jun Tue–Fri 9am–4pm, Sat noon–4pm, Sun noon–5pm; entrance fee; tel: 090-17 18 00).

An alternative to the main road along the coast from Umeå to the next place north, **Skellefteå**, an industrial centre, is to take the secondary road (364) inland, which is more interesting and very quiet. There are no dramatic panoramas, just a succession of pleasant rural views. You pass the **Bygdeträsket lake** and reach a smaller lake at **Burträsk ⑦**, about 100 km (60 miles) north of Umeå, which has an imposing village church and a very small open-air museum – "every community should have one" might well be the Swedish motto. Never mind: this museum serves good coffee and waffles (open in summer; free).

By now, you will have become so used to northern Sweden's quiet rural landscape that to arrive in **Piteå ⑧** is something of a culture shock. It lies just

Bags packed and ready to go. The north of Sweden is popular for summer hiking and fishing expeditions.

BELOW: the clear, clean waters of the north are an angler's paradise.

FISHING IN THE FAR NORTH

There is nothing quite like fishing against the impressive backdrop of Sweden's mountains. Creeping silently along a river bank and trying to tempt a shy trout or grayling to the fly is an unforgettable experience. Fishing is well organised in the north. If you are driving along the northeast coast there are plenty of opportunities to fish along the route, especially in the Piteälven, Kalixälven and Torneälven rivers; just ask at the nearest tourist office. Further afield, the Tjuonajokk fishing camp on the Kaitumälven river in northwest Lapland, for instance, is renowned for its grayling fishing. The Miekak fishing camp, 100 km (60 miles) northwest of Arjeplog (accessible by helicopter from Tjärnberg at Silvervägen, or by snowmobile in winter from Silvervägen), provides arguably the best char fishing in Lapland. At the northernmost extremity of Sweden, the fishing centre on Rostojaure lake is renowned for its char and grayling. It is accessible in summer only by helicopter.

Not surprisingly, transport can be expensive, but the cost of fishing permits is low compared with other countries. Permits can be bought at a number of outlets, including Tourist Information Offices and some petrol stations. The best month for fishing is usually August.

north of the Västerbotten-Norrbotten provincial boundary on a peninsula that dates back to the 17th century, and has a few narrow lanes and wooden houses to recall the past. So far so good, but now it has developed into an industrial centre with timber, paper and pulp industries and – more surprisingly – a popular holiday resort.

This big holiday centre, **Pite Havsbad**, has a candy-floss atmosphere with a mass of self-catering cabins, camping sites, a large hotel complex with an adventure swimming pool, and all kinds of entertainment (tel: 0911-327 00). It has more than 3.2 km (2 miles) of beach and is full of noise and people. The Norwegians love it, and migrate there in great flocks from the austere calm of their northern fjords.

From Piteå, the road leads northwest and follows the course of the Piteälven river through Älvsbyn and on to Bredsel and **Storforsen** ❾, 90 km (56 miles) away. This magnificent waterfall is said to be Europe's highest unfettered waterfall with a 81-metre (265-ft) drop.

Lulea: World Heritage site

Back to the coast and it is not far to **Luleå** ❿, the most northerly major town in Sweden. Today, it stands at the mouth of the Luleälven river, surrounded on three sides by water and fringed with islands. In olden times, the town was some 10 km (6 miles) further inland. It had been given its own charter by King Gustav II Adolf in 1621, but in 1649 the Crown decreed that trade had grown too large for that first small harbour and the town had to move.

The townspeople were reluctant to leave their homes but the Crown issued a decree forcing them to go. The king could not force the new town to develop

BELOW: shop in Gammelstad, the old town of Luleå.

quickly and, in 1742, when the intrepid botanist Linnaeus passed through Luleå on his Lapland journey, he dismissed it as "a pretty village".

The early shipyards closed when the first steamship appeared; then the discovery of iron ore in Lapland and the opening of the railways gave the town a chance to develop. The first steelworks were built in the 1940s, followed by a massive but stillborn project for a new steelworks on 250 hectares (618 acres) of reclaimed land. It was due for completion in 1980, but by then over-production of steel elsewhere made the new works a non-starter.

Though it has been dogged by a certain amount of misfortune, Luleå is today a pleasant town. Its museum, the **Norrbotten Museum** in Hermelin Park, provides a well-rounded picture of the twin strands of the province with the inclusion of a major collection of Sami artefacts (open Mon–Fri 10am–4pm, Sat–Sun noon–4pm; free; tel: 0920-24 35 00).

One happy legacy of the king's decision to move Luleå is that it left the old church town, **Gammelstad**, on its original site. Now the church village and the church itself have been placed on UNESCO's World Heritage list. It is a fascinating place to visit, with 400 small red-painted cottages surrounding the church. The cottages were built mainly in the 17th century and were used when people came in from the country to go to church at the major festivals, or when it was time to pay taxes to the sheriff (open all year; free; tel: 0920-25 43 10).

The 15th-century church at its centre has walls of red and grey granite. The altarpiece, carved in wood, and gilded, was made in Antwerp, and the chancel frescoes date from the 1480s. The triumphal crucifix is a remarkable example of medieval art, while the sandstone baptismal font is even older than the church itself. The ornate pulpit in baroque style was the work of a village joiner, Nils

Map on page 312

Dressed for the great outdoors. Northern Sweden lies under a blanket of snow from January to May.

BELOW: a window on the world in historic Luleå.

Map
on page
312

Fluur. The church is still used today on important religious occasions. Close to the original harbour is an open-air museum with farm buildings, cottages, stables, a log cabin, a croft and a fisherman's dwelling. It also includes one of the typical haysheds which are a feature of the farming landscape in Norrbotten. Once a necessity, hundreds survive today as relics from the past.

Border country

About 35 km (22 miles) inland from Luleå on the Luleälven river is a town once called the "Gibraltar of the North". **Boden** ⓫ has been a military town for many years and, at the end of the 19th century, was referred to as "one of the strongest fortresses of Europe – that is to say in the whole world". The reason for the great fortress was the loss of Finland to the Russians in 1809, which left Sweden fearful of an attempted invasion by its eastern neighbour.

Today, Boden remains the largest garrison town in Sweden and is the home of six regiments. **Garnisonsmuseet** (Garrison Museum) has much to reveal about Sweden's military history over the past 400 years, and it has a collection of weapons, uniforms and other militaria (open Jun–Aug: daily 11am–4pm).

Even now, Sweden has remained sensitive about military issues and a major slice of eastern Norrbotten is a defence area. This means restrictions on foreigners entering and staying in the designated area.

Sweden's easternmost town is **Haparanda** ⓬, which lies on the western side of the Torneälven river, and is another result of Sweden's losing the 1808–9 war. Along with Finland went the important Finnish town, Tornio. To compensate for that loss, the Swedes built Haparanda opposite Tornio on the Torneälven river which forms the border between the two countries for many miles. On the Swedish side it also skirts a largely uninhabited region of Norrbotten and Lapland. All these northern provinces, collectively called Norrland, have a distinctive northern terrain and, whether it be on mountain, lake or river, they offer endless outdoor pastimes, including canoeing, white-water rafting, and fishing.

This northern curve of the Gulf of Bothnia is a mixture of archipelago, rivers and wonderful scenery. It's worth taking road 400 to the north along the Torneälven river on the Swedish side into the Tornedalen valley. Make a stop at the **Kukkolaforsen waterfall**, 15 km (9 miles) from Haparanda, where there are excellent visitor facilities close to the falls.

Between Haparanda and Luleå lies **Kalix** ⓭, which has a medieval church from the 15th century, and in death the graveyard unites Russian and Swedish soldiers. Earlier Viking graves lie nearby at Sangis.

This is Sami country and 75 km (46 miles) inland from Kalix on the Kalixälven river is **Överkalix** ⓮, a typical Lapland township. There are fine views here from the top of the local mountain, **Brännaberget**, and, if you time your visit cleverly, you have the chance to see the glories of the Midnight Sun.

If you come at the end of June, you can see the spectacular traditional netting of the whitefish. The locals build rickety, long jetties out into the rapids where they use traditional *haaf* nets to catch not only whitefish, but also salmon. ❑

BELOW: taking a breather among the Sarek mountains.
RIGHT: on the Torneälven river at Kukkolaforsen.

INSIGHT GUIDES
TRAVEL TIPS

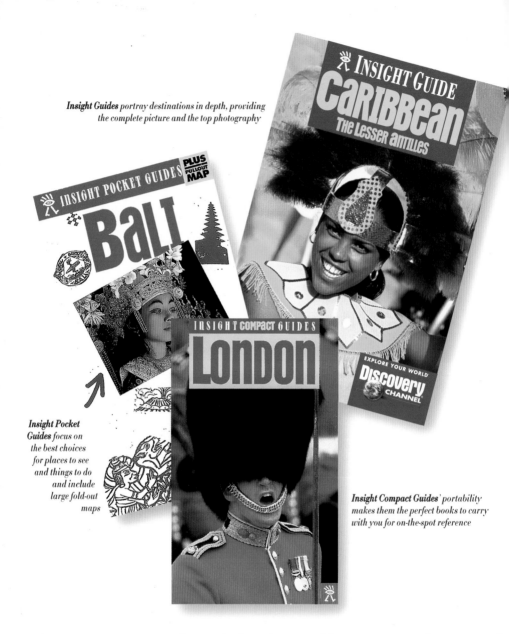

Insight Guides portray destinations in depth, providing the complete picture and the top photography

Insight Pocket Guides *focus on the best choices for places to see and things to do and include large fold-out maps*

Insight Compact Guides *portability makes them the perfect books to carry with you for on-the-spot reference*

Three types of guide for all types of travel

INSIGHT GUIDES Different people need different kinds of information. Some want *background information* to help them prepare for the trip. Others seek *personal recommendations* from someone who knows the destination well. And others look for *compactly presented data* for on-the-spot reference. With three carefully designed series, Insight Guides offer readers the perfect choice. Insight Guides will turn your visit into an experience.

The world's largest collection of visual travel guides